NYSTCE ATS-W 90

Elementary Assessment of Teaching Skills -- Written

Teacher Certification Exam

By: Sharon Wynne, M.S.

XAMonline, INC.
Boston

XAMonline, Inc.
25 First Street, Suite 106
Cambridge, MA 02141
Toll Free 1-800-509-4128
Email: info@xamonline.com
Web: www.xamonline.com
Fax: 1-617-583-5552

Library of Congress Cataloging-in-Publication Data
Wynne, Sharon A.
NYSTCE ATS-W Elementary Assessment of Teaching Skills – Written 90 Teacher Certification / Sharon A. Wynne.
ISBN: 978-1-60787-305-1, 1st edition
1. NYSTCE ATS-W Elementary Assessment of Teaching Skills – Written 90 2. Study Guides. 3. NYSTCE
4. Teachers' Certification & Licensure. 5. Careers

Disclaimer:
The opinions expressed in this publication are the sole works of XAMonline and were created independently from the National Education Association (NES), Educational Testing Service (ETS), or any State Department of Education, National Evaluation Systems or other testing affiliates. Between the time of publication and printing, state specific standards as well as testing formats and website information may change that are not included in part or in whole within this product. XAMonline develops sample test questions, and they reflect similar content as on real tests; however, they are not former tests. XAMonline assembles content that aligns with state standards but makes no claims nor guarantees teacher candidates a passing score. Numerical scores are determined by testing companies such as NES or ETS and then are compared with individual state standards. A passing score varies from state to state.

Printed in the United States of America   œ-1
NYSTCE ATS-W Elementary Assessment of Teaching Skills – Written 90
ISBN: 978-1-60787-305-1

TABLE OF CONTENTS

Section 1 About XAMonline

XAMonline – A Specialty Teacher Certification Company

Created in 1996, XAMonline was the first company to publish study guides for state-specific teacher certification examinations. Founder Sharon Wynne found it frustrating that materials were not available for teacher certification preparation and decided to create the first single, state-specific guide. XAMonline has grown into a company of over 1800 contributors and writers and offers over 300 titles for the entire PRAXIS series and every state examination. No matter what state you plan on teaching in, XAMonline has a unique teacher certification study guide just for you.

XAMonline – Value and Innovation

We are committed to providing value and innovation. Our print-on-demand technology allows us to be the first in the market to reflect changes in test standards and user feedback as they occur. Our guides are written by experienced teachers who are experts in their fields. And, our content reflects the highest standards of quality. Comprehensive practice tests with varied levels of rigor means that your study experience will closely match the actual in-test experience.

To date, XAMonline has helped nearly 600,000 teachers pass their certification or licensing exams. Our commitment to preparation exceeds simply providing the proper material for study - it extends to helping teachers **gain mastery** of the subject matter, giving them the **tools** to become the most effective classroom leaders possible, and ushering today's students toward a **successful future**.

Section 2 About this Study Guide

Purpose of this Guide
Is there a little voice inside of you saying, "Am I ready?" Our goal is to replace that little voice and remove all doubt with a new voice that says, "I AM READY. **Bring it on**!" by offering the highest quality of teacher certification study guides.

Organization of Content
You will see that while every test may start with overlapping general topics, each are very unique in the skills they wish to test. Only XAMonline presents custom content that analyzes deeper than a title, a subarea, or an objective. Only XAMonline presents content and sample test assessments along with **focus statements**, the deepest-level rationale and interpretation of the skills that are unique to the exam.

Title and field number of test
→Each exam has its own name and number. XAMonline's guides are written to give you the content you need to know for the specific exam you are taking. You can be confident when you buy our guide that it contains the information you need to study for the specific test you are taking.

Subareas
→These are the major content categories found on the exam. XAMonline's guides are written to cover all of the subareas found in the test frameworks developed for the exam.

Objectives
→These are standards that are unique to the exam and represent the main subcategories of the subareas/content categories. XAMonline's guides are written to address every specific objective required to pass the exam.

Focus statements
→These are examples and interpretations of the objectives. You find them in parenthesis directly following the objective. They provide detailed examples of the range, type, and level of content that appear on the test questions. **Only XAMonline's guides drill down to this level.**

How do We Compare with Our Competitors?
XAMonline – drills down to the focus statement level
CliffsNotes and REA – organized at the objective level
Kaplan – provides only links to content
MoMedia – content not specific to the test

Each subarea is divided into manageable sections that cover the specific skill areas. Explanations are easy-to-understand and thorough. You'll find that every test answer contains a rejoinder so if you need a refresher or further review after taking the test, you'll know exactly to which section you must return.

How to Use this Book

Our informal polls show that most people begin studying up to 8 weeks prior to the test date, so start early. Then ask yourself some questions: How much do you really know? Are you coming to the test straight from your teacher-education program or are you having to review subjects you haven't considered in 10 years? Either way, take a **diagnostic or assessment test** first. Also, spend time on sample tests so that you become accustomed to the way the actual test will appear.

This guide comes with an online diagnostic test of 30 questions found online at www.XAMonline.com. It is a little boot camp to get you up for the task and reveal things about your compendium of knowledge in general. Although this guide is structured to follow the order of the test, you are not required to study in that order. By finding a time-management and study plan that fits your life you will be more effective. The results of your diagnostic or self-assessment test can be a guide for how to manage your time and point you towards an area that needs more attention.

Week	Activity
8 weeks prior to test	Take a diagnostic test found at www.XAMonline.com
6-3 weeks prior to test	For each of these 4 weeks, choose a content area to study. You don't have to go in the order of the book. It may be that you start with the content that needs the most review. Alternately, you may want to ease yourself into plan by starting with the most familiar material.
2 weeks prior to test	Take the sample test, score it, and create a review plan for the final week before the test.
1 week prior to test	Following your plan (which will likely be aligned with the areas that need the most review) go back and study the sections that align with the questions you may have gotten wrong. Then go back and study the sections related to the questions you answered correctly. If need be, create flashcards and drill yourself on any area that you makes you anxious.

Section 3 About the NYSTCE Elementary Assessment of Teaching Skills - Written 90 (ATS-W)

What is the NYSTCE Elementary Assessment of Teaching Skills - Written 90 (ATS-W)?

The NYSTCE Elementary Assessment of Teaching Skills - Written 90 (ATS-W) is meant to assess mastery of the basic pedagogical knowledge and skills required to teach students in New York public schools. It is administered by Pearson Education on behalf of the New York Department of Education.

Often **your own state's requirements** determine whether or not you should take any particular test. The most reliable source of information regarding this is your state's Department of Education. This resource should have a complete list of testing centers and dates. Test dates vary by subject area and not all test dates necessarily include your particular test, so be sure to check carefully.

If you are in a teacher-education program, check with the Education Department or the Certification Officer for specific information for testing and testing timelines. The Certification Office should have most of the information you need.

If you choose an alternative route to certification you can either rely on our website at www.XAMonline.com or on the resources provided by an alternative certification program. Many states now have specific agencies devoted to alternative certification and there are some national organizations as well, for example:
National Association for Alternative Certification
http://www.alt-teachercert.org/index.asp

Interpreting Test Results

Contrary to what you may have heard, the results of the NYSTCE Elementary Assessment of Teaching Skills - Written 90 (ATS-W) are not based on time. More accurately, you will be scored on the raw number of points you earn in relation to the raw number of points available. Each question is worth one raw point. It is likely to your benefit to complete as many questions in the time allotted, but it will not necessarily work to your advantage if you hurry through the test.

Follow the guidelines provided by Pearson for interpreting your score. The web site offers a sample test score sheet and clearly explains how/whether the scores are scaled and what to expect if you have an essay portion on your test.

What's on the Test?

The NYSTCE Elementary Assessment of Teaching Skills - Written 90 (ATS-W) consists of approximately 80 multiple-choice questions and 1 constructed-response essay. The breakdown of the questions is as follows:

Category	Question Type	Approximate Percentage of the test
I: Student Development and Learning	Multiple choice	25%
II: Instruction and Assessment	Multiple choice	38%
III: The Professional Environment	Multiple choice	17%
IV: Instruction and Assessment	Constructed response	20%

Question Types

You're probably thinking, enough already, I want to study! Indulge us a little longer while we explain that there is actually more than one type of multiple-choice question. You can thank us later after you realize how well prepared you are for your exam.

1. **Complete the Statement.** The name says it all. In this question type you'll be asked to choose the correct completion of a given statement. For example: The Dolch Basic Sight Words consist of a relatively short list of words that children should be able to:
   a. Sound out
   b. Know the meaning of
   c. Recognize on sight
   d. Use in a sentence

   The correct answer is C. In order to check your answer, test out the statement by adding the choices to the end of it.

2. **Which of the Following.** One way to test your answer choice for this type of question is to replace the phrase "which of the following" with your selection. Use this example: Which of the following words is one of the twelve most frequently used in children's reading texts:
   a. There
   b. This
   c. The
   d. An

   Don't look! Test your answer. _____ is one of the twelve most frequently used in children's reading texts. Did you guess C? Then you guessed correctly.

3. **Roman Numeral Choices.** This question type is used when there is more than one possible correct answer. For example: Which of the following two arguments accurately supports the use of cooperative learning as an effective method of instruction?
   I. Cooperative learning groups facilitate healthy competition between individuals in the group.
   II. Cooperative learning groups allow academic achievers to carry or cover for academic underachievers.
   III. Cooperative learning groups make each student in the group accountable for the success of the group.

IV. Cooperative learning groups make it possible for students to reward other group members for achieving.

    A. I and II
    B. II and III
    C. I and III
    D. III and IV

Notice that the question states there are **two** possible answers. It's best to read all the possibilities first before looking at the answer choices. In this case, the correct answer is D.

4. **Negative Questions.** This type of question contains words such as "not," "least," and "except." Each correct answer will be the statement that does **not** fit the situation described in the question. Such as: Multicultural education is **not**

    a. An idea or concept
    b. A "tack-on" to the school curriculum
    c. An educational reform movement
    d. A process

Think to yourself that the statement could be anything but the correct answer. This question form is more open to interpretation than other types, so read carefully and don't forget that you're answering a negative statement.

5. **Questions That Include Graphs, Tables, or Reading Passages.** As ever, read the question carefully. It likely asks for a very specific answer and not broad interpretation of the visual. Here is a simple (though not statistically accurate) example of a graph question: In the following graph in how many years did more men take the NYSTCE exam than women?

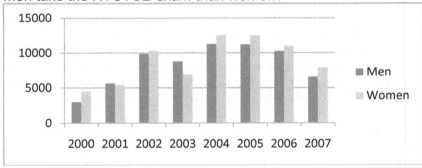

    a. None
    b. One
    c. Two
    d. Three

It may help you to simply circle the two years that answer the question. Make sure you've read the question thoroughly and once you've made your determination, double check your work. The correct answer is C.

Section 4 Helpful Hints

Study Tips

1. **You are what you eat.** Certain foods aid the learning process by releasing natural memory enhancers called CCKs (cholecystokinin) composed of tryptophan, choline, and phenylalanine. All of these chemicals enhance the neurotransmitters associated with memory and certain foods release memory enhancing chemicals. A light meal or snacks from the following foods fall into this category:

   - Milk
   - Nuts and seeds
   - Rice
   - Oats
   - Eggs
   - Turkey
   - Fish

   The better the connections, the more you comprehend!

2. **See the forest for the trees.** In other words, get the concept before you look at the details. One way to do this is to take notes as you read, paraphrasing or summarizing in your own words. Putting the concept in terms that are comfortable and familiar may increase retention.

3. **Question authority.** Ask why, why, why. Pull apart written material paragraph by paragraph and don't forget the captions under the illustrations. For example, if a heading reads *Stream Erosion* put it in the form of a question (why do streams erode? Or what is stream erosion?) then find the answer within the material. If you train your mind to think in this manner you will learn more and prepare yourself for answering test questions.

4. **Play mind games**. Using your brain for reading or puzzles keeps it flexible. Even with a limited amount of time your brain can take in data (much like a computer) and store it for later use. In ten minutes you can: read two paragraphs (at least), quiz yourself with flash cards, or review notes. Even if you don't fully understand something on the first pass, your mind stores it for recall, which is why frequent reading or review increases chances of retention and comprehension.

5. **The pen is mightier than the sword.** Learn to take great notes. A by-product of our modern culture is that we have grown accustomed to getting our information in short doses. We've subconsciously trained ourselves to assimilate information into neat little packages. Messy notes fragment the flow of information. Your notes can be much clearer with proper formatting. **The Cornell Method** is one such format. This method was popularized in *How to Study in College,* Ninth Edition, by Walter Pauk. You can benefit from the method without purchasing an additional book by simply looking the method up online. Below is a sample of how *The Cornell Method* can be adapted for use with this guide.

←— 2 ½" —→	←——————————————— 6" ———————————————→
Cue Column	**Note Taking Column**
	1. **Record:** During your reading, use the note-taking column to record important points.
	2. **Questions:** As soon as you finish a section, formulate questions based on the notes in the right-hand column. Writing questions helps to clarify meanings, reveal relationships, establish community, and strengthen memory. Also, the writing of questions sets the state for exam study later.
	3. **Recite:** Cover the note-taking column with a sheet of paper. Then, looking at the questions or cue-words in the question and cue column only, say aloud, in your own words, the answers to the questions, facts, or ideas indicated by the cue words.
	4. **Reflect:** Reflect on the material by asking yourself questions.
	5. **Review:** Spend at least ten minutes every week reviewing all your previous notes. Doing so helps you retain ideas and topics for the exam.
↑ 2" ↓	**Summary** After reading, use this space to summarize the notes from each page.

*Adapted from *How to Study in College,* Ninth Edition, by Walter Pauk, ©2008 Wadsworth

6. **Place yourself in exile and set the mood.** Set aside a particular place and time to study that best suits your personal needs and biorhythms. If you're a night person, burn the midnight oil. If you're a morning person set yourself up with some coffee and get to it. Make your study time and place as free from distraction as possible and surround yourself with what you need, be it silence or music. Studies have shown that music can aid in concentration, absorption, and retrieval of information. Not all music, though. Classical music is said to work best.

7. **Get pointed in the right direction.** Use arrows to point to important passages or pieces of information. It's easier to read than a page full of yellow highlights. Highlighting can be used sparingly, but add an arrow to the margin to call attention to it.

8. **Check your budget.** You should at least review all the content material before your test, but allocate the most amount of time to the areas that need the most refreshing. It sounds obvious, but it's easy to forget. You can use the study rubric above to balance your study budget.

> The proctor will write the start time where it can be seen and then, later, provide the time remaining, typically 15 minutes before the end of the test.

Testing Tips

1. **Get smart, play dumb.** Sometimes a question is just a question. No one is out to trick you, so don't assume that the test writer is looking for something other than what was asked. Stick to the question as written and don't overanalyze.

2. **Do a double take.** Read test questions and answer choices at least twice because it's easy to miss something, to transpose a word or some letters. If you have no idea what the correct answer is, skip it and come back later if there's time. If you're still clueless, it's okay to guess. Remember, you're scored on the number of questions you answer correctly and you're not penalized for wrong answers. The worst case scenario is that you miss a point from a good guess.

3. **Turn it on its ear.** The syntax of a question can often provide a clue, so make things interesting and turn the question into a statement to see if it changes the meaning or relates better (or worse) to the answer choices.

4. **Get out your magnifying glass.** Look for hidden clues in the questions because it's difficult to write a multiple-choice question without giving away part of the answer in the options presented. In most questions you can readily eliminate one or two potential answers, increasing your chances of answering correctly to 50/50, which will help out if you've skipped a question and gone back to it (see tip #2).

5. **Call it intuition.** Often your first instinct is correct. If you've been studying the content you've likely absorbed something and have subconsciously retained the knowledge. On questions you're not sure about trust your instincts because a first impression is usually correct.

6. **Graffiti.** Sometimes it's a good idea to mark your answers directly on the test booklet and go back to fill in the optical scan sheet later. You don't get extra points for perfectly blackened ovals. If you choose to manage your test this way, be sure not to mismark your answers when you transcribe to the scan sheet.

7. **Become a clock-watcher.** You have a set amount of time to answer the questions. Don't get bogged down laboring over a question you're not sure about when there are ten others you could answer more readily. If you choose to follow the advice of tip #6, be sure you leave time near the end to go back and fill in the scan sheet.

Do the Drill

No matter how prepared you feel it's sometimes a good idea to apply Murphy's Law. So the following tips might seem silly, mundane, or obvious, but we're including them anyway.

1. **Remember, you are what you eat, so bring a snack.** Choose from the list of energizing foods that appear earlier in the introduction.

2. **You're not too sexy for your test.** Wear comfortable clothes. You'll be distracted if your belt is too tight, or if you're too cold or too hot.

3. **Lie to yourself.** Even if you think you're a prompt person, pretend you're not and leave plenty of time to get to the testing center. Map it out ahead of time and do a dry run if you have to. There's no need to add road rage to your list of anxieties.

4. **Bring sharp, number 2 pencils.** It may seem impossible to forget this need from your school days, but you might. And make sure the erasers are intact, too.

5. **No ticket, no test.** Bring your admission ticket as well as **two** forms of identification, including one with a picture and signature. You will not be admitted to the test without these things.

6. **You can't take it with you.** Leave any study aids, dictionaries, notebooks, computers and the like at home. Certain tests **do** allow a scientific or four-function calculator, so check ahead of time if your test does.

7. **Prepare for the desert.** Any time spent on a bathroom break **cannot** be made up later, so use your judgment on the amount you eat or drink.

8. **Quiet, Please!** Keeping your own time is a good idea, but not with a timepiece that has a loud ticker. If you use a watch, take it off and place it nearby but not so that it distracts you. And **silence your cell phone.**

To the best of our ability, we have compiled the content you need to know in this book and in the accompanying online resources. The rest is up to you. You can use the study and testing tips or you can follow your own methods. Either way, you can be confident that there aren't any missing pieces of information and there shouldn't be any surprises in the content on the test.

If you have questions about test fees, registration, electronic testing, or other content verification issues please visit www.nystce.nesinc.com.

Good luck!
Sharon Wynne
Founder, XAMonline

DOMAIN I   STUDENT DEVELOPMENT AND LEARNING

COMPETENCY 001   UNDERSTAND HUMAN DEVELOPMENT,
                         INCLUDING DEVELOPMENTAL PROCESSES AND
                         VARIATIONS, AND USE THIS UNDERSTANDING
                         TO PROMOTE STUDENT DEVELOPMENT AND
                         LEARNING

Skill 1.1   Demonstrating knowledge of the major concepts, principles,
              and theories of human development (physical, cognitive,
              linguistic, social, emotional, and moral) as related to children
              from birth to grade six

Primary school teachers should have a broad knowledge and thorough understanding of the development that typically occurs during a student's formative years. More importantly, the teacher should understand how children learn best during each stage of development. The effective teacher applies knowledge of physical, social, and cognitive developmental patterns and of individual differences to meet the instructional needs of all students in the classroom. The most important premise of child development is that all domains of development (physical, social, and cognitive) are integrated. Development in each dimension is influenced by the other dimensions. Moreover, today's educator must also have knowledge of exceptionalities and how these exceptionalities affect all domains of a young child's development.

PHYSICAL DEVELOPMENT
It is important for the teacher to be aware of the physical stages of development and how changes to the child's physical attributes (which include internal developments, increased muscle capacity, improved coordination, and other attributes as well as obvious growth) affect the child's ability to learn. Factors determined by the physical stage of development include: ability to sit and attend, the need for activity, the relationship between physical coordination and self-esteem, and the degree to which physical involvement in an activity (as opposed to being able to understand an abstract concept) affects learning and the child's sense of achievement.

Early Childhood
Children ages 3.5–5 are typically referred to as preschoolers, and this age comprises the area of early childhood education. In their physicality, this age group begins to resemble miniature adults, rather than the physique of a baby. Arms and legs stretch to catch up with their torso and head, baby fat decreases, and their bodies become sleeker and ready for more complex activities. Within this age range, typical gross motor skills acquired include climbing stairs; catching, kicking, and throwing a ball; peddling; standing on one leg; jumping; and skipping. Fine motor skills include drawing a circle, triangle, square, basic

people, and large letters; zippering and buttoning; use of scissors; and twisting doorknobs and lids.

Once students enter kindergarten, they are referred to as grade-schoolers. Here, students refine the skills that they learned over the past few years, including running faster, more complex climbing, improved ball skills, and early exploration of organized sports. Fine motor development also progresses as students' drawings, lettering, and painting improves.

Early Adolescence
Early adolescence is characterized by dramatic physical changes, moving the individual from childhood toward physical maturity. Early, prepubescent changes are noted with the appearance of secondary sexual characteristics. Girls experience a concurrent rapid growth in height that occurs between the ages of about 9.5 and 14.5 years, peaking somewhere around 12 years of age. Boys experience a concurrent rapid growth in height that occurs between the ages of about 10.5 to 11 and 16 to 18, peaking around age 14.

The sudden and rapid physical changes that young adolescents experience typically cause this period of development to be one of self-consciousness, sensitivity, and concern over one's own body changes and excruciating comparisons between oneself and peers. Because physical changes may not occur in a smooth, regular schedule, adolescents may go through stages of awkwardness, both in terms of appearance and physical mobility and coordination.

COGNITIVE (ACADEMIC) DEVELOPMENT
Jean Piaget, a European scientist who studied cognitive development in the 20th century, developed many theories about the way humans learn. Most famously, he developed a theory about the stages of the development of human minds. The first stage is the **sensory-motor stage** that lasts until a child is in the toddler years. In this stage, children begin to understand their senses.

The next stage, called the **pre-operational stage**, is where children begin to understand symbols. For example, as they learn language, they begin to realize that words are symbols of thoughts, actions, items, and other elements in the world. This stage lasts into early elementary school.

The third stage is referred to as the **concrete operations stage**. This lasts until late elementary school. In this stage, children go one step beyond learning what a symbol is. They learn how to manipulate symbols, objects, and other elements. A common example of this stage is the ability to understand the displacement of water. In this stage, children can reason that a wide and short cup of water poured into a tall and thin cup of water can actually have the same amount of water.

The next stage is called the **formal operations stage**. It usually starts in adolescence or early teen years, and it continues on into adulthood. This stage allows for the development of abstract thinking, logic, critical thinking, hypothesis, systematic organization of knowledge, and other highly sophisticated thinking skills.

SOCIAL DEVELOPMENT

Children progress through a variety of social stages, beginning with an awareness of peers but a lack of concern for their presence. Young children engage in "parallel" activities playing alongside their peers without directly interacting with one another. During the primary years, children develop an intense interest in peers. They establish productive and positive social and working relationships with one another. This stage of social growth continues to increase in importance throughout the child's school years. It is necessary for the teacher to recognize the importance of developing positive peer group relationships and to provide opportunities and support for cooperative small group projects that not only develop cognitive ability but promote peer interaction.

Skill 1.2 **Identifying sequences (milestones) and variations of physical, cognitive, linguistic, social, emotional, and moral development in children from birth to grade six**

SEE also Skills 1.1 and 6.1

Teachers should have a broad knowledge and understanding of the phases of development which typically occur in each stage of life, and the teacher must be aware of how receptive children are to specific methods of instruction and learning during each period of development. It is important for the teacher to be aware of the physical stages of development and how changes to the child's physical attributes affect the child's ability to learn.

IDENTIFYING DELAYS IN COGNITIVE DEVELOPMENT

Early childhood and grade school is a critical time for learning as rapid cognitive and language development occur. Typical children begin to significantly develop language around age 2, and many other foundational aspects of learning occur at this time. Development certainly has many basic milestones in the early childhood years, and knowledge of what development is within a typical range versus what constitutes a delay is crucial for early childhood and elementary teachers. The earlier parents and teachers identify a delay, the more likely the child will make successful progress, many times eliminating the need for later special education services. Early intervention programs for delays such as speech, hearing, motor skills, social skills, and more are often available for parents and teachers.

IDENTIFYING THE MILESTONES OF COGNITIVE DEVELOPMENT

In early childhood and early elementary school years, children are in the learning stage known as pre-operational. In this stage (ages 2–7), students learn to represent objects by images, objects, signs, and words. Students this age remain quite ego-centric and have a hard time understanding that other people have a point of view or perspective.

Later in elementary school (around age 8), students begin to transition into the next stage of learning, known as the concrete operational stage. In this stage, intelligence is demonstrated through logical and systematic manipulation of symbols related to concrete objects. Operational thinking develops (mental actions that are reversible), egocentric thought gradually diminishes, and students begin to think concretely and logically about concepts and ideas.

At this stage of development, the student is becoming able to accept, process, comprehend, and retain more challenging concepts, materials, instruction, and skills. Learning from instruction through multiple perspectives is more effective as the student's mind is less focused on the self and the environment that supports the self. The increasing ability to use reason and think abstractly during this stage of development makes the mind more receptive to varied input and able to process this input without suffering intellectual "overload." But, of course, not all young minds are cognitively receptive to the same degree at the same age or grade level. Providing all students with the same knowledge base and the same skills can be challenging in a cognitively diverse classroom.

Around the beginning of middle school (age 11 through to high school), concrete operation thinkers begin to move toward the formal operational stage (generally, identified with full adolescence and adulthood), where intelligence is demonstrated through the logical use of symbols related to abstract concepts. Students can really begin to consider abstract concepts, representations, and various perspectives, probabilities, and ideologies. Students at this age are capable of creating hypotheses, testing them, anticipating outcomes, and engaging in higher levels of problem solving.

Skill 1.3   **Recognizing the range of individual developmental differences in children within any given age group from birth to grade six and the implications of this developmental variation for instructional decision making**

Those who study childhood development recognize that young students grow and mature in common, recognizable patterns, but at different rates that cannot be effectively accelerated. This can result in variance in the academic performance of different children in the same classroom. With the establishment of inclusion as a standard in the classroom, it is necessary for all teachers to understand that variation in development among the student population is another aspect of diversity within the classroom. This has implications for the ways in which instruction is planned and delivered and the ways in which students learn and are evaluated.

Knowledge of age-appropriate expectations is fundamental to the teacher's positive relationship with students and effective instructional strategies. Equally important is the knowledge of what is individually appropriate for the specific children in a classroom.

Developmentally oriented teachers approach classroom groups and individual students with a respect for their emerging capabilities. Developmentalists recognize that kids grow in common patterns but at different rates that usually cannot be accelerated by adult pressure or input. Developmentally oriented teachers know that variance in the school performance of different children often results from differences in their general growth.

The requirement for students within a diverse classroom to acquire the same academic skills (at the same levels) can sometimes be achieved with programmed learning instructional materials. While not widely available for every subject, at every level, a great deal of useful material is in publication. Professional teachers familiar with the format have often created their own modules for student use to be incorporated within their lesson planning.

SEE also Skills 1.4, 1.5, and 1.6

Skill 1.4   Identifying ways in which a child's development in one domain (physical, cognitive, linguistic, social, emotional, moral) may affect learning and development in other domains

UNDERSTANDING DOMAINS OF DEVELOPMENT

Child development does not occur in a vacuum. Each element of development impacts other elements of development. A significant premise in the study of child development holds that all domains of development (physical, social, and academic) are integrated. Development in each dimension is influenced by the others. For example, as cognitive development progresses, social development often follows.

When it is said that development takes place within domains, it is simply meant that different aspects of a human are undergoing change. For example, physical changes take place (e.g., body growth, sexuality); cognitive changes take place (e.g., better ability to reason); linguistic changes take place (e.g., a child's vocabulary develops further); social changes take place (e.g., figuring out identity); emotional changes take place (e.g., changes in ability to be concerned about other people); and moral changes take place (e.g., testing limits).

Developmental Advancement
Developmental advances within the domains occur neither simultaneously nor parallel to one another, necessarily. People often comment that adolescents develop slower in the physical domain than they do in the social or cognitive domain (e.g., they may think like teenagers, but they still look like children), however, the truth is that even in such cases, physical development is under progress—just not as evident on the surface. And as children develop physically, they develop the dexterity to demonstrate cognitive development, such as writing something on a piece of paper (in this case, this is cognitive development that only can be demonstrated by physical development). Or, as they develop emotionally, they learn to be more sensitive to others and therefore enhance social development.

What does this mean for teachers? The concept of latent development is particularly important. While teachers may not see some aspects of development present in their students, other areas of development may give clues as to a child's current or near-future capabilities. For example, as students' linguistic development increases, observable ability may not be present (i.e., a student may know a word but cannot quite use it yet). As the student develops emotionally and socially, the ability to use more advanced words and sentence structures develops because the student will have a greater need to express him or herself.

An important thing to remember about adolescent development within each of these domains is that they are not exclusive. For example, physical and emotional development are tied intricately, particularly when one feels awkward about his or her body, when emotional feelings are tied to sexuality, or when one feels that he or she does not look old enough (as rates of growth are obviously not similar). Moral and cognitive development often goes hand in hand when an adolescent gives reasons for behavior or searches for role models.

In general, by understanding that developmental domains are not exclusive, teachers can identify current needs of students better and they can plan for future instructional activities meant to assist students as they develop into adults.

Skill 1.5   Applying knowledge of developmental characteristics of learners from birth to grade six to evaluate alternative instructional goals and plans

ADDRESSING YOUNG LEARNERS
Until pre-adolescence, students do not think in abstract forms. They are able to understand symbols, but deep symbolism is not yet comprehended. For example, language is a symbol, and they can understand that certain words symbolize things, actions, emotions, etc. But they do not yet have the ability to see how symbolism works in a story as well as an adolescent would.

When it is said that young children are concrete thinkers, it means that they are driven by senses. In other words, they are very literal thinkers. If they can see something, hear something, or feel something, they are more likely to believe it—and learn it.

Therefore, the more teachers can utilize this concrete thinking, the better their students will master grade-level standards at this age. Take the example of math. Ever wonder why young children always count with their fingers? This is because even though they might be able to do it in their heads, seeing it (and feeling it, as they move their fingers) makes it more "real" to them. So, instead of teaching math through words and numbers on a chalkboard, teachers can be more effective at teaching math through **manipulatives**. By simply putting objects on a table, having students count the objects, taking away a certain number and having them re-count the left-over objects, students are more likely to understand the CONCEPT of subtraction.

Many reading teachers have learned that students can comprehend stories better if they get a chance to dramatize the story. In other words, they "act out" a story, and thereby learn what the words mean more clearly than they could have if they just read it and talked about it.

The whole concept of science laboratory learning in elementary school is founded on the idea that students will be more successful learning concepts if they use their hands, eyes, ears, noses, etc., in the learning process. Many concepts that would otherwise be very difficult for students to learn can be attained very quickly in a laboratory setting.

Skill 1.6 Selecting appropriate instructional strategies, approaches, and delivery systems to promote development in given learners from birth to grade six

SELECTING ACTIVITIES
The effective teacher is aware of students' individual learning styles and human growth and development theory and applies these principles in the selection and implementation of appropriate instructional activities.

Learning activities selected for younger students (below age eight) should focus on short time frames in highly simplified form. The nature of the activity and the content in which the activity is presented affects the approach that the students will take in processing the information. Younger children tend to process information at a slower rate than older children (age eight and older).

INSTRUCTIONAL PLANNING
Implementing such a child-centered curriculum is the result of very careful and deliberate planning. Well thought-out planning includes specifying behavioral objectives, specifying students' entry behavior (knowledge and skills), selecting

and sequencing learning activities so as to move students from entry behavior to objective, and evaluating the outcomes of instruction in order to improve planning.

Planning for instructional activities entails identification or selection of the activities the teacher and students will engage in during a period of instruction. Planning is a multifaceted activity which includes the following considerations:

- The determination of the order in which activities will be completed
- The specification of the component parts of an activity, including their order
- The materials to be used for each part
- The particular roles of the teacher and students
- Decisions about the amount of time to be spent on a given activity
- The number of activities to be completed during a period of instruction
- Judgment of the appropriateness of an activity for a particular situation
- Specifications of the organization of the class for the activity

Attention to learner needs during planning is foremost and includes identification of that which the students already know or need to know; the matching of learner needs with instructional elements such as content, materials, activities, and goals; and the determination of whether or not students have performed at an acceptable level following instruction.

CHILD-CENTERED TEACHING

The effective teacher selects learning activities based on specific learning objectives. Ideally, teachers should not plan activities that fail to augment the specific objectives of the lesson. Additionally, selected learning objectives should be consistent with state and district educational goals that focus on national educational goals (Goals 2000) and the specific strengths and weaknesses of individual students assigned to the teacher's class.

The effective teacher takes care to select appropriate activities and classroom situations in which learning is optimized. The classroom teacher should manipulate instructional activities and classroom conditions in a manner that enhances group and individual learning opportunities. For example, the classroom teacher can organize group learning activities in which students are placed in a situation in which cooperation, sharing ideas, and discussion occurs. Cooperative learning activities can assist students in learning to collaborate and share personal and cultural ideas and values in a classroom learning environment.

If an educational program is child-centered, then it will surely address the abilities and needs of the students because it will take its cues from students' interests, concerns, and questions. Making an educational program child-centered involves building on the natural curiosity children bring to school, and asking children what they want to learn.

Teachers help students to identify their own questions, puzzles, and goals, and then structure for them widening circles of experience and investigation of those topics. Teachers manage to infuse all the skills, knowledge, and concepts that society mandates into a child-driven curriculum. This does not mean passive teachers who respond only to students' explicit cues. Teachers also draw on their understanding of children's developmentally characteristic needs and enthusiasms to design experiences that lead children into areas they might not choose but that they do enjoy and that engage them. Teachers also bring their own interests and enthusiasms into the classroom to share and to act as a motivational means of guiding children.

COMPETENCY 002 UNDERSTAND LEARNING PROCESSES, AND USE THIS UNDERSTANDING TO PROMOTE STUDENT DEVELOPMENT AND LEARNING

Skill 2.1 Analyzing ways in which development and learning processes interact

Anyone who has been in an early childhood or elementary school classroom knows that students do not sit still and focus on one thing for too long. Some people joke that the age of a person equals the amount of time the person is willing to sit and listen for any one time. So, a kindergartener, under this premise, would only be able to sit and concentrate on one thing for five to six minutes.

Good teachers know how to capitalize on the need of children to move and change topics. Generally, young children should be changing academic activities every 15-20 minutes. This means that if a teacher wants to fill a block of two hours for literacy learning in the morning, the teacher should have about 6-8 activities planned. Here is an example:

1. Teacher has students write something to access background knowledge; in kindergarten, this might include just a picture, but in grade four, this might include a paragraph
2. Teacher might spend a few minutes asking students what they wrote about in a large group
3. Teacher might introduce a new book by doing a "book walk"—looking at the title, the pictures, etc.
4. Teacher reads book aloud as students follow along
5. Students do a pair-share where they turn to their neighbors to discuss a question
6. Students return to desks to do a comprehension activity on their own
7. Whole class discussion of what they wrote
8. Students go to centers to practice specific skills as teacher works with small groups of students
9. Teacher conducts a vocabulary activity with the whole class

Teachers who switch things around like this are more likely to keep their students' attention, engage their students more, and have a more behaved classroom. When children get bored, they obviously will start to not pay attention, and many will become disruptive. The key is to keep them interested in what they are learning.

Skill 2.2 **Analyzing processes by which students construct meaning and develop skills, and applying strategies to facilitate learning in given situations (e.g., by building connections between new information and prior knowledge; by relating learning to world issues and community concerns; by engaging students in purposeful practice and application of knowledge and skills; by using tools, materials, and resources)**

SEE also Skill 2.4.

BEHAVIORAL AND COGNITIVE LEARNING

First, teachers should realize that historically, there are two broad sides regarding the construction of meaning, the application of strategies, etc. One is behavioral learning. **Behavioral learning theory** suggests that people learn socially or through some sort of stimulation or repetition. The other broad theory is cognitive. **Cognitive learning theories** suggest that learning takes place in the mind, and that the mind processes ideas through brain mapping and connections with other material and experiences. In other words, with behaviorism, learning is somewhat external. We see something, for example, and then we copy it. With cognitive theories, learning is internal. For example, we see something, analyze it in our minds, and make sense of it for ourselves. Then, if we choose to copy it, we do, but we do so having internalized the process.

There are several cognitive educational learning theories that can be applied to classroom practices. One classic learning theory is Piaget's stages of development, which consists of four learning stages: sensory motor stage (from birth to age 2); pre-operation stages (ages 2 to 7 or early elementary); concrete operational (ages 7 to 11 or upper elementary); and formal operational (ages 11-high school). Piaget believed children passed through this series of stages to develop from the most basic forms of concrete thinking to sophisticated levels of abstract thinking. For more information on Piaget's stages of development, see Skill 1.1.

The **metacognition learning theory** deals with "the study of how to help the learner gain understanding about how knowledge is constructed and about the conscious tools for constructing that knowledge" (Joyce and Weil 1996). The cognitive approach to learning involves the teacher's understanding that teaching the student to process his/her own learning and mastery of skill provides the greatest learning and retention opportunities in the classroom. Students are taught to develop concepts and teach themselves skills in problem solving and critical thinking. The student becomes an active participant in the learning process, and the teacher facilitates that conceptual and cognitive learning process.

Skill 2.3   Demonstrating knowledge of different types of learning strategies (e.g., rehearsal, elaboration, organization, metacognition) and how learners use each type of strategy

LEARNING STRATEGIES

Learning strategies are methods of teaching content to students. There are many theories on how best to reach content objectives within a classroom. It is important for teachers to accumulate an effective "tool box," or a variety of strategies and tactics, in order to help both individual students and the entire classroom succeed. It is also important for teachers to utilize proper metacognition skills (or thinking about the mental processes of students) to review and modify learning strategies and tactics, create challenging goals and objectives, use appropriate assessments, and find out through experience and peer review what works best in certain situations.

The Behaviorist Model

As stated in Skill 2.2, the most basic learning strategy is the behaviorist model. In this model the teacher puts forth an objective that students should reach. Success is based on mastering the objective's knowledge or skills. In other words, students learn to master behaviors. This is often seen as a passive learning strategy where there is lectured content and students need to memorize and practice the content to succeed.

The Constructivist Model

SEE Skill 2.4 for information relating to the Constructivist Model.

Learning Tactics

While learning strategies are philosophies on how to best teach a single student or a group of students, all teachers use a variety of learning tactics to accomplish objectives. Some of these tactics include **rehearsal**, **elaboration**, **organization**, and **metacognition**. Learning tactics should be consistent with the learning strategy that the teacher has chosen.

For example, if a teacher prefers a behaviorist model for a particular group of students, s/he might use rehearsal, or mnemonic devices, to encourage memorization of vital concepts. Rehearsal is a tactic that relates to recitation of material in order to lay the groundwork for the basic knowledge needed to engage a topic. Most rote learning is done in this way. Mnemonic devices are used to memorize concepts by creatively grouping them together. A well-known mnemonic device is creating an acronym out of the concepts needing memorization. An example of this is PEMDAS for the order of mathematical operations (one performs the operations within parenthesis first, then figures the exponents; multiplication is done before division; lastly, one adds before subtracting). Behavioral tactics can also be as simple as teaching note-taking and organizational skills that will pay dividends throughout a student's education.

A tactic that encourages the constructivist learning strategy would be self-questioning: students create questions in order to direct their learning towards the things they most need to know. This tactic gives the student the chance to discover the components of a good primary question and then how to follow up with further clarifying questions that aim for more concise information. Another constructivist tactic is elaboration.

Elaboration relies on concepts the student already knows and is an excellent way to increase confidence. The student must expand or elaborate upon the target information in some prescribed fashion. Examples include creating an analogy (for instance, an election campaign might be like a "battle" in which two sides are trying to employ their own strengths and exploit their opponent's weaknesses and the outcome may affect large populations), or establishing a relationship (plant respiration is the opposite of human respiration).

Brain Based Learning

Recently developed, brain-based learning is a strategy related to the constructivist model. Based on a popular 1998 book by Eric Jensen, *Teaching with the Brain in Mind*, the brain-based model attempts to achieve the objectives of a school district's learning standards through both the child's search for meaning and pattern-recognition.

A common teaching tactic used that provides visual meaning and a discernible pattern is the graphic organizer. For example, Venn-Diagrams show differences and similarities between two objects; timelines exhibit a sequence of events; pyramid style organizers display importance or hierarchy. Graphic organizers present patterns that the brain can easily recognize and evaluate. A math-based variation of this brain-based learning tactic is to ask students to make a poster displaying all the mathematical operations they might use to get the answer 81. Students would then display their work and the class would tour the posters to learn cooperatively.

Project Based Learning

Project-based learning is a comprehensive learning strategy and takes careful planning, usually between two or more faculty members. Students participate in content input, guided and individual practice, projects, and assessments within an interdisciplinary array of skills from math, language arts, fine arts, geography, science, and technology.

Some teachers have labeled this the "middle school model" and, since middle schools and junior high schools are often separated into teams that divide the core subjects among four or five teachers who plan together frequently, the name is appropriate. However, elementary teachers who are responsible for all of their students' core subjects have also found great success with project-based learning. Connections between the core subjects can be made while the classroom studies central topics like the American Civil War, Alternative Energy

Sources, or The Diary of Anne Frank. Each unit might take a marking period or a semester, depending upon the school calendar and how creative faculty members can be.

Expeditionary learning schools center their academic year on project-based learning units and tied-in authentic experiences. A topic begins with a "kick-off" that might include a guest speaker or field trip, and finishes with a "culminating event" of student demonstrations in front of an audience of family members, school community, and the general public. Many tactics from other learning strategies are utilized among the core team of teachers in project-based learning and there is constant feedback and revision.

SEE Skill 2.4 for information about the learning strategies of differentiated instruction, constructivism, and cooperative learning.

Skill 2.4   Analyzing factors that affect students' learning (e.g., learning styles, contextually supported learning versus decontextualized learning), and adapting instructional practices to promote learning in given situations

SEE also Skill 12.2.

ADDRESSING LEARNING DIFFERENCES
No two students are alike. It follows, then, that no students *learn* alike. To apply a one-dimensional instructional approach is to impose learning limits on students. All students have the right to an education, but there cannot be a singular path to that education. A teacher must acknowledge the variety of learning styles and abilities among students within a class (and, indeed, the varieties from class to class) and apply multiple instructional and assessment processes to ensure that every child has appropriate opportunities to master the subject matter, demonstrate such mastery, and improve and enhance learning skills with each lesson.

DIFFERENTIATED INSTRUCTION
The effective teacher will seek to connect all students to the subject matter through multiple techniques, with the goal that each student, through their own abilities, will relate to one or more techniques and excel in the learning process. Differentiated instruction encompasses several areas:

- **Content**: What is the teacher going to teach? Or, better put, what does the teacher want the students to learn? Differentiating content means that students will have access to content that piques their interest about a topic, with a complexity that provides an appropriate challenge to their intellectual development.
- **Process**: A classroom management technique where instructional organization and delivery is maximized for the diverse student group.

These techniques should include dynamic, flexible grouping activities, where instruction and learning occurs both as whole-class, teacher-led activities, as well as peer learning and teaching (while teacher observes and coaches) within small groups or pairs.

- **Product**: The expectations and requirements placed on students to demonstrate their knowledge or understanding. The type of product expected from each student should reflect each student's own capabilities.

CONSTRUCTIVISM

For constructivist teachers, the belief is that students create their own reality of knowledge and how to process and observe the world around them. Students are constantly constructing new ideas, which serve as frameworks for learning and teaching.

Researchers have shown that the constructivist model is comprised of the four components:

1. Learner creates knowledge
2. Learner constructs and makes meaningful new knowledge to existing knowledge
3. Learner shapes and constructs knowledge by life experiences and social interactions
4. In constructivist learning communities, the student, teacher and classmates establish knowledge cooperatively on a daily basis

Constructivist learning for students is dynamic and ongoing. For constructivist teachers, the classroom becomes a place where students are encouraged to interact with the instructional process by asking questions and posing new ideas to old theories. The use of cooperative learning that encourages students to work in supportive learning environments using their own ideas to stimulate questions and propose outcomes is a major aspect of a constructivist classroom.

COOPERATIVE LEARNING

Cooperative learning situations, as practiced in today's classrooms, grew out of searches conducted by several groups in the early 1970's. Cooperative learning situations can range from very formal applications such as STAD (Student Teams-Achievement Divisions) and CIRC (Cooperative Integrated Reading and Composition) to less formal groupings known variously as "group investigation," "learning together," and "discovery groups." Cooperative learning as a general term is now firmly recognized and established as a teaching and learning technique in American schools.

Since cooperative learning techniques are so widely diffused in the schools, it is necessary to orient students in the skills by which cooperative learning groups can operate smoothly, and thereby enhance learning. Students who cannot interact constructively with other students will not be able to take advantage of the learning opportunities provided by the cooperative learning situations and will furthermore deprive their fellow students of the opportunity for cooperative learning.

These skills form the hierarchy of cooperation in which students first learn to work together as a group, so they may then proceed to levels at which they may engage in simulated conflict situations. This cooperative setting allows different points of view to be constructively entertained.

Most classrooms contain a mixture of the following:

- Differences among learners, classroom settings, and academic outcomes
- Biological, sociological, ethnicity, socioeconomic status, psychological needs, learning modalities, and styles among learners
- Differences in classroom settings that promote learning opportunities such as collaborative, participatory, and individualized learning groupings
- Expected learning outcomes that are theoretical, affective, and cognitive for students

APPLYING LEARNING THEORY IN THE CLASSROOM

No one theory will work for every classroom and a good approach is to incorporate a range of learning styles in a classroom. Still, under the guidance of any theory, good educators will differentiate their instructional practices to meet the needs of their students' abilities and interests using various instructional practices. Today, even though behavioral theories exist, most educators believe that children learn cognitively.

For example, when teachers introduce new topics by relating those topics to information students are already familiar with or exposed to (**prior knowledge**), they are expecting that students will be able to better integrate new information into their memories by attaching it to something that is already there. Cognitively, this makes a great deal of sense. Think of a file cabinet. When we already have files for certain things, it's easy for us to find a file and throw new information into it. When we are given something that does not fit into one of the pre-existing files, we struggle to know what to do with it. The same is true with human minds.

The teacher will, of course, have certain expectations regarding where the students will be physically and intellectually when he/she plans for a new class. However, there will be wide variations in the actual classroom. If he/she does not make the extra effort to understand where there are deficiencies and where there are strengths in the individual students, the planning will probably miss the mark, at least for some members of the class. This can be obtained through a review of student records, by observation, and by testing.

Skill 2.5   **Recognizing how various teacher roles (e.g., direct instructor, facilitator) and student roles (e.g., self-directed learner, group participant, passive observer) may affect learning processes and outcomes**

THE ROLES OF TEACHERS

Teaching consists of a multitude of roles. Teachers must plan and deliver instruction in a creative and innovating way so that students find learning both fun and intriguing. The teacher must also research various learning strategies, decide which to implement in the classroom, and balance that information according to the various learning styles of the students. Teachers must facilitate all aspects of the lesson including preparation and organization of materials, delivery of instruction, and management of student behavior and attention.

Simultaneously, the teacher must also observe for student learning, interactions, and on-task behavior while making mental or written notes regarding what is working in the lesson and how the students are receiving and utilizing the information. This will provide the teacher with immediate feedback as to whether to continue with the lesson, or if it is necessary to slow the instruction or present the lesson in another way. Teachers must also work collaboratively with other adults in the room and utilize them to maximize student learning. The teacher's job requires the teacher to establish a delicate balance among all these factors.

Handling the Balance

How the teacher handles this balance depends on the teaching style of the teacher and/or lesson. Cooperative learning will require the teacher to have organized materials ready, perhaps even with instructions for the students as well. The teacher should conduct a great deal of observations during this type of lesson. Direct instruction methods will require the teacher to have an enthusiastic, yet organized, approach to the lesson. When teaching directly to students, the teacher must take care to keep the lesson student-centered and intriguing while presenting accurate information.

There are a variety of ways a teacher can plan to implement instruction to enhance student learning. Hands-on lessons that keep students engaged are ideal for maintaining students' interest. The way a teacher groups and arranges students for such lessons is important to keeping students engaged.

Students can be taught the skills that lead to factual recall, and beginning to teach those skills at even very early grades will result in more successful students. It is important for teachers to vary their instructional techniques because experiencing a fact or an idea in several different ways or through multiple senses increases the ability to recall it.

ROLES IN THE CLASSROOM
In today's classrooms, the role of the teacher has evolved to more of a facilitator of learning, rather than the old-fashioned direct source of all information. In a learner-centered classroom, the teacher fosters learning by creating an information-rich atmosphere that is safe, structured, and organized. The teacher is still the leader, but in a different way than in the past—not in the sense that they *literally* lead the class each day, but that they lead the students, including their parents, to success.

So if the teacher's role has changed so much, it is expected that the student's role has changed as well. Students today are expected to do more than sit in silence and simply listen. In the mini-community effective teachers establish, the student now must take on the role of an active participant responsible for their own learning. The students are the researchers, the discussion leaders, the problem solvers, the question askers, the writers, the readers, the presenters, in the classroom today, which drastically impacts a higher level of learning and overall knowledge. Obviously, this role is smaller with the younger students, but good school systems will develop this student independence through staff development. Thus, it is a gradual shift to increased student independence as the years progress.

Skill 2.6 **Recognizing effective strategies for promoting independent thinking and learning (e.g., by helping students develop critical-thinking, decision-making, and problem-solving skills; by enabling students to pursue topics of personal interest) and for promoting students' sense of ownership and responsibility in relation to their own learning**

If a teacher can help students to take responsibility for their own ideas and thoughts, much has been accomplished. They will only reach that level in a non-judgmental environment, an environment that does not permit criticism of the ideas of others and that accepts any topic for discussion that is in the realm of appropriateness. Success in problem solving boosts students' confidence and makes them more willing to take risks, and the teacher must provide those opportunities for success.

DEVELOP SUCCESS-ORIENTED ACTIVITIES
Success-oriented activities are tasks that are selected to meet the individual needs of the student. During the time a student is learning a new skill, tasks should be selected so that the student will be able to earn a high percentage of correct answers during the teacher questioning and seatwork portions of the lesson. Later, the teacher should also include work that challenges students to apply what they have learned and stimulate their thinking.

Skill knowledge, strategy use, motivation, and personal interests are all factors that influence individual student success. The student who cannot be bothered with reading the classroom textbook may be highly motivated to read the rulebook for the latest video game. Students who did not master their multiplication tables will likely have problems working with fractions.

In the success-oriented classroom, mistakes are viewed as a natural part of the learning process. The teacher can also show that adults make mistakes by correcting errors without getting unduly upset. The students feel safe to try new things because they know that they have a supportive environment and can correct their mistakes.

Activities for Student Success
Activities that promote student success:

1. Are based on useful, relevant content that is clearly specified, and organized for easy learning
2. Allow sufficient time to learn the skill and is selected for high rate of success
3. Allow students the opportunity to work independently, self-monitor, and set goals
4. Provide for frequent monitoring and corrective feedback
5. Include collaboration in group activities or peer teaching

Students with learning problems often attribute their successes to luck or ease of the task. Their failures are often blamed on their supposed lack of ability, difficulty of the task, or the fault of someone else. Successful activities, attribution retraining, and learning strategies can help these students to discover that they can become independent learners. When the teacher communicates the expectation that the students can be successful learners and chooses activities that will help them be successful, achievement is increased.

CRITICAL THINKING SKILLS
A critical thinking skill is a skill target that teachers help students develop to sustain learning in specific subject areas that can be applied within other subject areas. The effective teacher uses advanced communication skills such as clarification, reflection, perception, and summarization as a means to facilitate communication and a community of learning.

Higher Order Thinking Skills
Bloom's taxonomy references six skill levels within the cognitive domain: knowledge, comprehension, application, analysis, synthesis, and evaluation. Higher-order thinking skills, often referred to as HOTS, refer to the top three levels of Bloom's Taxonomy: analysis, synthesis, and evaluation. They are the skills that most apply to critically thinking through information and not simply absorbing it. It is crucial for students to use and refine these skills because they are truly what enable us to learn more sophisticated content and apply our

learning to novel situations, skills that apply to life and work success beyond school.

Low Order Questioning

Low order questions (recall, knowledge, define, analyze, etc.) are useful to begin the process. They insure the student is focused on the required information and understands what needs to be included in the thinking process. For example, if the objective is for students to be able to read and understand the story "Goldilocks and the Three Bears," the teacher may wish to start with low order questions (i.e., "What are some things Goldilocks did while in the bears' home?" [Knowledge] or "Why didn't Goldilocks like the Papa Bear's chair?" [Analysis]).

Students use basic skills to understand things that are read such as a reading passage or a math word problem or directions for a project. However, students should also apply critical thinking skills to fully comprehend how what was read could be applied to their own life or how to make comparatives or choices based on the factual information given.

Using Higher Order Questioning in the Classroom

Teachers who want their educational objectives to use higher level thinking skills need to direct students to these higher levels on the taxonomy. Questioning is an effective tool to build up students to these higher levels. Through a series of questions, the teacher can move the students up the taxonomy. (For example, "If Goldilocks had come to your house, what are some things she may have used?" [Application], "How might the story have differed if Goldilocks had visited the three fishes?" [Synthesis], or "Do you think Goldilocks was good or bad? Why?" [Evaluation]). The teacher, through questioning, can control the thinking process of the class. As students become more involved in the discussion they are systematically being lead to higher level thinking.

TEACHER-DIRECTED TO SELF-DIRECTED ACTIVITY

Learning progresses in stages from initial acquisition, when the student needs a lot of teacher guidance and instruction, to adaptation, when the student can apply what he or she has learned to new situations outside the classroom. As students progress through the stages of learning, the teacher gradually decreases the amount of direct instruction and guidance and encourages the student to function independently. The ultimate goal of the learning process is to teach students how to be independent and apply their knowledge.

A summary of these states and their features appears here:

State	Teacher Activity	Emphasis
Initial Acquisition	• Provide rationale • Guidance • Demonstration • Modeling • Shaping • Cueing	• Errorless learning • Backward Chaining (working from the final product backward through the steps) • Forward Chaining (proceeding through the steps to a final product)
Advanced Acquisition	• Feedback • Error correction • Specific directions	• Criterion evaluation • Reinforcement and reward for accuracy
Proficiency	• Positive reinforcement • Progress monitoring • Teach self-management • Increased teacher expectations	• Increase speed or performance to the automatic level with accuracy • Set goals • Self-management
Maintenance	• Withdraw direct reinforcement • Retention and memory • Over learning • Intermittent schedule of reinforcement	• Maintain high level of performance • Mnemonic techniques • Social and intrinsic reinforcement
Generalization	• Corrective feedback	• Perform skill in different times and places
Adaptation	• Stress independent problem-solving	• Independent problem-solving methods • No direct guidance or direct instruction

COMPETENCY 003   UNDERSTAND HOW FACTORS IN THE HOME, SCHOOL, AND COMMUNITY MAY AFFECT STUDENTS' DEVELOPMENT AND READINESS TO LEARN; AND USE THIS UNDERSTANDING TO CREATE A CLASSROOM ENVIRONMENT WITHIN WHICH ALL STUDENTS CAN DEVELOP AND LEARN

Skill 3.1   Recognizing the impact of sociocultural factors (e.g., culture, heritage, language, socioeconomic profile) in the home, school, and community on students' development and learning

SEE Skill 5.2.

Skill 3.2   Analyzing ways in which student's personal health, safety, nutrition, and past or present exposure to abusive or dangerous environments may affect their development and learning in various domains (e.g., physical, cognitive, linguistic, social, emotional, moral) and their readiness to learn

PRENATAL CONCERNS
Issues of physical health might include the prenatal exposure to drugs, alcohol, or nicotine. In all cases, moderate to severe brain damage is possible; however, more subtle impairment can also occur (trouble with breathing, attention deficit disorder, etc.). For example, prenatal exposure to marijuana is harmful to the infant and has later developmental repercussions. It damages forming brain cells in an unborn fetus and harms existing brain cells in a student. Because drugs, alcohol, and nicotine can impair brain development, children exposed to such things in the womb may need significant extra classroom support. Some of these children will also need to be referred to the Special Education teacher in order to be tested for learning disabilities.

EARLY CHILDHOOD AND ELEMENTARY CHANGES
The early childhood and elementary years are both a time of rapid physical growth. Teachers must consider these tremendous changes and how they can affect learning in the classroom.

Nutrition and Sleep
At any age, but especially with younger students, day-to-day issues such as lack of sufficient sleep or nutrition can harm children. While a child who has had sleep disruptions or insufficient nutrition can bounce back easily when these are attended to, it is often the case that children living in environments where sleep and proper nutrition are not available will continue to struggle through childhood. Symptoms of a lack of nutrition and sleep most notably include a lack of

concentration, particularly in the classroom. Furthermore, children who lack sufficient sleep or nutrition may become agitated more easily than other children.

Through federal and local funds, many schools are able to provide free or reduced-price breakfasts and lunches for children; however, some children may not get a decent dinner, and during weekends and holidays, they may struggle even more.

ADOLESCENT CHANGES

Like younger students, students at the middle and early high school level are continually undergoing physical and emotional changes and development. No matter how well educators might try to prepare them for this, they have no point of reference within their own life experiences for such changes. Everything that is occurring to them is new and unfamiliar and often makes them uncomfortable about themselves and in the company of others. Often these physical, hormonal, and emotional changes will occur in spurts, moving some ahead of their peers and leaving some behind. In most cases, the individual feels different and often is treated as different by his or her peers. The student may feel socially awkward, and this may be reflected in schoolwork and especially in classroom participation. The teacher must be sensitive to the issues of a developing child and aware of the impact this may have on student learning, classroom decorum, and the cohesion among classmates which the teacher is trying to foster.

ABUSE

At any age and in any community, abuse can occur. Abuse can take the form of emotional and/or physical abuse, and it can severely increase the risk of lower academic achievement. Maltreated children experience such emotional trauma that it can lead to less focus and motivation in school (therefore, less academic learning), increased social problems, and lower emotional stability. Once lower achievement is realized by these students, they often continue along this path of failure and are more likely to display behavior problems and engage in risky behaviors as they age. Teachers must be able to recognize possible signs of abuse and know the proper approach in their school district for reporting possible cases of child abuse.

LACK OF AFFECTION AND ATTENTION

When children are emotionally neglected or have recently endured family upsets, their level of attention toward school will be greatly reduced. They may also show signs of jealousy towards other children or they may feel a sense of anger toward other children, the teacher, or their parents. Aggression is a very common behavior of emotionally neglected children.

When a child has had little verbal interaction, the symptoms can be similar to the symptoms of abuse or neglect. The child might have a "deer in the headlights" look and maintain a very socially awkward set of behaviors. In general, such a child will have a drastically reduced ability to express him or herself in words and often uses aggression as a tool to get his or her thoughts across.

Although cognitive ability is not lost due to such circumstances (abuse, neglect, emotional upset, lack of verbal interaction), the child will most likely not be able to provide as much intellectual energy as the child not experiencing these issues. Note though that the classroom can be seen as a "safe" place by a child, so it is imperative that teachers be attentive to the needs and emotions of their students.

SENSE OF SELF

Helping students to develop healthy self-images and self-worth are integral to the learning and development experiences. For students who are experiencing negative self-image and peer isolation, learning is not necessarily the top priority. When a student is attending school from a homeless shelter, is living through a parental divorce, or feeling a need to conform to fit into a certain student group, the student is being compromised and may be unable to effectively navigate the educational process or engage in the required academic expectations towards graduation or promotion to the next grade level or subject core level.

Most schools offer health classes that address issues around sexuality, self-image, peer pressure, nutrition, wellness, gang activity, drug engagement, and a variety of other relevant experiences. Some schools have contracted with outside agencies to develop collaborative partnerships to bring in after-school tutorial classes; often, these are gender and cultural specific groupings where students can deal authentically with integration of cultural and ethnic experiences and lifestyles. Drug intervention programs and speakers on gang issues have created dynamic opportunities for school communities to bring the "undiscussable" issues to the forefront.

WHEN TO BE CONCERNED

Lying, stealing, and fighting are atypical behaviors that most children may exhibit occasionally, but if a child lies, steals, or fights regularly or blatantly, these behaviors may be indicative of emotional distress. Emotional disturbances in childhood are not uncommon and take a variety of forms. Usually these problems show up in the form of uncharacteristic behaviors. Most of the time, children respond favorably to brief treatment programs of psychotherapy. At other times, disturbances may need more intensive therapy and are harder to resolve. All stressful behaviors need to be addressed, and any type of chronic antisocial behavior needs to be examined as a possible symptom of deep-seated emotional upset.

Skill 3.3   **Recognizing the significance of family life and the home environment for student development and learning (e.g., nature of the expectations of parents, guardians, and caregivers; degree of their involvement in the student's education)**

PARENTAL AND FAMILY INFLUENCES

Attitude, resources, and encouragement available in the home environment may be attributes for success or failure.

Family Income Level

Families with higher incomes are often able to provide increased opportunities for students. Students from lower income families may need to depend on the resources available from the school system and the community. These resources should be orchestrated by the classroom teacher in cooperation with school administrators and educational advocates in the community.

Family Educational Level

Family members with higher levels of education often serve as models for students, and have high expectations for academic success. And families with specific aspirations for children (often, regardless of their own educational background) encourage students to achieve academic success, and are most often active participants in the process.

Family Stability Level

A family in crisis (caused by economic difficulties, divorce, substance abuse, physical abuse, etc.) creates a negative environment that may have a profound impact on all aspects of a student's life and particularly his or her ability to function academically. The situation may require professional intervention. It is often the classroom teacher who will recognize a family in crisis situation and instigate an intervention by reporting on this to school or civil authorities.

Regardless of the positive or negative impacts on the student's education from outside sources, it is the teacher's responsibility to ensure that all students in the classroom have an equal opportunity for academic success. This begins with the teacher's statement of high expectations for every student and develops through planning, delivery, and evaluation of instruction that provides for inclusion and ensures that all students have equal access to the resources necessary for successful acquisition of the academic skills being taught and measured in the classroom.

Skill 3.4   **Analyzing how school-wide structures (e.g., tracking) and classroom factors (e.g., homogenous versus heterogeneous grouping, student-teacher interactions) may affect students' self-concept and learning**

HOMOGENEOUS GROUPING

Classroom climate is a significant influence on successful student learning. Interactions among and relationships between students are an important factor of a positive classroom climate. In past classroom practices, it was common for students to be grouped according to ability. This practice is sometimes referred to as tracking or homogenous grouping. For example, students who found math challenging would be in the "low" math group, average math students would be in the "grade-level" math group, and excelling math learners would make up the "advanced" group.

Drawbacks

This type of grouping can lead to problems with students' self-concept and motivation in class. Students who found themselves in the low group could feel ashamed or stupid. The label associated with these students is that they were difficult, incapable, and dim learners. At the same time, students in the advanced group may feel superior and boast their successes in front of other students, as well as stressed over the need to perform. In summary, this type of grouping typically leads to a combination of feelings including resentment, stress, inferiority, and failure; feelings that do not enhance learning.

HETEROGENEOUS GROUPING

It's not that teachers can never group students by ability. Used once in a while, this method does allow students to work at a comfortable level. However, teachers often find that heterogeneous grouping (grouping by mixed abilities) allows all students to feel success without the negative effects of homogenous groups. In mixed groups, students can learn from more advanced students, while advanced students can still be provided with opportunities to excel in an activity.

Cooperative learning is an excellent setting for heterogeneous groups as students work together to solve problems or complete activities while benefiting from all learning abilities. In this setting, all students feel they are successful in their learning, and feelings of confidence, friendship, and achievement are experienced.

POSITIVE SELF-CONCEPT

A positive self-concept for a child or adolescent is a very important element in terms of the students' ability to learn and to be an integral member of society. If students think poorly of themselves or have sustained feelings of inferiority, they probably will not be able to optimize their potential for learning. It is therefore part of the teacher's task to ensure that each student develops a positive self-concept.

A positive self-concept does not imply feelings of superiority, perfection, or competence/efficacy. Instead, a positive self-concept involves self-acceptance as a person and having a proper respect for oneself.

Students generally do not realize their own abilities and frequently lack self-confidence. Teachers can instill positive self-concept in children and thereby enhance their innate abilities by providing certain types of feedback. Such feedback includes attributing students' successes to their efforts and specifying what the student did that produced the success. Qualitative comments influence attitudes more than quantitative feedback such as grades.

Factors Affecting Positive Self-Concept

Many factors can affect how students perceive themselves including academics, appearance, peer acceptance, gender roles, sexuality, racial identity, and more. Around the onset of adolescence, factors such as physical appearance and a strong drive for autonomy become prominent in a student's mind. How an adolescent characterizes their body image is strongly influenced by family, culture, media, peers, and their own individual feelings.

Girls, especially, are subject to physical appearance pressures. Research shows that women's mass media magazines had more than 10 times more marketing advertisements promoting weight loss than men's magazines. When pressured with negative perceptions of their self-image and physical appearance, some young girls become prone to dangerous behaviors concerning their eating (such as bulimia, anorexia, dieting pills, etc.), their actions (rebellion, drugs, smoking, etc.) or other risky behaviors.

ENHANCING SELF-CONCEPT

Process Approach

Teachers may take a number of approaches to enhancement of self-concept among students. One such scheme is the process approach, which proposes a three-phase model for teaching. This model includes a sensing function, a transforming function, and an acting function. These three factors can be simplified into the words by which the model is usually given: **reach**, **touch**, and **teach**.

The sensing, or perceptual, function incorporates information or stimuli in an intuitive manner. The transforming function conceptualizes, abstracts, evaluates, and provides meaning and value to perceived information. The acting function chooses actions from several different alternatives to be set forth overtly. The process model may be applied to almost any curricular field.

Invitational Education

According to the invitational education approach, teachers and their behaviors may be inviting, or they may be disinviting. Inviting behaviors enhance self-concept among students, while disinviting behaviors diminish self-concept. Inviting teacher behaviors reflect an attitude of "doing with" rather than "doing to." Students are "invited" or "disinvited" depending on the teacher behaviors.

Invitational teachers exhibit the following skills (Biehler and Snowman, 394):

- Reaching each student (e.g., learning names, having one-to-one contact)
- Listening with care (e.g., picking up subtle cues)
- Being real with students (e.g., providing only realistic praise, "coming on straight")
- Being real with oneself (e.g., honestly appraising your own feelings and disappointments)
- Inviting good discipline (e.g., showing students you have respect in personal ways)
- Handling rejection (e.g., not taking lack of student response in personal ways)
- Inviting oneself (e.g., thinking positively about oneself)

Disinviting behaviors include those that demean students, as well as those that may be chauvinistic, sexist, condescending, thoughtless, or insensitive to student feelings. Inviting behaviors are the opposite of these, and characterize teachers who act with consistency and sensitivity.

Skill 3.5   Identifying effective strategies for creating a classroom environment that promotes student development and learning by taking advantage of positive factors (e.g., culture, heritage, language) in the home, school, and community and minimizing the effects of negative factors (e.g., minimal family support)

STRATEGIES FOR ASSESSING DIVERSITY NEEDS IN THE CLASSROOM

Diversity is a factor in virtually every classroom today. It is important for teachers to be aware that diversity applies to many areas of a student's life including race, socioeconomic status, ethnicity, religion, and individual abilities. Together, all of these variations provide for a unique set of students with each class and as teachers become aware of the increasing complexity of student makeup, as well as increase their knowledge of and experiences with various cultures, the teacher becomes more able to work with intercultural relationships.

Teachers must know how to inform themselves of their class's diverse needs. To do so, teachers must work to build a multicultural classroom. In doing so, they will learn about the backgrounds, interests, and needs of their students. First, be open and communicate with students in and out of class. Not only does this promote a positive learning environment, it shows the teacher is genuine and interested in really knowing the students. Another idea is to attend seminars regarding various backgrounds to be educated on various ethnicities, races, and religions.

Taking a genuine approach with students not only applies to their learning but to their well-being. The teacher-student relationship requires trust and care and so showing genuine care develops this trust between teachers and their students. This will play a role not only in academics but also in behavior and a teacher's responsiveness to student needs (academic, physical, emotional, and more). If a teacher has developed a trusting relationship with a child, the reasons for the child's behavior may come out. It might be that the child needs to tell someone what is going on and is seeking a confidant and a trusted teacher can intervene.

Understanding Cultural Learning Patterns
Another strategy to learn more about students is to understand cultural learning patterns. For example, some cultures encourage high degrees of questioning, debating, and criticizing as part of the learning process, while others revere strict listening and no speaking while learning. These various learning patterns may not be evident to some teachers and knowledge of this will help a teacher better understand students. Utilizing literature, music, customs, and art from various backgrounds demonstrates an appreciation for various cultures.

Also, teachers should be sure not to over-generalize with these patterns. Just because a student looks to be of Asian descent does not mean s/he adheres to that cultural learning pattern. That student may have grown up his/her whole life in America and his/her learning pattern would likely adhere to that of an American student instead.

Language is another factor. Teachers who attempt to learn even a word or two of a student's foreign language is conveying a respect for individual cultures and therefore increasing the student's perception that the teacher genuinely cares.

Teaching Diversity
The primary responsibility of the classroom teacher is to ensure that all aspects of the educational process, and all information necessary to master specified skills, are readily accessible by all students in the classroom. In the classroom, the teacher must actively promote inclusion and devise presentations which address commonalities among heterogeneous groups. In the development of lesson plans and presentation formats, this should be evident in the concept and in the language used (e.g., incorporating ideas and phrases that suggest "we" rather than "they" whenever possible).

The prescribed teaching material in a given subject area will usually provide an adequate format appropriate to the grade level and the diversity of a general student population. By assuring that any additional content or instructional aides used in classroom are thematically the same as the prescribed material, the teacher can usually assure these will also be appropriate. The teacher is the final arbiter regarding content, format, and presentation in the classroom, so the teacher must exercise judgment when reviewing all classroom materials, lesson plans, presentations, and activities against set criteria. For example:

- **Offensive**: Anything that might be considered derogatory regarding any individual or group; any comment or material which is insensitive to any nationality, religion, culture, race, family structure, etc.; Regardless the composition of a particular classroom, negativism about any group harbors an acceptance of such negativism and contributes to a "them" versus "us" attitude
- **Exclusive**: Anything which ignores or nullifies the needs, rights, or value of an individual or any group; anything which stratifies society, placing some group or groups above others in significance
- **Inappropriate**: Below or beyond the suitable comprehension level; imprecise, inadequate for mastery of specific skills within the subject matter; fails to provide for accurately measurable skill acquisition

THE TOTAL STUDENT ENVIRONMENT

The student's capacity and potential for academic success within the overall educational experience are products of her or his total environment: classroom and school system; home and family; and neighborhood and community. All of these segments are interrelated and can be supportive, one of the other, or divisive, one against the other. As a matter of course, the teacher will become familiar with all aspects of the system. This would include not only process and protocols but also the availability of resources provided to meet the academic, health and welfare needs of students. It is incumbent upon the teacher to look beyond the boundaries of the school system to identify additional resources as well as issues and situations which will effect (directly or indirectly) a student's ability to succeed in the classroom. These resources include:

- Libraries, museums, zoos, planetariums, etc.
- Clubs, societies and civic organizations, community outreach programs of private businesses and corporations and of government agencies
- Local speakers and presenters
- Departments of social services operating within the local community

These can provide background and program information relevant to social issues which may be impacting individual students. And this can be a resource for classroom instruction regarding life skills, at-risk behaviors, etc. Initial contacts for resources outside of the school system will usually come from within the system itself: from administration, teacher organizations, department heads, and other colleagues.

ELL STUDENTS AND DIVERSITY

Because ELL students are often grouped in classes that take a different approach to teaching English than those for native speakers, it is easy to assume that they all present the same needs and characteristics. Nothing could be further from the truth, even in what they need when it comes to learning English. It is important that their backgrounds and personalities be observed just as with native speakers.

Personalized learning communities provide supportive learning environments that address the academic and emotional needs of students. As socio-cultural knowledge is conveyed continuously in the interrelated experiences shared cooperatively and collaboratively in student groupings and individualized learning, the current and future benefits will continue to present the case and importance of understanding the "whole" child, inclusive of the social and the cultural context.

Skill 3.6   Analyzing ways in which peer interactions (e.g., acceptance versus isolation, bullying) may promote or hinder a student's development and success in school, and determining effective strategies for dealing with peer-related issues in given classroom situations

BULLYING

Increasingly, schools are finding they need to take action to address stereotyping, prejudice, and bullying among students. A number of factors lead to bullying behavior. Stereotypes and prejudice are major contributors, along with personal characteristics and life experiences of the bullying student. These may include poor social skills, distorted self-perceptions, problems with aggression and impulse control, and previous victimization experiences.

Certain characteristics and personality traits of other individuals may serve as magnets for prejudice and stereotyping. Some of these characteristics are based on membership in a specific group such as gender, race, ethnicity, religion, physical ability, sexual orientation, and age. Stereotypes abound in our culture regarding these characteristics, and they are frequently brought into the school setting and used as the basis for teasing and bullying. However, such stereotypes are not the only source of bias. Anything that makes a person different in the eyes of the perceiver—anything out of the "norm"—can trigger ridicule, ostracism, hate, and violence. Some of these perceptual biases are:

- Attractive versus unattractive people
- Thin versus obese individuals
- Effeminate males versus masculine males
- Masculine females versus feminine females
- "In" group versus "out" group (i.e., "cool" versus "not cool")

The presence of difference, in and of itself, is not a problem in the larger world or the school setting. In fact, in a positive school environment, such differences are acknowledged and appreciated. The important issue, however, is the way individuals who are perceived as different are treated, and how that treatment affects the social and emotional wellbeing of the targeted individuals.

There is evidence to suggest that this type of stereotyping directly affects a student's self-esteem. Stereotyping and its effects can begin as early as the first time a child enters school and may continue throughout life. As a result of excessive teasing or bullying, the targeted individual may:

- Believe there is something wrong with him or her and consider him- or herself a "loser"
- Develop emotional problems connected with the perceived inferiority
- Manifest a lack of motivation and desire to excel, with an attitude of "it doesn't matter what I do as I never do anything right"
- Display personality problems
- Begin to feel that life isn't worth living and contemplate suicide
- Begin to harbor thoughts of violence against the perpetrators of the perceived insult
- In extreme cases, carry out an act of violence against him- or herself or others

If not educated to accept differences among people, the perpetrator of the stereotyping, prejudice, or other bullying activities is likely to:

- Escalate the activity
- Enlist others to engage in the activity
- Become firm in their belief that the targeted individual is undesirable
- Feel superior to the targeted individual or groups and justify his or her actions
- Become resistant to changing attitudes and incorporate them into a way of life
- Resort to violence after justifying the violence in his or her mind

Programs to combat stereotyping, prejudice, and biases should be part of the school curriculum. Although the labeling of entire groups of people is irrational, the school must respond rationally and create programs to address these issues. Students can be taught to respect the rights of others through programs of cooperation and conflict resolution.

SCHOOL VIOLENCE

In 2005, the Centers for Disease Control and Prevention did a national survey of high school students' risk behaviors and reported the following information in relation to school violence:

- 13.6 percent reported being in a physical fight on school property in the twelve months preceding the survey
- 18.2 percent of male students and 8.8 percent of female students reported being in a physical fight on school property in the twelve months preceding the survey
- 29.8 percent of students reported having property stolen or deliberately damaged on school property
- 6.0 percent did not go to school on one or more days in the thirty days preceding the survey because they felt unsafe at school or on their way to or from school
- 6.5 percent reported carrying a weapon (gun, knife, or club) on school property on one or more days in the thirty days preceding the survey
- 7.9 percent reported being threatened or injured with a weapon on school property one or more times in the twelve months preceding the survey

(To see the CDC survey, go to this site: www.cdc.gov/ncipc/dvp/YV_DataSheet.pdf)

We are all familiar with the school shootings that occur once in a while. However, the above data reflect the equally troubling and perhaps more relevant facts regarding everyday violence in schools. A major factor contributing to violence in schools is the acceptance of violence as a "normal" reaction to perceived injustices. Media depictions of violence may convey a perception that violent retaliation is "normal" and common. Easy access to guns and other weapons and the effect of both drug abuse and the way the drug culture permeates the larger culture also may contribute to school violence.

In the school setting, administrators, teachers, counselors and support staff have the responsibility to make the school a safe place for all students. Clear policies that delineate safety and guide behavior are useful in working toward this goal. Policies should articulate appropriate behavior on school property and at school events with regard to the following topics, as well as others:

- Weapons
- Homicidal and/or suicidal intent
- Use of drugs and alcohol
- Self-harm
- Sexual harassment
- Bullying
- Violent threats

However, policies are not enough. Preventing violence and resolving conflicts in interpersonal relations are fundamentally related.

CONFLICT RESOLUTION

Programs of violence prevention must be accompanied by programs of constructive conflict resolution so that students can learn methods of positive interactions with others, including those who are different. Not only do these programs help create a safe environment in the schools, but they also teach students the skills to resolve future conflicts in their careers, families, and communities as adults. A program of violence prevention and conflict resolution acknowledges that, while destructive and violent conflicts may be out of control in our society, we can strive to minimize them in any particular school, home, or other setting.

The conflict resolution program should:

- Create an atmosphere of cooperation
- Have a component of peer mediation training that teaches negotiation, mediation, and arbitration skills to students and teachers
- Include units in academic classes on methods of negotiation, mediation, and arbitration

MONITORING AND RESOLVING CONFLICT

Whenever a teacher sees a situation in which two students are involved in a conflict of any sort, immediate action needs to be taken. The students should immediately be removed from each other and from harm's way. The teacher or another third party can then encourage the students to work out their conflict by creating a safe and non-threatening environment, where the problem can be discussed calmly and discreetly. Students should be reminded of the school rules that under no circumstances will this type of behavior be allowed or condoned on school property.

Students need to learn that when they are trying to resolve conflicts, it helps to have a plan in order to solve the problem. There are three basic steps that need to be followed in order to develop strong resolution skills. Students need to define the problem. They can then brainstorm possible solutions for fixing the problem. Choosing the best possible answer and then acting on it is the final step in the conflict resolution process. In order for students to monitor their own behavior, they need to be aware of the fact that all parties involved need to agree to work it out in a reasonable manner. There should be no name calling, fist fighting, or arguing between the students. Students need to act calmly and rationally in these types of situations.

By teaching students to use their own conflict resolution skills in handling disagreements in school situations, they can be better prepared to overcome these same types of problems that may occur in their everyday lives.

Skill 3.7 **Demonstrating knowledge of health, sexuality, and peer-related issues for students (e.g., self-image, physical appearance and fitness, peer-group conformity) and the interrelated nature of these issues; and recognizing how specific behaviors related to health, sexuality, and peer issues (e.g., eating disorders, drug and alcohol use, gang involvement) can affect development and learning**

RISKY BEHAVIORS AND EMOTIONAL DISTRESS

Risky behaviors, including (but not limited to) cigarette/drug/alcohol abuse, gangs, and sexual activity, are most likely to emerge during the middle or high school years. However, this does not mean that elementary school children are exempt from exploring or being exposed to such behaviors. According to the Institute of Youth Development (www.youthdevelopment.org), many children experience their first encounters with drugs, cigarettes, and sexual activity by age 12 (and sometimes even younger). It is possible that children as young as sixth grade (or perhaps even younger) may be exploring risky behaviors.

Effects of Risky Behaviors

Researchers have shown that when students engage in risky behaviors, it often negatively impacts their learning and development. Academically, students tend to start struggling and failing earlier, which further results in a lack of commitment to school. Socially, students demonstrate anti-social behaviors, begin to have trouble with friends, and start to display behavioral issues. These negative outcomes then impact their physical, emotional, and further cognitive development.

In middle-level students, decision-making skills are often deficient. This, coupled with erroneous messages from the media, the community and even the family, can make at-risk behavior appear attractive, acceptable, and desirable. As young people mature and are put in a position of making more choices, independent of adult advice or supervision, they will be faced with making choices regarding involvement in "at-risk" behaviors.

Reasons for Risky Behaviors

While young people are often self-conscious and perceive deficits in themselves when compared to their peers, they also want to be accepted by their peers. Some adolescents (and even pre-adolescents) will deliberately adopt certain behaviors as a statement to their peers that they are "special." In practice, this can range from acting-out, or mild, antisocial behavior, to the adoption of at-risk behaviors that can impede physical, emotional, and intellectual development, restrict appropriate social development, impair judgment and functionality, and possibly impair health or even become life-threatening.

Although peer acceptance or making a statement before one's peers may be the motivation, involvement in at-risk behaviors will quite often put the young individual's future at risk. Choosing behaviors that society deems as unacceptable places the individual outside of the "norm". As that individual's peers continue to mature and develop socially and intellectually, he or she may be perceived as an outsider—and he or she may come to share and accept this perception. Unfortunately, this negative reinforcement may result in continued or increased involvement in at-risk behaviors and the consequences are many. Academically, the consequences of this are reflected in the high drop-out rate for students who became involved in at-risk behaviors during early adolescence.

Signs of Emotional Distress

All students demonstrate some behaviors that may indicate emotional distress from time to time since all children experience stressful periods within their lives. However, the emotionally healthy students can maintain control of their own behavior even during stressful times. Teachers need to be mindful that the difference between typical stressful behavior and severe emotional distress is determined by the frequency, duration, and intensity of stressful behavior.

Lying, stealing, and fighting are atypical behaviors that most children may exhibit occasionally, but if a child lies, steals, or fights regularly or blatantly then these behaviors may be indicative of emotional distress. Lying is especially common among young children who feel the need to avoid punishment or seek a means to make themselves feel more important. As children become older, past the ages of six or seven, lying is often a signal that the child is feeling insecure. These feelings of insecurity may escalate to the point of being habitual or obvious and then may indicate that the child is seeking attention because of emotional distress. Fighting, especially among siblings, is a common occurrence. However, if a child fights, is unduly aggressive, or is belligerent towards others on a consistent basis, teachers and parents need to consider the possibility of emotional problems.

HELPING STUDENTS

How can a teacher know when a child needs help with his/her behavior? The child will indicate by what they do that they need and want help. Breaking rules established by parents, teachers, and other authorities or destroying property can signify that a student is losing control, especially when these behaviors occur frequently. Other signs that a child needs help may include frequent bouts of crying, a quarrelsome attitude, and constant complaints about school, friends, or life in general. Anytime a child's disposition, attitude, or habits change significantly, teachers and parents need to seriously consider the existence of emotional difficulties.

Emotional disturbances in childhood are not uncommon and take a variety of forms. Usually these problems show up in the form of uncharacteristic behaviors. Most of the time, children respond favorably to brief treatment programs of psychotherapy. At other times, disturbances may need more intensive therapy and are harder to resolve. All stressful behaviors need to be addressed, and any type of chronic antisocial behavior needs to be examined as a possible symptom of deep-seated emotional upset.

Behaviors indicating a tendency toward the use of drugs and/or alcohol usually are behaviors that suggest low self-esteem. Such behaviors might be academic failure, social maladaptation, antisocial behavior, truancy, disrespect, chronic rule breaking, aggression and anger, and depression. The student tending toward the use of drugs and/or alcohol will exhibit losses in social and academic functional levels that were previously attained. He may begin to experiment with substances. The adage, "Pot makes a smart kid average and an average kid dumb," is right on the mark. In some families, substance abuse is a known habit of the parents. Thus modeled, the children may assume this to be acceptable behavior, making it very difficult to convince them that drugs and alcohol are not good for them.

COMPETENCY 004   UNDERSTAND LANGUAGE AND LITERACY DEVELOPMENT, AND USE THIS KNOWLEDGE IN ALL CONTENT AREAS TO DEVELOP THE LISTENING, SPEAKING, READING, AND WRITING SKILLS OF STUDENTS, INCLUDING STUDENTS FOR WHOM ENGLISH IS NOT THEIR PRIMARY LANGUAGE

Skill 4.1   Identifying factors that influence language acquisition and analyzing ways students' language skills affect their overall development and learning

LEARNING APPROACH

Early theories of language development were formulated from learning theory research. The assumption was that language development evolved from learning the rules of language structures and applying them through imitation and reinforcement. The learning approach also assumed that linguistic, cognitive, and social developments were independent of each other. Thus, children were expected to learn language from patterning after adults who spoke and wrote Standard English. No allowance was made for communication through child jargon, idiomatic expressions, or grammatical and mechanical errors resulting from too strict adherence to the rules of inflection (*childs* instead of *children*) or conjugation (*runned* instead of *ran*). No association was made between physical and operational development and language mastery.

LINGUISTIC APPROACH

Studies spearheaded by Noam Chomsky in the 1950s formulated the theory that language ability is innate and develops through natural human maturation as environmental stimuli trigger the acquisition of syntactical structures appropriate to each exposure level. This is known as the linguistic approach. The assumption of a hierarchy of syntax downplayed the significance of semantics. Because of the complexity of syntax and the relative speed with which children acquire language, linguists attributed language development to biological rather than cognitive or social influences.

COGNITIVE APPROACH

Researchers in the 1970s proposed that language knowledge derives from both syntactic and semantic structures. Drawing on the studies of Piaget and other cognitive learning theorists, supporters of the cognitive approach maintained that children acquire knowledge of linguistic structures after they have acquired the cognitive structures necessary to process language.

For example, joining words for specific meaning necessitates sensory motor intelligence. The child must be able to coordinate movement and recognize objects before he or she can identify words to name the objects or word groups to describe the actions of these objects. Children must have developed the mental abilities for organizing concepts as well as performing concrete operations, predicting outcomes, and theorizing before they can assimilate and verbalize complex sentence structures, choose vocabulary for particular nuances of meaning, and examine semantic structures for tone and manipulative effect.

SOCIOCOGNITIVE APPROACH

Other theorists in the 1970s proposed that language development results from sociolinguistic competence. This theory finds that the different aspects of linguistic, cognitive, and social knowledge are interactive elements of total human development. Emphasis on verbal communication as the medium for language expression resulted in the inclusion of speech activities in most language arts curricula.

Unlike previous approaches, the sociocognitive approach allows that determining the appropriateness of language in given situations for specific listeners is as important as understanding semantic and syntactic structures. By engaging in conversation, children at all stages of development have opportunities to test their language skills, receive feedback, and make modifications. As a social activity, conversation is as structured by social order as grammar is structured by the rules of syntax. Conversation satisfies the learner's need to be heard, to be understood, and to influence others. Thus, his or her choices of vocabulary, tone, and content are dictated by the ability to assess the linguistic knowledge of his or her listeners. The learner is constantly applying cognitive skills in using language as a form of social interaction. Although the capacity to acquire language is inborn, a child would not pass beyond grunts and gestures without an environment in which to practice language.

Of course, the varying degrees of environmental stimuli to which children are exposed at all age levels create a slower or faster development of language. Some children are prepared to articulate concepts and recognize symbolism by the time they enter fifth grade, either because they have been exposed to challenging reading and conversations with well-spoken adults at home, or in their social groups. Others are still trying to master the sight recognition skills and are not yet ready to combine words in complex patterns.

SECOND LANGUAGE LEARNER

One of the most important things to know about the differences between L1 (first language) and L2 (second language) acquisition is that people usually will master L1, but they will almost never be fully proficient in L2. However, if children can be trained in L2 before about the age of seven, their chances at full mastery will be much higher.

Children learn language with little effort, which is why they can be babbling at one year and speaking with complete, complex ideas just a few years later. It is important to know that language is innate, meaning that our brains are ready to learn a language from birth. Yet a lot of language learning is behavioral, meaning that children imitate adults' speech.

L2 acquisition is much harder for adults. Multiple theories of L2 acquisition have been developed. One of the more notable ones comes from Jim Cummins. Cummins argues that two types of language usually need to be acquired by students learning English as a second language: Basic Interpersonal Communication Skills (BICS) and Cognitive Academic Language Proficiency (CALP).

BICS is general, everyday language used to communicate simple thoughts, whereas CALP is the more complex, academic language used in school. It is harder for students to acquire CALP, and many teachers mistakenly assume that students can learn complex academic concepts in English if they have already mastered BICS. The truth is that CALP takes much longer to master, and in some cases, particularly with little exposure in certain subjects, it may never be mastered.

Another set of theories is based on Stephen Krashen's research in L2 acquisition. Most people understand his theories based on five principles:

1. **The acquisition-learning hypothesis**: There is a difference between learning a language and acquiring it. Children "acquire" a first language easily—it's natural. But adults often have to "learn" a language through coursework, studying, and memorizing. One can acquire a second language, but often it requires more deliberate and natural interaction within that language.
2. **The monitor hypothesis**: The learned language "monitors" the acquired language. In other words, this is when a person's "grammar check" kicks in and keeps awkward, incorrect language out of a person's L2 communication.
3. **The natural order hypothesis**: This theory suggests that learning grammatical structures is predictable and follows a "natural order."
4. **The input hypothesis**: Some people call this "comprehensible input." This means that a language learner will learn best when the instruction or conversation is just above the learner's ability. That way, the learner has the foundation to understand most of the language, but still will have to figure out, often in context, what that extra more difficult element means.
5. **The affective filter hypothesis**: This theory suggests that people will learn a second language when they are relaxed, have high levels of motivation, and have a decent level of self-confidence.

Teaching students who are learning English as a second language poses some unique challenges, particularly in a standards-based environment. The key is realizing that no matter how little English a student knows, the teacher should teach with the student's developmental level in mind. This means that instruction should not be "dumbed-down" for ESOL students. Different approaches should be used, however, to ensure that these students (a) get multiple opportunities to learn and practice English and (b) still learn content.

Many ESOL approaches are based on social learning methods. By being placed in mixed level groups or by being paired with a student of another ability level, students will get a chance to practice English in a natural, nonthreatening environment. Students should not be pushed in these groups to use complex language or to experiment with words that are too difficult. They should simply get a chance to practice with simple words and phrases.

In teacher-directed instructional situations, visual aids, such as pictures, objects, and video are particularly effective at helping students make connections between words and items with which they are already familiar.

ESOL students may need additional accommodations with assessments, assignments, and projects. For example, teachers may find that written tests provide little to no information about a student's understanding of the content. Therefore, an oral test may be better suited for ESOL students. When students are somewhat comfortable and capable with written tests, a shortened test may actually be preferable; take note that they will need extra time to translate.

Skill 4.2 Identifying expected stages and patterns of second-language acquisition, including analyzing factors that affect second-language acquisition

SEE also Skill 4.1.

THE FIVE STAGES OF SECOND-LANGUAGE DEVELOPMENT
There is wide agreement that there are generally five stages of second-language development.

The first stage is **pre-production**. While these students may actually understand what someone says to them (for the most part), they have a much harder time talking back in the target language. Teachers must realize that if a student cannot "produce" the target language, it does not mean that they aren't learning. Most likely, they are. They are taking it in, and their brains are trying to figure out what to do with all the new language.

The second phase is **early production**. This is where the student can actually start to produce the target language. It is quite limited, and teachers most likely should not expect students to produce eloquent speeches during this time.

The third phase is **emergent speech or speech emergence**. Longer, more complex sentences are used, particularly in speech—and in social situations. But remember that students aren't fully fluent in this stage, and they cannot handle complex academic language tasks.

The fourth phase is **intermediate fluency**. This is where more complex language is produced. Grammatical errors are common.

The fifth stage is **advanced fluency**. While students may appear to be completely fluent, though, they will still need academic and language support from teachers.

Many people say that there are prescribed amounts of time by which students should reach each stage. However, keep in mind that it depends on the level at which students are exposed to the language. For example, students who get opportunities to practice with the target language outside of school may have greater ease in reaching the fifth stage quicker. In general, though, it does take years to reach the fifth stage, and students should never be expected to have complete mastery within one school year.

Skill 4.3   Identifying approaches that are effective in promoting English Language Learners' development of English language proficiency, including adapting teaching strategies and consulting and collaborating with teachers in the ESL program

Most of us think that learning a language strictly involves drills, memorization, and tests. While this is a common method used (some people call it a structural, grammatical, or linguistic approach), it certainly does not work for all.

COMMONLY USED SECOND LANGUAGE TEACHING METHODS
Although dozens of methods have been developed to help people learn additional languages, these are some of the more common approaches used in today's K-12 classrooms.

Cognitive Approach
Cognitive approaches to language learning focus on concepts. While words and grammar are important, when teachers use the cognitive approach, they focus on using language for conceptual purposes—rather than learning words and grammar for the sake of simply learning new words and grammatical structures. This approach focuses heavily on students' learning styles, and it cannot necessarily be pinned down as having specific techniques. Rather, it is more of a philosophy of instruction.

Functional Approach
Many approaches are noted for their motivational purposes. In a general sense, when teachers work to motivate students to learn a language, they do things to help reduce fear and to assist students in identifying with native speakers of the target language. A very common method is often called the functional approach.

In this approach, the teacher focuses on communicative elements. For example, a first grade English as a Second Language (ESOL) teacher might help students learn phrases that will assist them in finding a restroom, asking for help on the playground, etc. Many functionally based adult ESOL programs help learners with travel-related phrases and words.

Total Physical Response
Another very common motivational approach is Total Physical Response. This is a kinesthetic approach that combines language learning and physical movement. In essence, students learn new vocabulary and grammar by responding with physical motion to verbal commands. Some people say it is particularly effective because the physical actions help to create good brain connections with the words.

In general, the best methods do not treat students as if they have a language deficit. Rather, the best methods build upon what students already know, and they help to instill the target language as a communicative process rather than a list of vocabulary words that have to be memorized.

THE IMPORTANCE OF CONSISTENCY
In addition to these methods, it is important that when second language learners have multiple teachers, that teachers communicate and collaborate in order to provide a great level of consistency. It is particularly difficult for second language learners to go from one class to the next, where there are different sets of expectations and varied methods of instruction, and still focus on the more complex elements of learning language.

When students have higher levels of anxiety regarding the learning of a second language, they will be less likely to focus on the language; rather, they will be focusing on whatever it is that is creating their anxiety. This does not mean that standards and expectations should be different for these students in all classes; it simply means that teachers should have common expectations so that students know what to expect in each class and don't have to think about the differences between classes.

Another hugely important reason for teachers to collaborate, particularly with the ESOL specialists, is to ensure that students are showing consistent development across classes. Where there is inconsistency, teachers should work to uncover what it is that is keeping the student from excelling in a particular class.

YOUNG SECOND LANGUAGE LEARNERS
The most important concept to remember regarding the difference between learning a first language and a second one is that, if the learner is approximately age seven or older, learning a second language will occur very differently in the learner's brain than it would in a younger student.

An innate language-learning function exists in young children and it appears to go away as they mature. Learning a language before age seven is almost guaranteed, with relatively little effort. The mind is like a sponge, and it soaks up language very readily. Some theorists, including the famous linguist Noam Chomsky, argue that the brain has a *universal grammar* and that only vocabulary and very particular grammatical structures, related to specific languages, need to be introduced in order for a child to learn a language. In essence, a child's mind has slots that language fills in, which is definitely not the case with learning a second language after about seven years old.

OLDER SECOND LANGUAGE LEARNERS
Learning a second language as a pre-adolescent, adolescent or adult requires quite a bit of translation from the first language to the second. Vocabulary and grammar particulars are memorized, not necessarily internalized (at least, as readily as a first language). In fact, many (though not all) people who are immersed in a second language never fully function as fluent in the language. They may appear to be totally fluent, but often there will be small traits that are hard to pick up and internalize.

It is fairly clear that learning a second language successfully does require *fluency* in the first language. This is because, as stated above, the second language is translated from the first in the learner's mind. First language literacy is also a crucial factor in second language learning, particularly second language literacy.

When helping second language learners make the "cross-over" in language fluency or literacy from first language to second language, it is important to help them identify strategies they use in the first language and apply those to the second language. It is also important to note similarities and differences in phonetic principals in the two languages. Sometimes it is helpful to encourage students to translate; other times, it is helpful for them to practice production in the target language. In either case, teachers must realize that learning a second language is a slow and complicated process.

Skill 4.4 **Recognizing the role of oral language development, including vocabulary development, and the role of the alphabetic principle, including phonemic awareness and other phonological skills, in the development of English literacy; and identifying expected stages and patterns in English literacy development**

SPEECH OR LANGUAGE DELAYS
Understanding the development of language in young children can provide information on delays or differences. Parents and teachers must understand the difference between developmental speech, word development, and language delays/differences that may prevent oral language acquisition. Teachers and

parents who have concerns about a child's language development should be proactive in addressing them. Early intervention is critical.

Age/Language Acquisition Guidelines

- Children at the age of 2 should have speech patterns that are about 70 percent intelligible.
- Children at the age of 3 should have an increased 10 percent speech pattern that is about 80 percent intelligible.
- Children at the age of 4 should have an increased 20 percent speech pattern that is about 90 percent intelligible.
- Children at the age of 5 should have a speech pattern that is 100 percent intelligible.
- Children over the age of 5 will develop speech patterns that continue at 100 percent intelligibility with increased vocabulary.

STIMULATING DEVELOPMENT OF CHILDREN'S ORAL LANGUAGE SKILLS
In order to stimulate the development of their oral language skills, children should be exposed to a challenging environment that is rich in opportunities. Teachers should remain focused on oral language skills throughout the day, even while teaching other subjects.

Activities That Encourage Development of Oral Language Skills

- Encourage meaningful conversation
- Allow dramatic playtime
- Let children share personal stories
- Sing the alphabet song
- Teach the art of questioning
- Read rhyming books
- Play listening games
- Encourage sharing of information

PHONOLOGICAL AND PHONEMIC AWARENESS

Phonics involves studying the rules and patterns found in language. By age 5 or 6, children can typically begin to use phonics to begin to understand the connections between letters, their patterns, vowel sounds (i.e., short vowels, long vowels) and the collective sounds they all make.

Phonemic awareness is the ability to break down and hear separate and/or different sounds and distinguish between the sounds one hears. These terms are different; however, they are interdependent. Phonemic awareness is required to begin studying phonics, when students will need to be able to break down words into the smalls units of sound, or phonemes, to later identify syllables, blends, and patterns. Phonological awareness is a broader term that includes phonemic awareness.

Methods for Teaching Phonemic Awareness

Since the ability to distinguish between individual sounds, or phonemes, within words is a prerequisite to association of sounds with letters and manipulating sounds to blend words (a fancy way of saying "reading"), the teaching of phonemic awareness is crucial to emergent literacy. Children need a strong background in phonemic awareness in order for phonics instruction to be effective.

- Clapping syllables in words
- Distinguishing between a word and a sound
- Using visual cues and movements to help children understand when the speaker goes from one sound to another
- Incorporating oral segmentation activities which focus on easily distinguished syllables rather than sounds
- Singing familiar songs (e.g., "Happy Birthday," "Knick-Knack, Paddy Wack") and replacing key words in it with words with a different ending or middle sound (oral segmentation)
- Dealing children a deck of picture cards and having them sound out the words for the pictures on their cards or calling for a picture by asking for its first and second sound

ALPHABETIC PRINCIPLE

The alphabetic principle, sometimes called graphophonemic awareness, describes the understanding that written words are composed of patterns of letters that represent the sounds of spoken words. The alphabetic principle has two parts:

- Words are made up of letters and each letter has a specific sound.
- The correspondence between sounds and letters leads to phonological reading.

Since the English language is dependent on the alphabet, being able to recognize and sound out letters is the first step for beginning readers. Decoding is essential. Critical skills that students need to learn are:

- letter–sound correspondence
- how to sound out words
- how to decode text to make meaning

Strategies for Teaching the Alphabetic Principle

Multisensory structured language education uses visual, auditory, and kinesthetic cues simultaneously to enhance memory and learning.

- **Quilt book:** Students can piece together pictures of objects whose name begins with the same letter of the alphabet.
- **Rhyme time:** Students participate in reciting a rhyme, identifying the words that all begin with the same sound.
- **Letter path:** Use masking tape to outline a large letter on the floor. As the students follow the path of the letter, have them name words that begin with that letter
- **Shape game:** Call out a letter. Have the students arrange themselves to form the shape of that letter.

Skill 4.5   Identifying factors that influence students' literacy development, and demonstrating knowledge of research-validated instructional strategies for addressing the literacy needs of students at all stages of literacy development, including applying strategies for facilitating students' comprehension of texts before, during, and after reading, and using modeling and explicit instruction to teach students how to use comprehension strategies effectively

SEE also Skill 4.4.

The point of comprehension instruction is not necessarily to focus just on the text(s) students are using at the very moment of instruction, but rather to help them learn the strategies that they can use independently with any other text.

MONITORING AND FACILITATING COMPREHENSION

Before Reading

Making predictions
One theory or approach to the teaching of reading that gained currency in the late 1960s and the early 1970s was the importance of asking *inferential* and *critical thinking* questions of the reader meant to challenge and engage the children in the text. This approach to reading went beyond the literal level of what was stated in the text to an inferential level of using text clues to make predictions and to a critical level of involving the child in evaluating the text. While asking engaging and thought-provoking questions is still viewed as part of the teaching of reading, it is only viewed currently as a component of the teaching of reading.

Prior knowledge
Literary response skills are partially dependent on prior knowledge. Effective comprehenders of text, whether they are adults or children, use prior knowledge *plus* the ideas from the printed text for reading comprehension. Prior knowledge can be defined as all of an individual's prior experiences, education, and development that precede his or her entrance into a specific learning situation or

his or her attempts to comprehend a specific text. Sometimes, prior knowledge can be erroneous or incomplete. Obviously, if there are misconceptions in a child's prior knowledge, these must be corrected so that the child's overall comprehension skills can continue to progress. Even kindergarteners display prior knowledge, which typically includes their accumulated positive and negative experiences both in and out of school. Prior knowledge activities and opportunities might range from traveling with family, watching television, visiting museums, and visiting libraries to staying in hospitals, visiting prisons, and surviving poverty.

During Reading

Graphic organizers
Graphic organizers solidify, in a chart format, a visual relationship among various reading and writing ideas. The content of a graphic organizer may include:

- Sequence
- Timelines
- Character traits
- Fact and opinion
- Main idea and details
- Differences and likenesses (generally done using a Venn diagram of interlocking circles, a KWL Chart, etc).

These charts and formats are essential for providing scaffolding for instruction through activating pertinent prior knowledge.

KWL strategy
KWL charts are exceptionally useful for reading comprehension, as they outline what children KNOW, what they WANT to know, and what they've LEARNED after reading. Students are asked to activate prior knowledge about a topic and further develop their knowledge about a topic using this organizer. Teachers often opt to display and maintain KWL charts throughout a text to continually record pertinent information about students' reading.

What do I KNOW?	What do I WANT to know?	What did I LEARN?

When the teacher first introduces the KWL strategy, the children should be allowed sufficient time to brainstorm what they all actually know about the topic. The children should have a three-columned KWL worksheet template for their journals, and there should be a chart to record the responses from class or group discussion. The children can write under each column in their own journal; they should also help the teacher with notations on the chart. This strategy involves the children in actually gaining experience in note taking and in having a concrete record of new data and information gleaned from the passage.

Depending on the grade level of the participating children, the teacher may also want to channel them into considering categories of information they hope to find out from the expository passage. For instance, they may be reading a book on animals to find out more about the animals' habitats during the winter or about the animals' mating habits.

When children are working on the middle (the *What I want to know* section of their KWL strategy sheet), the teacher may want to give them a chance to share what they would like to learn further about the topic and help them to express it in question format.

KWL can even be introduced as early as second grade with extensive teacher discussion support. It not only serves to support the child's comprehension of a particular expository text, but it also models for children a format for note taking. Additionally, when the teacher wants to introduce report writing, the KWL format provides excellent outlines and question introductions for at least three paragraphs of a report.

Cooper (2004) recommends this strategy for use with thematic units and with reading chapters in required science, social studies, or health textbooks. In addition to its usefulness with thematic unit study, KWL is wonderful for providing the teacher with a concrete format to assess how well children have absorbed pertinent new knowledge within the passage (by looking at the third L section). Ultimately it is hoped that students will learn to use this strategy, not only under explicit teacher direction with templates of KWL sheets, but also on their own by informally writing questions they want to find out about in their journals and then going back to their own questions and answering them after the reading.

Note taking

Older children take notes in their reading journals, while younger children and those more in need of explicit teacher support contribute their ideas and responses as part of the discussion in class. Their responses can be recorded on an experiential chart.

After Reading

Connecting texts

The concept of *readiness* is generally regarded as a developmentally based phenomenon. Various abilities, whether cognitive, affective, or psychomotor, are perceived to be dependent upon the mastery or development of certain prerequisite skills or abilities. Readiness, then, implies that the necessary prior knowledge, experience, and readiness prerequisites should be present before the child engages in the new task.

Readiness for subject area learning is dependent not only on prior knowledge but also on affective factors such as interest, motivation, and attitude. These factors are often more influential on student learning than the pre-existing cognitive base.

When texts relate to a student's life, to other reading materials, or to additional areas of study, they become more meaningful and relevant to students' learning. Students enjoy seeing reading material that they can connect to on a deeper level.

Discussing the text

Discussion is an activity in which the children concentrate on a particular text. Among the prompts, the teacher-coach might suggest that the children focus on words of interest they encountered in the text. These can also be words that they heard if the text was read aloud. Children can be asked to share something funny or upsetting or unusual about the words they have read. Through this focus on children's responses to words as the center of the discussion circle, peers become more interested in word study.

Using illustrations in a text

Illustrations can be key supports for emergent and early readers. Teachers should not only use wordless stories (books which tell their narratives through pictures alone), but can also make targeted use of Big Books for read-alouds, so that young children become habituated in the use of illustrations as an important component for constructing meaning. The teacher should model for the child how to reference an illustration for help in identifying a word in the text the child does not recognize.

Of course, children can also go on a picture walk with the teacher as part of a mini-lesson or guided reading and anticipate the story (narrative) using the pictures alone to construct meaning.

Skill 4.6   **Recognizing similarities and differences between the English literacy development of native English speakers and English Language Learners, including how literacy development in the primary language influences literacy development in English, and applying strategies for helping English Language Learners transfer literacy skills in the primary language to English**

SEE Skills 4.1 and 4.3.

Skill 4.7   **Using knowledge of literacy development to select instructional strategies that help students use literacy skills as tool for learning; that teach students how to use, access, and evaluate information from various resources; and that support students' development of content-area reading skills**

The educational community has not done the best job at transitioning students into reading tasks that require accessing information, making real-world judgments, or comprehending directions. Typically, children are taught to read with fiction, and then suddenly, are handed science and social science textbooks. Teachers believe the students will be able to handle the material successfully.

JUDGING SOURCES

While it is a bit of an exaggeration to say that teachers do not use nonfiction in younger grades, it is true that many students are completely unprepared to use textbooks with complete ease. Furthermore, when teachers start to assign research projects in upper elementary, middle school, and/or high school, they forget that students not only struggle with comprehending nonfiction sources, they also struggle with assessing the reliability of sources. This is why, in these days where students are often better at using the Internet than some of their teachers, the sources of students' research projects are not always reliable. While they can easily navigate around the web, they do not always have the ability to decide whether a website is professional or not.

The reason for this is simple: inexperience with having to judge sources, combined with the lack of instruction regarding the proper selection of sources. To go a bit deeper, another reason for this is that students do not always know strategies for reading content-area material.

Example of Student Challenges in Judging Sources

Let's take middle school subjects, for example. The English-Language Arts teacher, who instructs students in the elements of fiction, such as character, setting, and plot, is teaching her students strategies for understanding fiction. Likewise, that same teacher who conducts lessons on rhyme and imagery in poetry is teaching her students the strategies for reading poetry. When do students get the opportunity to study the ways in which we come to understand the material in the science textbook or the math textbook?

Too often, we assume that they will naturally be able to read those materials. And too often, teachers then find that our students are completely lost in a science textbook. With today's textbooks, the struggle to make sense of the material goes further: to supposedly keep students' attention, textbooks contain flashy graphics, side-bars with somewhat related information, discussion questions, vocabulary entries, etc. Surprisingly, some students simply do not know which parts of the text are required reading and which are peripheral.

Strategies to Help Students

To improve this situation, it is strongly recommended that teachers explicitly teach the strategies needed to make sense of nonfiction sources. Some of the strategies are as follows:

- **Text structure**: This refers to both the arrangement of a book (e.g., chapters, sub-headings, etc.) as well as the method of paragraphs (e.g., a paragraph that introduces a concept and explains it, versus one that compares and contrasts one concept with another).
- **Summarization**: This is much harder for students than it may seem. Too often, students believe that summarization is simply the re-telling of information that has been read. In actuality, summarization requires that the student identify the most important details, identify the main point, and highlight the pieces of a text that give light to that main point.
- **Source identification**: Although this isn't a term that gets used too much, the concept is very important. Teachers must instruct students explicitly in methods of determining whether a website, for example, is reliable or not. Methods for doing so include discussing author credentials, page layout, website links, etc.
- **Vocabulary**: Teachers need to train students to look up words they are unfamiliar with or use textbook-provided glossaries. When students are unfamiliar with vocabulary used in textbooks, comprehension is much slower.

- **Text annotation**: Students will be more active readers if they interact with the text they are reading in some fashion. Marking texts can help students identify for themselves what concepts they are already familiar with, what concepts they are unclear about, or what concepts interest them.
- **Background knowledge**: Students who find a way to activate background knowledge will be far more successful with reading nonfiction than those who do not. This is because background knowledge serves as a place to organize and attach new knowledge more quickly.

While there are many more strategies that can be used, remember students need explicit instruction in understanding and accessing nonfiction material.

COMPETENCY 005   UNDERSTAND DIVERSE STUDENT POPULATIONS, AND USE KNOWLEDGE OF DIVERSITY WITHIN THE SCHOOL AND THE COMMUNITY TO ADDRESS THE NEEDS OF ALL LEARNERS, TO CREATE A SENSE OF COMMUNITY AMONG STUDENTS, AND TO PROMOTE STUDENTS' APPRECIATION OF AND RESPECT FOR INDIVIDUALS AND GROUPS

Skill 5.1   Recognizing appropriate strategies for teachers to use to enhance their own understanding of students (e.g., learning about students' family situations, cultural backgrounds, individual needs) and to promote a sense of community among diverse groups in the classroom

SEE also Skill 5.2.

PROMOTING A SENSE OF COMMUNITY

The bridge to effective learning for students begins with a collaborative approach by all stakeholders that support the educational needs of students. Underestimating the power and integral role of the community institutions in impacting the current and future goals of students can carry high stakes for students beyond the high school years who are competing for college access, student internships, and entry level jobs in the community. Researchers have shown that school involvement and connections with community institutions yield greater retention rates of students graduating and seeking higher education experiences. The current disconnect and autonomy that has become commonplace in today's society must be reevaluated in terms of promoting tomorrow's citizens.

When community institutions provide students and teachers with meaningful connections and input, the commitment is apparent in terms of volunteering, loyalty and professional promotion. Providing students with placements in leadership positions such as the ASB (Associated Student Body); the PTSA (Parent Teacher Student Association); school boards; neighborhood sub-committees addressing political or social issues; or government boards that impact and influence school communities creates an avenue for students to explore ethical, participatory, collaborative, transformational leadership that can be applied to all areas of a student's educational and personal life.

Community liaisons provide students with opportunities to experience accountability and responsibility and learn how effective organizations use communication and teamwork to accomplish goals and objectives. Teaching students skills of inclusion and creating public forums that represent student voice fosters student interest and access to individual opinions and increases understanding of the world around them.

Skill 5.2   Applying strategies for working effectively with students from all cultures, students of both genders, students from various socioeconomic circumstances, students from homes where English is not the primary language, and students whose home situations involve various family arrangements and lifestyles

CULTURAL AND SOCIOECONOMIC ISSUES
A positive environment, where open, discussion-oriented, non-threatening communication among all students can occur, is a critical factor in creating an effective learning culture. The teacher must take the lead and model appropriate actions and speech and intervene quickly when a student makes a misstep and offends (often inadvertently) another.

Communication issues that the teacher in a diverse classroom should be aware of include:

- Be sensitive to terminology and language patterns that may exclude or demean students. Regularly switch between the use of "he" and "she" in speech and writing. Know and use the current terms that ethnic and cultural groups use to identify themselves (e.g., "Latinos" [favored] vs. "Hispanics" [not favored]).
- Be aware of body language that is intimidating or offensive to some cultures, such as direct eye contact, and adjust accordingly.
- Monitor your own reactions to students to ensure equal responses to males and females, as well as differently-performing students.
- Don't "protect" students from criticism because of their ethnicity or gender. Likewise, acknowledge and praise all meritorious work without singling out any one student. Both actions can make all students hyper-aware of ethnic and gender differences and cause anxiety or resentment throughout the class.
- Emphasize the importance of discussing and considering different viewpoints and opinions. Demonstrate and express value for all opinions and comments, and lead students to do the same.

Possible Cultural and Language Issues
Most class rosters will consist of students from a variety of cultures. Teachers should get to know their students (of all cultures) so that they may incorporate elements of their cultures into classroom activities and planning. Also, getting to know about a student's background/cultural traditions helps to build a rapport with each student, as well as further educate the teacher about the world in which he or she teaches.

For students still learning English, teachers must make every attempt to communicate with that student daily. Whether it is with another student who speaks the same language, word cards, computer programs, drawings, or other methods, teachers must find ways to encourage each student's participation. The teacher must also be sure the appropriate language services begin for the student in a timely manner.

Possible Socioeconomic Issues
Teachers must also consider students from various socioeconomic backgrounds. Teachers should watch these students carefully for signs of malnutrition, fatigue, and possible learning disorders. In many cases, however, these students are just as likely as anyone else to work well in a classroom. Unfortunately, sometimes students from lower SES backgrounds may need help deriving a homework system or perhaps need more attention on study or test-taking skills. Difficulties sometimes occur with these students when it comes to completing homework consistently. For example, access to technology and media may vary greatly within the student population. In planning classroom work, homework assignments and other projects, the teacher must take this into account.

DEALING WITH THESE ISSUES
First, be knowledgeable about the resources available to the students within the school, the library system, and the community. Be sure that any issues which might restrict a student's access (physical impediments, language difficulties, expenses, etc.) are addressed. Secondly, never plan for work or assignments where every student would not have equal access to information and technology. As in all aspects of education, each student must have an equal opportunity to succeed. Teachers should encourage these students as much as possible and offer positive reinforcements when they meet or exceed classroom expectations.

Skill 5.3   **Applying strategies for promoting students' understanding and appreciation of diversity and for using diversity that exists within the classroom and the community to enhance all student's learning**

SEE also Skill 3.5

According to Campbell, Campbell, and Dickinson (1992) *Teaching and Learning through Multiple Intelligences,* "The changing nature of demographics is one of the strongest rationales for multicultural education in the United States." The Census Bureau predicts a changing demographic for the American population and school communities that will include a forecast between 1990 and 2030, that "while the white population will increase by 25%, the African American population will increase by 68%, the Asian-American, Pacific Island, and American Indian by 79%, and the Hispanic-American population by 187%." Reinforcing the learning beyond the classroom must include a diversity of instructional and learning strategies for any adult role models in a student's life.

CLASSROOM DIVERSITY

Diversity in the classroom includes race, ethnicity, gender, and varying socioeconomic situations but also includes students who are physically or intellectually challenged or who have exceptionalities. All students must be included in the learning process and all students can contribute and add value to the learning process. Acceptance of diversity and any specific requirements necessary to aid individuals to accomplish on a par with classmates, must be incorporated in lesson planning, teacher presentation, and classroom activities.

Oftentimes, students absorb the culture and social environment around them without deciphering contextual meaning of the experiences. When provided with a diversity of cultural contexts, students are able to adapt and incorporate multiple meanings from cultural cues vastly different from their own socioeconomic backgrounds. Socio-cultural factors provide a definitive impact on a students' psychological, emotional, affective, and physiological development, along with a students' academic learning and future opportunities.

METHODS FOR TEACHING DIVERSITY

Teachers must establish a classroom climate that is culturally respectful and engaging for students. In a culturally sensitive classroom, teachers maintain equity and fairness in student interactions and curriculum implementation. Teachers are responsible for including cultural and diverse resources in their curriculum and instructional practices. Exposing students to culturally sensitive room decorations and posters that show positive and inclusive messages is one way to demonstrate inclusion of multiple cultures.

Artifacts that could reflect teacher/student sensitivity to diversity might consist of the following:

- Student portfolios reflecting multicultural/multiethnic perspectives
- Journals and reflections about field trips/guest speakers from diverse cultural backgrounds
- Printed materials and wall displays from multicultural perspectives
- Parent/guardian letters in a variety of languages reflecting cultural diversity
- Projects that include cultural history and diverse inclusions
- Disaggregated student data reflecting cultural groups
- Classroom climate of professionalism that fosters diversity and cultural inclusion

Teachers must create personalized learning communities where every student is a valued member and contributor of the classroom experiences. In classrooms where socio-cultural attributes of the student population are incorporated into the fabric of the learning process, dynamic interrelationships are created that enhance the learning experience and the personalization of learning. When students are provided with numerous academic and social opportunities to share cultural incorporations into the learning, everyone in the classroom benefits from bonding through shared experiences and having an expanded viewpoint of a world experience and culture that vastly differs from their own.

PERSONALIZED LEARNING COMMUNITIES

In personalized learning communities, relationships and connections between students, staff, parents, and community members promote lifelong learning for all students. School communities that promote an inclusion of diversity in the classroom, community, curriculum, and connections enable students to maximize their academic capabilities and educational opportunities. Setting school climates that are inclusive of the multicultural demographic student population create positive and proactive mission and vision themes that align student and staff expectations.

The following factors enable students and staff to emphasize and integrate diversity in student learning:

- Inclusion of multicultural themes in curriculum and assessments
- Creation of a learning environment that promotes multicultural research, learning, collaboration, and social construction of knowledge and application
- Providing learning tasks that emphasize student cognitive, critical thinking, and problem-solving skills
- Learning tasks that personalize the cultural aspects of diversity and celebrate diversity in the subject matter and student projects
- Promotion of intercultural, positive, social, peer interrelationships and connections

Teachers communicate diversity in instructional practices and experiential learning activities that create curiosity in students who want to understand the interrelationship of cultural experiences. Students become self-directed in discovering the global world in and outside the classroom. Teachers understand that when diversity becomes an integral part of the classroom environment, students become global thinkers and doers.

In the intercultural communication model, students are able to learn how different cultures engage in both verbal and nonverbal modes of communicating meaning. Students who become multilingual in understanding the stereotypes that have defined other cultures are able to create new bonding experiences that will typify a more integrated global culture. Students who understand how to effectively communicate with diverse cultural groups are able to maximize their own learning experiences by being able to transmit both verbally and non-verbally cues and expectations in project collaborations and in performance-based activities.

The learning curve for teachers in intercultural understanding is exponential in that they are able to engage all learners in the academic process and learning engagement. Teaching students how to incorporate learning techniques from a cultural aspect enriches the cognitive expansion experience since students are able to expand their cultural knowledge bases.

Skill 5.4   Analyzing how classroom environments that respect diversity promote positive student experiences

SEE also Skill 5.3.

BENEFITS OF TEACHING DIVERSITY
Researchers continue to show that personalized learning environments increase the learning effect for students; decrease drop-out rates among marginalized students; and reduce unproductive student behavior that can result from constant cultural misunderstandings or miscues between students. Promoting diversity of learning and cultural competency in the classroom for students and teachers creates a world of multicultural opportunities and learning.

When students are able to step outside their comfort zones and share the world of a homeless student or empathize with an English Language Learner (ELL) student who has just immigrated to the United States and is learning English for the first time and is still trying to keep up with the academic learning in an unfamiliar language; then students grow exponentially in social understanding and cultural connectedness.

COMPETENCY 006   UNDERSTAND THE CHARACTERISTICS AND NEEDS OF STUDENTS WITH DISABILITIES, DEVELOPMENTAL DELAYS, AND EXCEPTIONAL ABILITIES (INCLUDED GIFTED AND TALENTED STUDENTS); AND USE THIS KNOWLEDGE TO HELP STUDENTS REACH THEIR HIGHEST LEVELS OF ACHIEVEMENT AND INDEPENDENCE

Skill 6.1   Demonstrating awareness of types of disabilities, developmental delays, and exceptional abilities and of the implications for learning associated with these differences

UNDERSTANDING DISABILITIES

The classification of student exceptionalities and disabilities in education is a categorical system; it organizes special education into categories. Within the categories are subdivisions that may be based on the severity or level of support services needed. Having a categorical system allows educators to differentiate and define types of disabilities, relate treatments to certain categories, and concentrate research and advocacy efforts. The disadvantage of the categorical system is the labeling of groups or individuals. Critics of labels say that labeling can place the emphasis on the label and not the individual needs of the child.

The following table summarizes the categories of disabilities and major characteristics of their definitions under IDEA.

Classification	Characteristics
Autism*	Impairment in social interaction and communication accompanied by restricted repetitive and stereotyped patterns of behavior, interests, and activities, occurring before age 3.
Deaf	Impairment in processing linguistic information with or without hearing aids that has an adverse impact on educational performance.
Deaf-blind	Hearing and visual impairments causing communication, developmental, and education problems too severe to be met in programs solely for deaf or blind children
Hard of Hearing	Permanent or fluctuating hearing impairment that adversely affects educational performance but is not included in the definition of deafness
Mentally Retarded	Significantly sub average general intellectual functioning with deficits in adaptive behavior,

Classification	Characteristics
	manifested during the developmental period, and adversely affecting educational performance
Multi handicapped	Combination of impairments, excluding deaf-blind children, that cause educational problems too severe to be serviced in programs designed for a single impairment
Orthopedically Impaired	Severe orthopedic impairment that adversely affects educational performance resulting from birth defects, disease (e.g., polio), or other causes (e.g., amputation, burns)
Other Health Impaired	Medical conditions such as heart conditions, tuberculosis, rheumatic fever, nephritis, asthma, sickle cell anemia, hemophilia, epilepsy, lead poisoning, leukemia, or diabetes. (IDEA listing). Other health conditions may be included if they are so chronic or acute that the child's strength, vitality, or alertness is limited.
Seriously Emotionally Disturbed (Does not include children who are socially maladjusted unless they are also classified as seriously emotionally disturbed.)	Schizophrenia, and conditions in which one or more of these characteristics is exhibited over a long period of time and to a marked degree: (a) inability to learn not explained by intellectual, sensory, or health factors, (b) inability to build or maintain satisfactory interpersonal relationships, (c) inappropriate types of behavior or feelings, (d) general pervasive unhappiness or depression, (e) tendency to develop physical symptoms or fears associated with personal or school problems.
Specific Learning Disability	Disorder in one or more basic psychological processes involved in understanding or in using spoken or written language that manifests itself in an imperfect ability to listen, think, speak, read, write, spell, or to do mathematical calculations. They cannot be attributed to visual, hearing, physical, intellectual, or emotional handicaps, or cultural, environmental, or economic disadvantage.
Speech Impaired	Communication disorder such as stuttering, impaired articulation, voice impairment, or language impairment adversely affecting educational performance.

Classification	Characteristics
Visually Handicapped (Partially sighted or blind)	Visual impairment, even with correction, adversely affecting educational performance

Autism was added as a separate category of disability in 1990 under P. L. 101-476. This addition was not a change in the law but a clarification. The law previously covered students with autism, but now the law identifies them as a separate and distinct class entitled to the law's benefits.

It should also be noted that there is no classification for gifted children under IDEA. Funding and services for gifted programs are left up to the individual states and school districts. Therefore, the number of districts providing services and the scope of gifted programs varies among states and school districts.

DEVELOPMENTAL DELAYS

Children develop at rapidly different rates and therefore there is always a range in what is considered "typical" development. It is very important for teachers to be familiar with the range of typical development so that concerns regarding delays and/or impairments can be identified and addressed early.

The term "developmental delay" refers to a significant lag in a student's cognitive, physical, social, behavioral, or emotional development. Cognitive delays can include delays in both verbal and non-verbal domains (e.g., verbal communication, mathematical reasoning, logical reasoning, visual processing, auditoring processing, memorization, etc.). Physical delays refer to delays in gross and/or fine motor skills (e.g., the inability to stand up straight, walk normally, play simple sport-like activities, hold a pencil). In very young children (i.e, infants and toddlers), physical delays include limitations in milestones such as sitting up, crawling, or walking. Social delays refer to a lag in a child's ability to relate to others. Behavioral delays can include a slower progression into and then out of the more egocentric toddler stage or may include atypical behaviors (e.g., handflapping). Emotional delays revolve around a student's understanding and ability to convey feelings.

Some developmental delays may exist in isolation, such as a specific language impairment, while others are more global in nature (e.g., mental retardation). Likewise, delays might relate to specific disabilities that can stay with a child the rest of his or her life (everything from problems with eyesight to autism) or learning disabilities (everything from attention deficit disorder to dyslexia). They might also be things that fade as a child gets older or can be addressed with remediation and/or therapy (such as problems with motor skills).

Dealing with Delays

Generally, teachers and parents should know the range of attributes that develop over time in children. There is usually no cause for alarm, as many children do develop skills later in childhood (and certain domains may be developed later than others). When concern regarding the need for intervention does arise, it may be because the teacher observes a child struggling with certain tasks as compared to peers. This may be noted via observation of student behaviors, student frustration, work samples, or by student report. The fear or presence of bullying can also be a harsh reality for the student who is struggling with a developmental delay. The teacher must be aware of peer interactions in order to ensure that all children are fully protected.

When in doubt, the teacher should privately discuss any concern regarding a student with a special education teacher or school psychologist first. That professional may be able to assist the teacher in determining whether it would be important to evaluate the child, or whether it would be important to contact the parent to ask questions, seek clarification, or point out a potential delay. Very often though, parents will be aware of the delay and the child will be able to receive special accomodations in the classroom. Teachers should be forewarned about this by the special education personnel prior to the beginning of the schoolyear.

Skill 6.2   Applying criteria and procedures for evaluating, selecting, creating, and modifying materials and equipment to address individual special needs, and recognizing the importance of consulting with specialists to identify appropriate materials and equipment, including assistive technology, when working with students with disabilities, developmental delays, or exceptional abilities

SEE also Skill 15.2.

INSTRUCTIONAL ADAPTATIONS

Instructional alternatives to help students with learning problems may be referred to as compensatory techniques, instructional adaptations, accommodations, or modifications. A problem-solving approach to determining what modifications should be made centers around the following:

1. The requirements of the course (often state or local standards and objectives)
2. The requirement(s) that the student is not meeting
3. Factors interfering with the student's meeting the requirements
4. Identification of possible modifications or accommodations

Many of the adaptations and modifications helpful to students with disabilities can be seen in terms of Cummins' (1994) analysis of the cognitive demands of a task or lesson. Such adaptations can be designed to either lighten the cognitive burden of a task or make it easier for the student to carry that burden. Lessons or tasks that have a lot of context for a student will be easier for that student than tasks with little or no context.

Cognitive demand is a measure of how much information must be processed quickly. A cognitively demanding task requires processing lots of information all at once or in rapid succession and is more demanding or difficult. Cognitively undemanding tasks or lessons present only single pieces of information or concepts to process, and they separate tasks or lessons into discrete, small steps. When making changes to accommodate students with special needs, it is helpful to focus on changes that will move the task or lesson from a cognitively demanding, low context arena to one of high context and reduced cognitive demand.

Adaptations or changes designed to help the student(s) meet the requirements of a class or standard can take place in a number of areas of curriculum and settings such as: the learning environment, methods of instruction and presentation, materials and texts, lesson content, assessment and testing, use of assistive technology, and staff collaboration.

ADAPTING THE OVERALL INSTRUCTIONAL ENVIRONMENT
The teacher can modify the classroom instructional environment in several ways.

Individual Student Variables
Some students with disabilities benefit from sitting close to the teacher or away from windows. Others (with ADHD, for example) might benefit from wiggle seats or fiddle objects, others from an FM system or cubicles that reduce distractions. Seating that reduces distractions serves also to reduce the cognitive load of lessons, by removing the need for the students to block distractions themselves.

Classroom Organization
Many students with learning disabilities benefit from a highly structured environment in which physical areas are clearly labeled and a schedule for the day prominently displayed. Individual schedule charts can be useful if some students follow different schedules, such as leaving for a resource room or specialized therapy periodically. Such schedules reduce the cognitive load required to simply get through the day, and provide increased context for the student navigating the daily routine.

The teacher can also vary grouping arrangements (e.g., large group, small group, peer tutoring, or learning centers) with student needs in mind. Five basic types of grouping arrangements are typically used in the classroom:

Large Group with Teacher
Examples of appropriate activities include show and tell, discussions, watching plays or movies, brainstorming ideas, and playing games. The advantage of large-group instruction is that it is time-efficient and prepares students for higher levels of secondary and post-secondary education settings. However, with large groups, instruction cannot be as easily differentiated or tailored to individual student needs or learning styles.

When students with special needs are included in large group instruction, care must be taken to conduct the activity with their needs in mind. For example, if a particular student may have a limited recall or understanding of a subject, it can be useful to ask the student a concrete question or let the student answer before anyone else so his/her answer is not "taken" by someone else. Choral responses regarding key points can help provide context and support for students with some disabilities, as well.

Small Group Instruction
Small group instruction usually includes 5 to 7 students and is recommended for teaching basic academic skills such as math facts or reading, and for introducing many abstract content area concepts. This model is especially effective for students with learning problems. Composition of the groups should be flexible to accommodate different rates of progress through instruction. Some of the advantages of teaching in small groups are that the teacher is better able to tailor the instruction to the special needs of certain students, to provide feedback, monitor student progress, and give more individual attention and praise. With small groups, the teacher must provide a steady pace for the lesson, provide questions and activities that allow all to participate, and include lots of positive praise. Small groups can also make differentiated instruction easier and more practical.

One Student with Teacher
One-to-one tutorial teaching can be used to provide extra assistance to individual students. Such tutoring may be scheduled at set times during the day or provided as the need arises. The tutoring model is typically found more often in elementary and resource classrooms than in secondary settings, and is particularly effective for students with certain disabilities.

Peer Tutoring
In an effective peer tutoring arrangement, the teacher trains the peer tutors and matches them with students who need extra practice and assistance. In addition to academic skills, the arrangement can help both students work on social skills such as cooperation and self-esteem. Both students may be working on the same material or the tutee may be working to strengthen areas of weakness. The teacher determines the target goals, selects the material, sets up the guidelines, trains the student tutors in the rules and methods of the sessions, and monitors and evaluates the sessions. Care must be taken, however, to avoid that appearance that some students are smarter than others and that the "smarter" students have more work because of the "slower" students. It can be very helpful if the teacher can find something that allows the tutee in one situation to act as tutor in another.

Cooperative Learning
Cooperative learning differs from peer tutoring in that students are grouped in teams or small groups and the methods are based on teamwork, individual

accountability and team reward. Individual students are responsible for their own learning and share of the work, as well as the group's success. As with peer tutoring, the goals, target skills, materials, and guidelines, are developed by the teacher. Teamwork skills may also need to be taught. By focusing on team goals, all members of the team are encouraged to help each other as well as improve their individual performance. When students with disabilities are included in such cooperative teams it is imperative that the teacher arrange the tasks so that there is something substantive and important for each member of the group to contribute.

METHODS OF PRESENTATION OF SUBJECT MATTER

The teacher can vary the method of presentation of new material in many ways depending upon the specific needs of the students. Students with learning disabilities will often benefit from hands-on, multimodal presentation and interaction with new concepts and materials. It is helpful if the goal of the lesson, and the most important points are clearly stated at the start. Students with learning disabilities also benefit from material that is presented one concept at a time. Advance organizers and other instructional devices can:

- Connect information to what is already known (increases context)
- Make abstract ideas more concrete (reduces cognitive demand)
- Capture students' interest in the material
- Help students organize the information and visualize the relationships (increases context and reduces demand)

Organizers can be such visual aids as diagrams, tables, charts, guides, or verbal cues that alert students to the nature and content of the lesson. Organizers may be used:

- Before the lesson to alert the student to the main point of the lesson, establish a rationale for learning, and activate background information.
- During the lesson to help students organize information, keep focused on important points, and aid comprehension.
- At the close of the lesson to summarize and remember important points

INSTRUCTIONAL MATERIALS

In many school systems the textbooks and primary instructional materials have been chosen by the school, though the teacher may also be able to select additional materials. Although specialized materials for certain special needs (e.g., large print or CDs for students with visual disabilities or Dyslexia) may be available, it is usually necessary for the teachers to modify instructional materials and texts for their students with special needs. It may be necessary to enlarge the print on a worksheet or text not available in large print, or to provide additional diagrams or rearrange text on the page for students with organizational difficulties. Students with certain visual or writing difficulties may not be able to copy math problems from a book, or may need larger numbers or space for their work.

Though the specific modifications will depend upon individual student needs, one of the most common requirements will be finding or revising text for learners who cannot read at grade level or who have difficulty comprehending what they read in content areas such as science and social studies. The most common specific learning disabilities involve reading difficulties. In order for such students to have equal access to the grade level curriculum in content areas, it is often necessary to revise printed material so students can access it at their reading comprehension level. Whether selecting published materials, or revising them for the students, these guidelines should be followed in order to increase context, reduce cognitive demand, and provide content material that students with learning disabilities can access.

- Avoid complex sentences with many relative clauses.
- Avoid the passive tense.
- Try to make the topic sentence the first sentence in a paragraph.
- Make sure paragraphs have a concluding sentence that restates the topic sentence in another way.
- Use simple, declarative sentences that have only one main idea or concept at a time.
- Use simple, single syllable, concrete words rather than more complex words (e.g., "an arduous journey" should be "a hard trip").
- Eliminate nonessential information in favor of the main concepts necessary to teach.
- Try to use only one tense in all the sentences.
- Add diagrams and illustrations whenever possible and deliver information through labels rather than complete sentences.
- Whenever possible, include multisensory elements and multimodalities in the presentation.
- Avoid unfamiliar names and terms that will "tie up" the students' cognitive efforts (e.g., while the student is trying to figure out how to read the name "Aloicious" he/she will miss the point of the sentence; change the name to "Al").

Skill 6.3   **Identifying teacher responsibilities and requirements associated with referring students who may have special needs and with developing and implementing Individualized Education Plans (IEPS), and recognizing appropriate ways to integrate goals from IEPs into instructional activities and daily routines**

SEE also Skills 6.2 and 6.4.

IDENTIFICATION
Identification of a student's learning problem occurs when comparisons are made between a given student's academic and behavioral characteristics and those of the peer population. All children and youth exhibit behaviors that deviate from normative expectations at times. But overall, it is the intensity of the behavior, the degree to which it is shown, and the frequency and length of time that it persists or has occurred that is significant.

INTERVENTION
Once a student is identified as being at-risk academically or socially, remedial interventions are attempted within the regular classroom. Federal legislation requires that sincere efforts be made to help the child learn in the regular classroom.

In some states, school-based teams of educators are formed to solve learning and behavior problems in the regular classroom. These teams are created to make professional suggestions about curricular alternatives and instructional modifications. These teams may be composed of a variety of participants, including regular education teachers, building administrators, guidance counselors, special education teachers, and the student's parent(s). The team composition varies based on the type of referral, the needs of the student, and availability of educational personnel and state requirements.

REFERRAL
Referral is the process through which a teacher, a parent, or some other person formally requests an evaluation of a student to determine eligibility for special education services. The decision to refer a student may be influenced by the following:

- Student characteristics, such as the abilities, behaviors, or skills (or lack thereof) that students exhibit;
- Individual differences among teachers, in their beliefs, expectations, or skill in dealing with specific kinds of problems;
- Expectations for assistance with a student who is exhibiting academic or behavioral learning problems;
- Availability of specific kinds of strategies and materials;
- Parents' request for referral or opposition to referral; and
- Institutional factors that may facilitate or constrain teachers in making referral decisions. Fewer students are referred when school districts have complex procedures for referral, psychological assessments are backlogged for months, special education classes are filled to capacity, or principals and other administrators do not fully recognize the importance of special services.

EVALUATION

If instructional modifications in the regular classroom have not proven successful, a student may be referred for multidisciplinary evaluation. The evaluation is comprehensive and includes:

- Norm and criterion-referenced tests (e.g., IQ and diagnostic tests)
- Curriculum-based assessment
- Systematic teacher observation (e.g., behavior frequency checklist)
- Samples of student work
- Parent interviews

The purpose of the evaluation is twofold: to determine eligibility for special education services and to identify a student's strengths and weaknesses in order to plan an individual education program (IEP).

The wording in federal law is very explicit about the manner in which evaluations must be conducted and about the existence of due process procedures that protect against bias and discrimination. Provisions in the law include the following:

- The testing of children in their native or primary language unless it is clearly not feasible to do so
- The use of evaluation procedures selected and administered to prevent cultural or ethnic discrimination
- The use of assessment tools validated for the purpose for which they are being used (e.g., achievement levels, IQ scores, adaptive skills)
- Assessment by a multidisciplinary team using several pieces of information to formulate a placement decision

Furthermore, parental involvement must occur in the development of the child's educational program. According to the law, parents must:

- Be notified before initial evaluation or any change in placement by a written notice in their primary language describing the proposed school action, the reasons for it, and the available educational opportunities
- Consent, in writing, before the child is initially evaluated

Parents may then:

- Request an independent educational evaluation if they feel the school's evaluation is inappropriate
- Request an evaluation at public expense if a due process hearing decision is that the public agency's evaluation was inappropriate
- Participate on the committee that considers the evaluation, placement, and programming of the student

All students referred for evaluation for special education should have on file the results of a relatively current vision and hearing screening. This will determine the adequacy of sensory acuity and ensure that learning problems are not due to a vision and/or hearing problem.

ELIGIBILITY

Eligibility is based on criteria defined in federal law or state regulations, which vary from state to state. Evaluation methods correspond with eligibility criteria for the special education classifications. For example, a multidisciplinary evaluation for a student being evaluated for intellectual disabilities would include the individual's intellectual functioning, adaptive behavior, and achievement levels. Other tests are based on developmental characteristics exhibited (e.g., social, language, and motor).

A student evaluated for learning disabilities is given reading, math, and spelling achievement tests, an intelligence test to confirm average or above average cognitive capabilities, and tests of written and oral language ability. Tests need to show a discrepancy between potential and performance. Classroom observations and samples of student work (such as impaired reading ability or impaired writing ability) also provide indicators of possible learning disabilities.

Eligibility for services in behavior disorders requires documented evidence of social deficiencies or learning deficits that are not because of intellectual, sensory, or physical conditions. Therefore, any student undergoing multidisciplinary evaluation for this categorical service is usually given an intelligence test, diagnostic achievement tests, and social and/or adaptive inventories. Results of behavior frequency lists, direct observations, and anecdotal records collected over an extended period often accompany test results.

Additional information frequently used when making decisions about a child's eligibility for special education include the following:

- Developmental history
- Past academic performance
- Medical history or records
- Neurological reports
- Classroom observations
- Speech and language evaluations
- Personality assessment
- Discipline reports
- Home visits
- Parent interviews
- Samples of student work

If considered eligible for special education services, the child's disability should be documented in a written report stating specific reasons for the decision.

Three-year reevaluations (Triennials) of a student's progress are required by law and determine the growth and changing needs of the student. During the re-evaluation, continued eligibility for services in special education must be assessed using a range of evaluation tools similar to those used during the initial evaluation. All relevant information about the student is considered when making a decision about continued eligibility or whether the student no longer needs the service and is ready to begin preparing to exit the program. If the student is deemed ready to exit the program, then planning for the transition must occur.

INDIVIDUAL EDUCATION PLAN
Before placement can occur, the multidisciplinary team must develop an Individualized Education Plan (IEP), a child-centered educational plan that is tailored to meet individual needs. IEPs acknowledge each student's requirement for a specially designed educational program.

The following three purposes are identified by Polloway, Patton, Payne, and Payne (1989):

1. IEPs outline instructional programs. They provide specific instructional direction, which eliminates any pulling together of marginally related instructional exercises
2. IEPs function as the basis for evaluation
3. IEPs facilitate communication among staff members, teachers, and parents, and to some extent, teachers, and students

Development of the IEP follows initial identification, evaluation, and classification. The educational plan is evaluated and rewritten at least annually. An IEP is a binding legal document and both the school system and the teacher are responsible for seeing that its conditions are met. An IEP also follows the child from school to school when the child moves.

Skill 6.4   Demonstrating knowledge of basic service delivery models (e.g., inclusion models) for students with special needs, and identifying strategies and resources (e.g., special education staff) that help support instruction in inclusive settings

INCLUSION, MAINSTREAMING, AND LEAST RESTRICTIVE ENVIRONMENT
Inclusion, mainstreaming, and least restrictive environment are interrelated policies under the IDEA, with varying degrees of statutory imperatives.

- **Inclusion**: the right of students with disabilities to be placed in the regular classroom

- **Lease restrictive environment**: the mandate that children be educated to the maximum extent appropriate with their nondisabled peers
- **Mainstreaming**: a policy where disabled students can be placed in the regular classroom, as long as such placement does not interfere with the student's educational plan

INDIVIDUALS WITH DISABILITIES ACT AND CHILD STUDY TEAMS

Collaborative teams play a crucial role in meeting the needs of all students, and they are an important step in helping to identify students with special needs. Under the Individuals with Disabilities Act (IDEA), which federally mandates special education services in every state, it is the responsibility of public schools to ensure consultative, evaluative and, if necessary, prescriptive services to children with special needs.

In most school districts, this responsibility is handled by a collaborative group of professionals called the Child Study Team (CST). If a teacher or parent suspects a child is experiencing academic, social or emotional problems a referral can be made to the CST. The CST will review the student's case and situation through meetings with the teacher and parents or guardians. The CST will determine what evaluations or tests are necessary, if any, and will also discuss the results. Based on these results, the CST will suggest a plan of action if one is necessary.

ACADEMIC INTERVENTION PLAN

One plan of action is an Academic Intervention Plan (AIP). An AIP consists of additional instructional services that are provided to the student in order to help them better achieve academically. Often these plans are developed if the student has met certain criteria (such as scoring below the state reference point on standardized tests or performing more than two levels below grade-level).

504 PLAN

Another plan of action is a 504 plan. A 504 plan is a legal document based on the provisions of the Rehabilitation Act of 1973 (which preceded IDEA). A 504 plan is a plan of instructional services to assist students with special needs in a regular education classroom setting. When a student's physical, emotional, or other impairments (such as Attention Deficit Disorder) impact his or her ability to learn in a regular education classroom setting, that student can be referred for a 504 meeting. Typically, the CST and perhaps even the student's physician or therapist will participate in the 504 meeting and review the student's specific needs to determine if a 504 plan will be written.

INDIVIDUALIZED EDUCATION PLAN (IEP)

Finally, a child referred to CST may qualify for an Individualized Education Plan (IEP). An IEP is a legal document that delineates the specific, adapted services a student with disabilities will receive. An IEP differs from a 504 plan in that the child must be identified for special education services to qualify for an IEP, and all students who receive special education services must have an IEP. Each IEP must contain statements pertaining to the student's present performance level, annual goals, related services and supplementary aids, testing modifications, a projected date of services, and assessment methods for monitoring progress. At least once each year, the CST and guardians must meet to review and update a student's IEP.

According to IDEA, each IEP must contain the following:

- A statement of the present levels of educational performance of the child
- A statement of annual goals, including short-term instructional objectives
- A statement of the specific educational services to be provided to the child, and the extent to which the child will be able to participate in regular educational programs
- The projected date for initiation and anticipated duration of such services
- Appropriate objective criteria and evaluation procedures and schedules for determining, on at least an annual basis, whether instructional objectives are being achieved
- Instructional and program accommodations and supports that must be provided throughout the educational settings and, specifically, in state and district mandated testing
- A clear rationale for any placement that involves nonparticipation in any part of the general education classroom
- Transition services, as appropriate and needed

WORKING WITH IEPS

All teachers and staff who interact with a child on an IEP are required to follow the dictates of the IEP. In addition to goals and objectives, the IEP will specify what accommodations or instructional modifications are to be provided to the child. Accommodations usually concern *access* to the curriculum. A child with accommodations to access the curriculum will follow the same grade level standards and goals as general education students, and be graded on the same scale. Modifications usually refer to changes that significantly alter the standards, content, instructional level, or performance level required of the student. This means the student will be graded differently than grade peers. Whatever terminology is used, these distinctions are important, and it is the teacher's responsibility to be familiar with all aspects of the IEP, so as to ensure compliance with it.

First and foremost, teachers must be familiar with what is stated in their students' IEPs. For example, some IEPs have explicit strategies that teachers should use to help the students learn effectively. Additionally, teachers may want to provide additional attention to these students to ensure that they are progressing effectively. Sometimes, it may be necessary to reduce or modify assignments for students with disabilities. For example, if a teacher were to assign fifteen math problems for homework, for particular students, the assignment might be more effective if it is five problems for the students with disabilities. Teachers can use multiple strategies, group students in flexible situations, and pair them with others who can be of greater assistance.

RESOURCES

Special education teachers, resource specialists, school psychologists, and other special education staff are present on school campuses to be resources for students who have special educational needs. Occasionally, new teachers fear that when a resource specialist seeks to work with them, it means that the resource specialist does not think they are doing an adequate job in dealing with students with Individualized Education Plans (IEPs). Quite the contrary is true. Many IEPs require that resource specialists work in students' general education classrooms. Considering that school is more than just about the learning of content standards—that it is often about socialization and the development of citizens for a democratic society—it is both counterproductive and unfair to exclude students from regular classrooms, even if they need some individualized assistance from a special education resource teacher.

Skill 6.5   Demonstrating knowledge of strategies to ensure that students with special needs and exceptional abilities are an integral part of the class and participate to the greatest extent possible in all classroom activities

Per federal law, students with disabilities should be included as much as possible in the general education curriculum of their schools. While this may be difficult for new teachers (likewise, it may be difficult for new teachers to include gifted students in the general education curriculum), it is extremely important to do so.

INCLUDING SPECIAL NEEDS STUDENTS IN THE CLASSROOM

Flexible Grouping

Flexible grouping is a unique strategy to ensure that students with special needs are fully accommodated. While flexible grouping can indeed involve groups for various learning activities that will change (depending on the activity, or just depending on the need to rotate groups), when teachers consistently build in various group structures in order to accommodate various learning needs, their students will get varied and multiple opportunities to talk about, reflect upon, and question new learning. In some cases, teachers may wish to pair students with special needs with other students who are proficient in particular subjects; at other times, they may desire to pair students with others who have similar levels of proficiency.

Behavior Issues

Behavior issues often cause students with special needs to be excluded from full class participation. It is important for teachers to note that often, students with special needs do not want to be excluded, and often, they do not want to be "bad." Rather, they are seeking attention, or they are bored. In either case, classroom activities must be developed with these concerns in mind. All students, in fact, will be more engaged with hands-on, real-world learning activities. Often, when teachers give students even small amounts of choice, such as letting them choose one of three topics to write about, students feel empowered. Students with special needs are no different.

Being "Caught Up"

Finally, many students with special needs want to stay "caught up" with the rest of the class, but occasionally, they cannot. In such cases, it is imperative that teachers find ways that will allow these students to know that they are on the same page as the rest of the class. Reducing the amount of work for students with special needs is often productive; pairing such students with more proficient students can also be assistive.

Students with Exceptional Abilities

Students with exceptional abilities can be a great challenge for teachers. It is very unfair to assume that since these students already "get it" that they can be ignored. These students need to continue to learn, even if it is above and beyond the rest of the class. Furthermore, they will often resent being so much smarter than the rest of the class because they are "called on" more or they are treated as if they do not need any attention. First, while these students are a fantastic resource for the rest of the class, being a resource is not their role in the classroom. They are there to learn, just like the rest of the class. They occasionally need different work to engage them and stimulate their minds. They do not simply need more work; this is unfair to them, and it is insulting.

DOMAIN II   **INSTRUCTION AND ASSESSMENT**

COMPETENCY 007   **UNDERSTAND HOW TO STRUCTURE AND MANAGE A CLASSROOM TO CREATE A SAFE, HEALTHY, AND SECURE LEARNING ENVIRONMENT**

Skill 7.1   **Analyzing relationships between classroom management strategies (e.g., in relation to discipline, student decision making, establishing and maintaining standards of behavior) and student learning, attitudes, and behaviors**

CLASSROOM MANAGEMENT

Classroom management plans should be in place when the school year begins. Developing a management plan requires a proactive approach. A proactive approach involves:

- Deciding what behaviors will be expected of the class as a whole
- Anticipating possible problems
- Teaching the behaviors early in the school year
- Implementing behavior management techniques that focus on positive procedures that can be used at home as well at school

Establishing Rules

It is important to involve the students in the development of the classroom rules. The benefits include:

- It lets the students understand the rationale for the rules
- It allows the students to assume responsibility for the rules because they had a part in developing them; when students get involved in helping establish the rules, they will be more likely to assume responsibility for following them

Once the rules are established, enforcement and reinforcement for following the rules should begin right away.

Establishing Consequences and Rewards

Consequences should be introduced when the rules are introduced, clearly stated, and understood by all of the students. The severity of the consequence should match the severity of the offense and must be enforceable. The teacher must apply the consequence consistently and fairly, so the students will know what to expect when they choose to break a rule.

Like consequences, students should understand what rewards to expect for following the rules. The teacher should never promise a reward that cannot be delivered, and follow through with the reward as soon as possible. Consistency and fairness is also necessary for rewards to be effective. Students will become frustrated and give up if they see that rewards and consequences are not delivered timely and fairly.

Displaying the Classroom Management Plan

About four to six classroom rules should be posted where students can easily see and read them. These rules should be stated positively, and describe specific behaviors so they are easy to understand. Certain rules may also be tailored to meet target goals and IEP requirements of individual students. (For example, a new student who has had problems with leaving the classroom may need an individual behavior contract to assist him or her with adjusting to the class rule about remaining in the assigned area.) As the students demonstrate the behaviors, the teacher should provide reinforcement and corrective feedback.

Reviewing the Classroom Management Plan

Periodic "refresher" practice can be done as needed, for example, after a long holiday or if students begin to "slack off." A copy of the classroom plan should be readily available for substitute use, and the classroom aide should also be familiar with the plan and procedures.

The teacher should clarify and model the expected behavior for the students. In addition to the classroom management plan, a management plan should be developed for special situations, (i.e., fire drills) and transitions (i.e., going to and from the cafeteria). Periodic review of the rules, as well as modeling and practice, may be conducted as needed, such as after an extended school holiday.

Things Not To Do

Procedures that use social humiliation, withholding of basic needs, pain, or extreme discomfort should never be used in a behavior management plan. Emergency intervention procedures used when the student is a danger to himself or others are not considered behavior management procedures. Throughout the year, the teacher should periodically review the types of interventions being used assess their effectiveness and make revisions as needed.

BEHAVIOR MANAGEMENT THEORIES

One of the more influential behavior management theories is from B.F. Skinner. Skinner's theories have been put into practice in school systems in an assortment of ways. However, parents and teachers both have rewarded students for good behavior long before B.F. Skinner's theories were well-known. Skinner believed immediate praise should be offered to students, instantaneous feedback should be given, and rewards given to encourage proper behavior in the classroom. Teachers wanting to put into action a reinforcement system in their classrooms might use strategies such as a "token economy" as an incentive for positive behaviors.

A second theory that is often used in today's classroom is the **student-centered approach.** This theory encourages independent thinking in order that students choose their own appropriate behavior for the situation. Another theory is the **moderate approach.** In this approach are the combinations of humanist and behaviorists belief systems. Students need to have a sense of belonging and feel important in their environment. This will increase their sense of self-worth in order to improve their behavior, and ultimately their academic achievements.

A final theory is the **assertive discipline approach** which has a positive discipline system. This system has a clear indication of the rules, frequent reminders of the rules, and clear indication of consequences. This behavioral management method aspires to create a positive discipline system that reinforces the teacher's authority to teach and control in order to guarantee a safe setting which is the best possible environment for student learning.

BEHAVIOR MANAGEMENT TECHNIQUES

Listed below are some behavior management plan strategies for increasing desired behavior:

- **Prompt:** A prompt is a visual or verbal cue that assists the child through the behavior shaping process. In some cases, the teacher may use a physical prompt such as guiding a child's hand. Visual cues include signs or other visual aids. Verbal cues include talking a child through the steps of a task. The gradual removal of the prompt as the child masters the target behavior is called fading.
- **Modeling:** In order for modeling to be effective, the child must first be at a cognitive and developmental level to imitate the model. Teachers are behavior models in the classroom, but peers are powerful models as well, especially in adolescence. A child who does not perceive a model as acceptable will not likely copy the model's behavior. This is why teachers should be careful to reinforce appropriate behavior and not fall into the trap of attending to inappropriate behaviors. Children who see that the students who misbehave get the teacher's constant attention will most likely begin to model those students' behaviors.
- **Contingency Contracting:** Also known as the Premack Principle or "Grandma's Law," this technique is based on the concept that a preferred behavior that frequently occurs can be used to increase a less preferred behavior with a low rate of occurrence. In short, performance of X results in the opportunity to do Y, such as getting 10 minutes of free time for completing the math assignment with 85% accuracy.
  - Contingency contracts are a process that continues after formal schooling and into the world of work and adult living. Contracts can be individualized, developed with input of the child, and accent positive behaviors. Contingencies can also be simple verbal contracts, such as the teacher telling a child that he or she may earn a treat or special activity for completion of a specific academic

activity. Contingency contracts can be simple daily contracts or more formal, written contracts.

- o Written contracts last for longer periods of time, and must be clear, specific, and fair. Payoffs should be deliverable immediately after the student completes the terms of the contract. An advantage of a written contract is that the child can see and re-affirm the terms of the contract. By being actively involved in the development of the contract with the teacher and/or parent, the child assumes responsibility for fulfilling his share of the deal. Contracts can be renewed and renegotiated as the student progresses toward the target behavior goal.
- **Token Economy:** A token economy mirrors our money system in that the students earn tokens ("money") that are of little value in themselves but can be traded for tangible or activity rewards, just as currency can be spent for merchandise. Using stamps, stickers, stars, or point cards instead of items like poker chips decrease the likelihood of theft, loss, and noise in the classroom.

Here are some tips for a token economy:

- Keep the system simple to understand and administer
- Develop a reward "menu" which is deliverable and varied
- Decide on the target behaviors
- Explain the system completely and in positive terms before beginning the economy
- Periodically review the rules
- Price the rewards and costs fairly, and post the menu where it will be easily read
- Gradually fade to a variable schedule of reinforcement

These behavioral management theories are not all inclusive nor do they stand alone. They may overlap or even combine themselves into one cohesive learning theory. Ultimately, each teacher will need to establish the best behavioral management belief system that works for them and their class. Teachers need to keep in mind that each class will be different and behavior management systems will need to be adapted accordingly.

Skill 7.2   Recognizing issues related to the creation of a classroom climate (e.g., with regard to shared values and goals, shared experiences, patterns of communication)

SEE also Skills 2.5 and 14.5.

COMMUNICATING BEHAVIOR EXPECTATIONS

Student behavior expectations should be taught with the teacher explaining the rules and discussing the consequences of nonconformity. The severity of the consequence should equal the severity of the wrongdoing and must be quickly enforced by the teacher or the principal.

Clear, consistent class rules go a long way to preventing inappropriate behavior. Effective teachers give immediate feedback to students regarding their behavior or misbehavior. If there are consequences, they should be as close as possible to the outside world, especially for adolescents. Consistency, especially with adolescents, reduces the occurrence of power struggles and teaches them that predictable consequences follow for their choice of actions.

Listed below are examples of rules of expected behavioral standards at the various developmental levels.

Early Childhood

1. Raise your hand
2. Keep hands and objects to yourself
3. Clean up your area
4. Be kind and show respect
5. Listen carefully

Young Elementary

1. Follow directions the first time given
2. Raise your hand and wait for permission to talk
3. Do not leave your seat while the teacher is teaching
4. Stay on task
5. Pay attention

Middle School

1. Raise your hand to speak
2. Stay in your seat
3. Speak appropriately to adults and peers
4. No profanity, name calling, or teasing
5. Behave appropriately
6. Keep your hands and feet to yourself
7. No physical or verbal disruption

PRAISE

Teachers should make ample use of praise. When good behavior is noted, these should be noted and acknowledged right away. This can be in the form of a smile, a nod, or even a "thumbs up." Just remember that classroom behavior management expectations are skills that teachers acquire and perfect over time.

Tips to Remember

- The first few days are the most important ones of the year
- Never get into a power struggle with your students
- Not every student will like you
- Do not make any rules for your class with which you are not willing to follow through on

CLASSROOM CLIMATE

Teachers must take the time to know each student as an individual, and demonstrate a sincere interest in each student. For example, it is important to know the correct spelling and pronunciation of each student's name, and any preference in how the student would like to be addressed. Plan time for interaction in the classroom; time when the teacher and the class can become familiar with each student's interests and experiences. This will help the teacher and the students avoid making assumptions based on any individual's background or appearance.

To create this environment, teachers must first model how to welcome and consider all points of view for the students. The teacher should positively affirm students for offering their ideas in front of the other students. Even if somewhat amiss, the teacher should receive the idea while perhaps offering a modification or corrected statement (for more factual pieces of information). The idea is for students to feel confident and safe in being able to express their thoughts or ideas. Only then will students be able to engage in independent discussions that consider and respect everyone's statements.

Student-student and teacher-student interactions play a significant role in a positive classroom climate. When interactions among classroom members are encouraging, learning becomes a more natural and genuine process. Cold or routine interactions discourage questioning, critical thinking and useful discussion.

A teacher's enthusiasm can significantly impact a student's desire to learn. Research indicates that as teachers become significantly more enthusiastic, students exhibit increased on-task behavior.

Not only does the teacher need to be enthusiastic while teaching, he or she needs to model his or her own enthusiasm for gaining knowledge. For example, the teacher should be reading during silent reading time. Or, if a question is asked that the teacher does not know the answer to, the teacher should get excited about finding out the right answer while modeling how to do so with the students.

Skill 7.3 **Demonstrating knowledge of basic socialization strategies, including how to support social interaction and facilitate conflict resolution among learners, and applying strategies for instructing students on the principles of honesty, personal responsibility, respect for others, observance of laws and rules, courtesy, dignity, and other traits that will enhance the quality of their experiences in, and contributions to, the class and the greater community**

SEE also Skills 2.4 and 14.2 for information on cooperative learning.

SEE Skill 3.6 for information on peer interactions and conflict resolution.

HIGH EXPECTATIONS

Teachers must set the bar high for learning in their classrooms. Academic integrity consists of five core values that are instrumental in managing student behavior and for promoting appropriate behavior in the classroom. Honesty requires truthfulness at all times on the part of the student. Students should be aware of that fact that cheating is not allowed and will not be tolerated in the classroom. Trust is an important issue that should be encouraged between teacher and student. If a problem arises within the classroom, a student should feel comfortable in discussing it with the teacher. Students should treat other students with fairness and understanding. Respect is an extremely important value that needs to be taught to all students concerning race, ethnicity, and diversity. Students should be taught to be understanding of others around them that might hold differing viewpoints than their own. Students should be held responsible and accountable for their actions and deeds.

Skill 7.4 **Organizing a daily schedule that takes into consideration and capitalizes on the developmental characteristics of learners**

THE IMPORTANCE OF ROUTINES

There are a number of things that hinder teachers from beginning instruction immediately. Some examples are attendance and discipline (getting students to settle down). Analysts have found that if class is delayed for 10 minutes each day, almost two months of instruction is lost over the school year. Punctuality leads to more on-task time, which results in greater subject matter retention among the students. Therefore, it is very important to begin class on time. Effective teachers have pre-determined plans to deal with these distractions.

Eliminating Wasted Time

Dealing with the daily task of attendance can be done efficiently and quickly with the use of a seating chart. A teacher can spot absentees in seconds by noting the empty seats, rather than calling each student's name, which could take as long as five minutes. Another timesaving technique is to laminate the seating chart. This allows the teacher to make daily notes right on the chart. The teacher may also efficiently keep track of who is volunteering and who is answering questions.

Effective teachers use class time efficiently. This results in higher student subject engagement and will likely result in more subject matter retention. One way teachers use class time efficiently is through a smooth transition from one activity to another; this activity is also known as "management transition." Management transition is defined as "teacher shifts from one activity to another in a systemic, academically oriented way."

CLASSROOM SCHEDULING

Young children are continually developing physically, emotionally, and intellectually. Even among peers in a classroom setting there can be diverse levels of development. The classroom teacher must plan according to the norm, allowing for exceptions that ensure the inclusion of all students in the education process.

Not only do young children need variety to avoid boredom and remain interested and motivated, but they require a mix of physical and mental activities broken by restful periods where their minds and bodies can adjust and prepare for further activities. As a teacher would not lecture to an early elementary class for an entire hour, she or he would also not expect them to play a game requiring physical exertion for an hour or more. In planning each module of instruction, the teacher must anticipate the physical and intellectual demands necessary for the students to meet the lesson objectives and incorporate limitations which will provide variety in activities and avoid stressing the students' capacity to attend, retain, remain interested and acquire skills.

Guidelines for allocating time by activity type and varying activities within the lesson module may be provided to the teacher within the school system and are usually available at the departmental level. But even guidelines may need to be tempered by common sense and specific classroom experience to ensure that young students are not stressed by demands beyond their current developmental levels and yet are working, learning, and achieving to their full potential.

An organized daily schedule helps children know what to expect during their day, which can reduce confusion in the class and also gives young students the structure they need. Scheduling blocks of time is ideal for large group activities or allowing students to work in reading, science, or math centers. Since many students have short attention spans and are not able to fully concentrate or sit still for long periods of time, scheduling reading activities and group projects into manageable blocks of time is an ideal way to regulate the attention levels of the students.

By having blocks of time set aside for group projects and activity centers, teachers have more time to develop key concepts and incorporate creativity into instruction, and this also allows for more in-depth study time for the students. Teachers that incorporate learning centers into their daily class schedules promote student independence, which causes students to become more responsible, through self-discovery. This also allows time for teachers to work one-on-one with students or in small groups as well.

Block (Modular) Scheduling

Block scheduling refers to organizing academic days to have fewer, but longer, class periods that allow teachers great amounts of time with which to work with students, plan activities that delve deeper, and therefore, boost academic achievement. Block scheduling is typically introduced in the later school years (middle school and higher) but can certainly be utilized, at least for part of the day, in elementary classrooms. For example, regular education teachers who have the same students for the majority of the day could certainly attempt to layout all the Language Arts activities together to create a "Literacy Block" where activities merge reading, writing, and spelling lessons.

Blocks of time devoted to learning centers and group projects may range from 30 minutes to 45 minutes. Students may be unable to fully concentrate if more time is allotted and will become fidgety and lose focus. Teachers should allow a passing time of 10 minutes between each schedule block of learning. Students will need time to re-focus and prepare for the next scheduled activity.

The advantages of block scheduling include teachers having more time with individual students; longer cooperative activities and/or labs can be completed; students have less information to handle at a time so can better focus on and process the information they receive; teachers can vary instruction for students with different abilities; students can retake failed classes; and fewer textbooks are required.

4x4 and A/B Schedules

One common schedule is the 4x4 schedule, where students have four academic classes per day that last for 90 minutes each. Classes meet for one semester, and so there are two 4x4 schedules in a year. An A/B schedule also has four, 90-minute academic classes per day, but has a total of eight classes that are held over the course of two days. An A/B schedule would last an entire academic year. With a trimester schedule, students take two to three core courses each trimester, over 60 days. Within these schedules, most schedules also incorporate traditional amounts of time for lunch, extracurricular activities, and "specials."

A sample A/B schedule for an elementary school is shown below. Time for lunch, recess and specials are incorporated into additional time for core subjects and would be only a portion of the large block of time.

Time	Day A	Day B	Day A	Day B	Day A
8:45 -			Math /	Library	
10:15 -	Math	Spelling		Spelling	Math
	Science	Reading / Art	Science	Reading	Science / Computers
11:45 -	Lunch /	Lunch /	Lunch / Recess	Lunch / Recess	
12:30 -	Reading /				Lunch / Recess
2:00 -		History	Reading	History	Reading
	Writing	Lang. Arts	Writing	Math / Music	Writing

Criticism of Block Scheduling
Some critics state not enough research has been conducted to support block scheduling. In addition, some arguments for not relying entirely on block scheduling include:

- Students loose continuity, and possibly a lot of instruction, if a student is absent or if school is out for a holiday

- Poor planning could result in not enough material for the longer time block, and over the course of a year, this could result in a lot of lost instructional time
- Difficult to cover ample material for advanced classes, and on the other side, the long instructional times are difficult for young and/or special needs children
- If a student has an "off" semester (i.e., distracted with a heavy sports schedule, family issue, etc), this could result in that student missing the majority of a subject for the year

Although some educators feel it is not significantly beneficial for students, many educators feel block scheduling heightens morale and encourages the use of innovative teaching methods that perhaps would not be used in a traditional timeframe.

Skill 7.5   **Evaluating, selecting, and using various methods for managing transitions (e.g., between lessons, when students enter and leave the classroom), and handling routine classroom tasks and unanticipated situations**

TRANSITIONS AND SEQUENCING

One factor that contributes to efficient management of transition is the teacher's management of instructional material. Effective teachers gather their materials during the planning stage of instruction. Doing this, a teacher avoids flipping through things looking for the items necessary for the current lesson. Momentum is lost and student concentration is broken when this occurs. Smooth transitions can also contribute to improving student behavior in the classroom. When a teacher handles movement between activities (or redirects a student who is off-task back to on-task work) well, s/he decreases opportunities for student inattention and misconduct.

Effective teachers deal with daily classroom procedures efficiently and quickly because then students will spend the majority of class time engaged in academic tasks that will likely result in higher achievement. Various studies have shown that the high-achieving classrooms spend less time on off-task behavior. For example, C.W. Fisher, et al, in a 1978 study, found that in the average classroom, students spent about eight minutes per hour engaged in off-task behavior. However, this was reduced to about four minutes in high-achieving classrooms. Therefore, effective teachers spend less time on daily housekeeping chores.

Furthermore, effective teachers maintain a business-like atmosphere in the classroom. This leads to the students getting on-task quickly when instruction begins. There are many ways effective teachers begin instruction immediately. One method is through the use of over-head projectors. The teacher turns-on the overhead the second class begins, and the students begin taking notes. The teacher is then free to circulate for the first few minutes of class and settle down individual students as necessary. Having a routine that is followed regularly at the beginning of class allows the students to begin without waiting for teacher instruction.

Additionally, teachers who keep students informed of the sequencing of instructional activities maintain systematic transitions because the students are prepared to move on to the next activity. For example, the teacher says, "When we finish with this guided practice together, we will turn to page twenty-three and each student will do the exercises. I will then circulate throughout the classroom helping on an individual basis. Okay, let's begin." Following an example such as this will lead to systematic smooth transitions between activities because the students will be turning to page twenty-three when the class finishes the practice without a break in concentration.

Group Fragmentation

Another method that leads to smooth transitions is to move students in groups and clusters rather than one by one. This is called "group fragmentation." For example, if some students do seat work while other students gather for a reading group, the teacher moves the students in pre-determined groups. Instead of calling the individual names of the reading group, which would be time consuming and laborious, the teacher simply says, "Will the blue reading group please assemble at the reading station. The red and yellow groups will quietly do the vocabulary assignment I am now passing out." As a result of this activity, the classroom is ready to move on in a matter of seconds rather than minutes.

Interruptions

Effective teachers have rules that deal with controlled interruptions, such as students who are tardy to class or who do not have their supplies. For example, when a student returns to class after being absent, he or she places his or her parent note in the box on the teacher's desk designated for this. The student then proceeds to the side counter where extra copies of yesterday's work are located. The student takes the work and sits down to begin today's class work. The student is aware that the teacher will deal with individual instructions during seatwork time when it will not disrupt the class momentum.

ORGANIZED MATERIALS

Additionally, effective teachers have highly planned lessons with all materials in order prior to class. If a teacher is going to utilize a chart or a map in a lesson, the chart or map is already prepared and in place in the classroom before class begins. Furthermore, all materials are copied and in order ready to pass out as needed. This results in the efficient distribution of materials and leads to less off-task time.

These effective organizational and management routines minimize time wasted in the classroom. As discussed above, minimizing distractions, housekeeping and transitions allows for increased instructional time that will positively affect student learning in the classroom.

SEE Skill 2.1 for methods of scheduling a lesson for young children.

Skill 7.6 Analyzing the effects of the physical environment, including different spatial arrangements, on student learning and behavior

TEACHING MANAGEMENT SKILLS

Teachers have a responsibility to help students learn how to manage time and organize their learning environments for maximum effectiveness. Classrooms are great places for children to learn responsibility and good citizenship. Teachers of young children can help students learn how to behave appropriately and take care of their surroundings by providing them with opportunities to practice ownership, chores, and leadership. Many high school and college-aged students reflect on the fact that they were never taught how to do these things in earlier grade levels, and often, they struggle into adulthood without these skills.

CLASSROOM SETUP

The physical setting of the classroom contributes a great deal toward the propensity for students to learn. An adequate, well-built, and well-equipped classroom will invite students to learn. This has been called "invitational learning." A classroom must have adequate physical space so students can conduct themselves comfortably. Some students are distracted by windows, pencil sharpeners, doors, etc. Some students prefer the front, middle, or back rows. Classrooms with warmer subdued colors contribute to students' concentration on task items. Neutral hues for coloration of walls, ceiling, and carpet or tile are generally used in classrooms so distraction due to classroom coloration may be minimized.

In the modern classroom, there is a great deal of furniture, equipment, supplies, appliances, and learning aids to help the teacher teach and students learn. The classroom should be provided with furnishings that fit the purpose of the classroom. The kindergarten classroom may have a reading center, a playhouse, a puzzle table, student work desks/tables, a sandbox, and any other relevant learning/interest areas. A middle school or high school classroom may have desks/tables, a content-specific library, a writing station, and a manipulative/project station (particularly for math and science classes).

Whatever the arrangement of furniture and equipment may be the teacher must provide for adequate traffic flow. Rows of desks must have adequate space between them for students to move and for the teacher to circulate. All areas must be open to line-of-sight supervision by the teacher.

Environment

First, teachers should arrange classrooms in ways that students can access materials. However, materials should be arranged in ways that maintain cleanliness. Messy classrooms show students that teachers do not care enough to provide students with clean, safe environment in which to learn. It also presents a negative image to parents, principals, and other teachers.

As children learn to clean up after themselves, they should be taught how to appropriately divide responsibilities (so, if a group of three students are working with blocks together, all three should divide up materials to put away). They should also learn how to put materials back in an organized fashion. So, for example, the first time blocks are put away, the teacher should show how to sort by shapes and size. The teacher can quiz students as a group about which items belong together and which items do not belong together.

SAFETY AND MAINTENANCE

In all cases, proper care must be taken to ensure student safety. Furniture and equipment should be situated safely at all times. No equipment, materials, boxes, etc., should be placed where there is danger of falling over. Doors must have entry and exit accessibility at all times.

The teacher has the responsibility to report any items of classroom disrepair to maintenance staff. Broken windows, falling plaster, exposed sharp surfaces, leaks in ceiling or walls, and other items of disrepair present hazards to students. Another factor that must be considered is adequate lighting. Report any inadequacies in classroom illumination. Florescent lights placed at acute angles often burn out faster. A healthy supply of spare tubes is a sound investment.

Local fire and safety codes dictate entry and exit standards. In addition, all corridors and classrooms should be wheelchair accessible for students and others who use them. Older schools may not have this accessibility.

Another consideration is adequate ventilation and climate control. Some classrooms in some states use air conditioning extensively. Sometimes it is so cold as to be considered a distraction. Specialty classes such as science require specialized hoods for ventilation. Physical Education classes have the added responsibility for shower areas and specialized environments that must be heated such as pool or athletic training rooms.

COMPETENCY 008   UNDERSTAND CURRICULUM DEVELOPMENT, AND APPLY KNOWLEDGE OF FACTORS AND PROCESSES IN CURRICULAR DECISION MAKING

Skill 8.1   Applying procedures used in classroom curricular decision making (e.g., evaluating the current curriculum, defining scope and sequence)

CURRICULUM DEVELOPMENT

Curriculum development today must consider many factors including:

- Alignment
- Scope
- Sequence
- Design

First, curriculum must be aligned to state standards, state and local assessments, and district and school goals. **Curriculum alignment** simply means that there is reflection in the curriculum of these elements. In other words, what students learn should reflect state requirements. Usually, this also means that what students' learn is tested on state assessments.

Second, **curriculum scope** is the "horizontal" aspect of curriculum. For example, if a topic of study in a biology class is invertebrate animals, the scope would define everything that must be taught for students to adequately understand this concept.

While on the other hand, **curriculum sequence** is the outline of what should be taught before and after a particular subject. So, for example, a sequence in math might suggest that students should learn addition and subtraction before multiplication and division. Likewise, basic math topics, like those just described, should be taught before decimals and fractions. A sequence would put all of these elements into an appropriate order.

Curriculum design considers the progression from the beginning of a unit of study to the end of the same unit of study. First, curriculum should be designed with the end in mind. What do you want students to know and be able to do when finished? How would they prove that they know the material or have the skill? If that information has been defined, it is much easier to design a curriculum. Too often, curricula is designed only considering forward steps in a process without concern for what students should be getting out of the curriculum.

As a teacher implements a curriculum, the teacher should be familiar with these three main components:

Main components of curriculum:

- The philosophy or principal aims of the curriculum—in other words, what the curriculum wants students to get out of it
- The knowledge base of the curriculum—If teachers are not deeply familiar with what they are teaching to students, they will be very ineffective at getting students to learn it
- The plan, scope, and sequence of the curriculum—-What would students have learned prior? Where will they go next?

Skill 8.2   Evaluating curriculum materials and resources for their effectiveness in addressing the developmental and learning needs of given students

INSTRUCTIONAL MATERIALS & RESOURCES
Student-centered classrooms contain not only textbooks, workbooks, and literature materials but also rely heavily on a variety of audio-visual equipment and computers. There are tape recorders, language masters, filmstrip projectors, and laser disc players to help meet the learning styles of the students.

Regardless of what the material is, teachers must make sure that the materials used in their classrooms are:

- Accurate
- Age-appropriate
- Useful
- Current (relatively); if mandated materials are somewhat outdated, it is possible to supplement them with other learning materials that offer more current perspectives
- Readable
- Easy to use (especially software, videos, and websites)
- Has connections to the curriculum

These ideas evaluate the materials from the teacher's point of view, but be sure to also evaluate from the student's perspective. Some questions to consider are:

- Will this interest my students?
- Will this offer a new perspective?
- Does this promote critical thinking?
- Does this promote interdisciplinary learning?
- What types of learning strategies are involved?
- Does this touch upon multiple intelligences?
- Is learning interactive and hands-on?

Most communities support agencies which offer assistance in providing the necessities of special needs people including students. Teachers must know how to obtain a wide range of materials including school supplies, medical care, clothing, food, adaptive computers and books (such as Braille), eye glasses, hearing aids, wheelchairs, counseling, transportation, etc.

Skill 8.3 Applying strategies for modifying curriculum based on learner characteristics

BRAIN-BASED LEARNING
Some of the most prominent learning theories in education today include brain-based learning. Supported by recent brain research, brain-based learning suggests that knowledge about the way the brain retains information enables educators to design the most effective learning environments. As a result, researchers have developed 12 principles that relate knowledge about the brain to teaching practices. These 12 principles are:

1. The brain is a complex adaptive system
2. The brain is social
3. The search for meaning is innate
4. We use patterns to learn more effectively
5. Emotions are crucial to developing patterns
6. Each brain perceives and creates parts and whole simultaneously
7. Learning involves focused and peripheral attention
8. Learning involves conscious and unconscious processes
9. We have at least two ways of organizing memory
10. Learning is developmental
11. Complex learning is enhanced by challenge (and inhibited by threat)
12. Every brain is unique

(Caine & Caine, 1994, Mind/Brain Learning Principles)

Educators can use these principles to help design methods and environments in their classrooms to maximize student learning.

MULTIPLE INTELLIGENCE THEORY
The Multiple Intelligent Theory, developed by Howard Gardner, suggests that students learn in (at least) seven different ways. These include visually/spatially, musically, verbally, logically/mathematically, interpersonally, intrapersonally, and bodily/kinesthetically.

As children develop into adults their specific learning abilities and personal interests will become more and more apparent. Particularly in adolescence, students will determine which areas of school they enjoy and which areas they do not. Often, this has to do with the subjects at which they succeed.

If a student has linguistic intelligence, that student might have an easier time with reading comprehension, writing, or learning new languages. If a student has kinesthetic intelligence, he or she might be skilled in art (as many visual arts require good hand-eye movement). If a student has spatial intelligence, he or she might be able to develop a map of a location easily. If a student has strong interpersonal intelligence, he or she might be good at "reading" other people's moods or helping them through problems.

What this means for teachers is that if one type of intelligence or thinking style is prized in the classroom over another, many students will be unsuccessful. This is unfair to students as all types of intelligence are valued in the real world and all types are important. However, when students are judged on their mathematics and reading skills alone, for example, the other areas in which they might excel are ignored.

Addressing Multiple Intelligences
How do teachers demonstrate commitment to all types of intelligences and learning styles? What teachers can do is to first alternate the ways that lessons are taught and knowledge is assessed. If teachers alternate lessons, this allows some students to be very successful at an activity but then exposes other students to that type of thinking.

Secondly, teachers can give students choices. When students are given choices (on how the learn certain things or how they prove that they know something), they further develop the skills of adult thinking. This allows them to assess their knowledge on their own and then assess which style of thinking will best demonstrate mastery. Teachers may be very impressed with how well students perform in this type of environment. Furthermore, it helps to develop responsibility.

It is also crucial to keep in mind that students' abilities to engage in abstract thinking and reasoning develop over time; and, that all students will not develop these skills at exactly the same time. Piaget's theory of cognitive development suggests that it is not until the Formal Operational stage, which begins around age 11 and continues into adulthood, that students begin to think abstractly.

MODIFYING CURRICULA BASED ON LEARNER CHARACTERISTICS
The effective teacher will seek to connect all students to the subject matter using multiple techniques. The goal should be that each student, through their own abilities, will relate to one or more techniques and excel in the learning process. While all students need to have exposure to the same curriculum, not all students need to have the curriculum taught in the same way. Differentiation is the term used to describe the variations of curriculum and instruction that can be provided to an entire class of students.

The following are three primary ways to differentiate:

- **Content**—the specifics of what is learned. This does not mean that whole units or concepts should be modified. However, within certain topics, specifics can be modified.
- **Process**—the route to learning the content. This means that not everyone has to learn the content in exactly the same method.
- **Product**—the result of the learning. Usually, a product is the end result or assessment of learning. For example, not all students are going to demonstrate complete learning on a quiz; likewise, not all students will demonstrate complete learning on a written paper.

The following are two keys to successful differentiation:

- Knowing what is essential in the curriculum. Although certain things can be modified, other things must remain intact in a specific order. Disrupting central components of a curriculum can actually damage a student's ability to learn something successfully.
- Knowing the needs of the students. While this can take quite some time to figure out, it is very important that teachers pay attention to the interests, tendencies, and abilities of their students so that they understand how each of their students will best learn.

Many students will need certain concepts explained in greater depth; others may pick up on concepts rather quickly. For this reason, teachers will want to adapt the curriculum in a way that allows students with the opportunity to learn at their own pace, while also keeping the class together as a community. While this can be difficult, the more creative a teacher is with the ways in which students can demonstrate mastery, the more fun the experience will be for students and teachers. Furthermore, teachers will reach students more successfully as they will tailor lesson plans, activities, groupings, and other elements of curriculum to each student's need.

Skill 8.4 Applying strategies for integrating curricula (e.g., incorporating interdisciplinary themes)

When the teacher actively and frequently models viewing from multiple perspectives as an approach to learning in the classroom, the students not only benefit through improved academic skill development, they also begin to adopt this approach for learning and contemplating as a personal skill. This ability to consider a situation, issue, problem, or event from multiple viewpoints is a skill that will serve the individual well throughout his or her academic career and beyond.

THEMATIC UNITS
Interdisciplinary and thematic instruction, by definition and design, provide for teaching from perspective. Examples of effective, readily available instructional units are displayed below.

Discovering Your World by Anita Yeoman
This integrated unit introduces students to various countries as they plan a trip around the world. The unit is very flexible and can be adapted for any middle-level grade and time period. It consists of detailed suggestions for planning a "journey" according to the needs of each class. Worksheets for planning an itinerary, making passports and calculating distances are included, together with peer and self evaluation sheets and tracking sheets. Students will utilize research skills as they learn about language, history, geography and culture of the countries they "visit" on their world trip.

Let's Create an Island by Philip Richards
In this unit, students will create an island, following a set of suggestions, deciding on such things as its location, topography, climate, population, employment, form of government, leisure activities, education, etc. It enables students to learn important geographic, scientific and civic concepts in a manner that is enjoyable and imaginative. For each activity a concept is taught as a class activity, followed by independent exercises to reinforce what has been taught. The students then this use this knowledge when creating their own island. Unit includes tracking sheets, suggestions for teaching the unit, a rubric for evaluation, and an answer key. Grades 6–9.

Cool Character by Charlotte Wilcox, Sharon, Toothman, Linda Hatfield
The objective of this unit, intended for grade 6, is to teach character education through the integration of different subject areas, primarily Health, English/Language Arts, Science, and Social Studies. This unit meets the following National Standards:
- **Language Arts:**
  - ○ Gathers and uses information for research purposes
  - ○ Demonstrates competence in the general skills and strategies of the writing process
  - ○ Demonstrates competence in speaking and listening as tools for learning
- **Social Studies:**
  - ○ Understands the importance of Americans sharing and supporting certain values, beliefs, and principles of American constitutional democracy
  - ○ Understands economic, social, and cultural developments in the contemporary United States
- **Health:**
  - ○ Knows how to maintain mental and emotional health
  - ○ Understands the fundamental concepts of growth and development

COMPETENCY 009   UNDERSTAND THE INTERRELATIONSHIP
                   BETWEEN ASSESSMENT AND INSTRUCTION
                   AND HOW TO USE FORMAL AND INFORMAL
                   ASSESSMENT TO LEARN ABOUT STUDENTS,
                   PLAN INSTRUCTION, MONITOR STUDENT
                   UNDERSTANDING IN THE CONTEXT OF
                   INSTRUCTION, AND MAKE EFFECTIVE
                   INSTRUCTIONAL MODIFICATIONS

Skill 9.1   Demonstrating understanding that assessment and instruction must be closely integrated

PURPOSES OF ASSESSMENT
Assessment is observing an event and making a judgment about its status of success. There are seven purposes of assessment:

- To assist student learning
- To identify students' strengths and weaknesses
- To assess the effectiveness of a particular instructional strategy
- To assess and improve the effectiveness of curriculum programs
- To assess and improve teaching effectiveness
- To provide data that assists in decision making
- To communicate with and involve parents

MAKING INSTRUCTIONAL DECISIONS BASED ON ASSESSMENT RESULTS
Assessment is key to providing differentiated and appropriate instruction to all students, and this is the area in which teachers will most often use assessment. Teachers should use a variety of assessment techniques to determine the existing knowledge, skills, and needs of each student. Depending on the age of the student and the subject matter under consideration, diagnosis of readiness may be accomplished through pretest, checklists, teacher observation, or student self-report. Diagnosis serves two related purposes—to identify those students who are not ready for the new instruction and to identify for each student what prerequisite knowledge is lacking.

Student assessment is an integral part of the teaching-learning process. Identifying student, teacher, or program weaknesses is only significant if the information so obtained is used to remedy those concerns. Lesson materials and lesson delivery must be evaluated to determine relevant prerequisite skills and abilities. The teacher must be capable of determining whether a student's difficulties lie with the new information, with a lack of significant prior knowledge, or with a core learning disability that must be addressed with specialized lesson plans or accommodations. The ultimate goal of any diagnostic or assessment endeavor is improved learning. Thus, instruction is adapted to the needs of the learner based on assessment information.

Skill 9.2   **Demonstrating familiarity with basic assessment approaches, including the instructional advantages and limitations of various assessment instruments and techniques (e.g., portfolio, teacher-designed classroom test, performance assessment, peer assessment, student self-assessment, teacher observation, criterion-referenced test, norm-referenced test)**

TYPES OF ASSESSMENT

Assessment types can be categorized in a number of ways, most commonly in terms of what is being assessed, how the assessment is constructed, or how it is to be used. It is important to understand these differences so as to be able to correctly interpret assessment results.

Formal vs. Informal

This variable focuses on how the assessment is constructed or scored. Formal assessments are assessments such as standardized tests or textbook quizzes; objective tests that include primarily questions for which there is only one correct, easily identifiable answer. These can be commercial or teacher made assessments, given to either groups or individuals. Informal assessments have less objective measures, and may include anecdotes or observations that may or may not be quantified, interviews, informal questioning during a task, etc. An example might be watching a student sort objects to see what attribute is most important to the student, or questioning a student to see what he or she found confusing about a task.

Standardized Tests

Formal tests that are administered to either groups or individuals, in a specifically prescribed manner, with strict rules to keep procedures, scoring, and interpretation of results uniform in all cases. Such tests allow comparisons to be made across populations, ages or grades, or over time for a particular student. Intelligence tests and most diagnostic tests are standardized tests.

Norm Referenced vs. Criterion Referenced

This distinction is based on the standard to which the student's performance is being compared. Norm referenced tests establish a ranking and compare the student's performance to an established norm, usually for age or grade peers. What the student knows is of less importance than how similar the student's performance is to a specific group. Norm referenced tests are, by definition, standardized. Examples include intelligence tests and many achievement tests. Norm referenced tests are often used in determining eligibility for special needs services.

Criterion referenced tests measure a student's knowledge of specific content, usually related to classroom instruction. The student's performance is compared to a set of criteria or a preestablished standard of information the student is expected to know. On these tests, what the student knows is more important than how he or she compares to other students. Examples include math quizzes at the end of a chapter, or some state mandated tests of specific content. Criterion referenced tests are used to determine whether a student has mastered required skills.

Group vs. Individual Assessments
This variable simply refers to the manner of presentation, whether given to a group of students or on a one to one basis. Group assessments can be formal or informal, standardized or not, criterion or norm referenced. Individual assessments can be found in all these types as well.

Authentic Assessments
Authentic assessments are designed to be as close to real life as possible so they are relevant and meaningful to the student's life. They can be formal or informal, depending upon how they are constructed. An example of an authentic test item would be calculating a 20 percent sales discount on a popular clothing item after the student has studied math percentages.

Rating Scales and Checklists
Rating scales and checklists are generally self-appraisal instruments completed by the student or observation-based instruments completed by teacher or parents. The focus is frequently on behavior or affective areas such as interest, motivation, attention or depression. These tests can be formal or informal and some can be standardized and norm referenced. Examples of norm referenced tests of this type would be ADHD rating scales or the Behavior Assessment System for Children.

ADVANTAGES AND DISADVANTAGES

Disadvantages of Formal Assessment
There are some disadvantages to formal assessment that need to be considered. Formal assessments do not always provide a full picture of a student's capabilities. They tend have multiple choice questions and/or some written format, and they rarely challenge the student to originate their own answer, showing their depth of understanding. These tests require strict rules and circumstances for implementation, and they are difficult for students who have a hard time sitting for long periods. They are unlikely to show oral, visual, or creative abilities in students, and some experts consider these tests culturally biased. In addition, these tests can neglect the students who have solid potential but need a little support to make the most of their education. Teachers must keep in mind that formal assessment is one component of assessment and must be combined with other types of assessment for a more accurate representation of students' abilities.

While the efficacy of the standardized tests that are being used nationally has come under attack recently, they are actually the only device for comparing where an individual student stands with a wide range of peers. They also provide a measure for a program or a school to evaluate how their own students are doing as compared to the populace at large. Even so, they should not be the only measure upon which decisions are made or evaluations drawn. There are many other instruments for measuring student achievement that the teacher needs to consult and take into account.

Disadvantages of Informal Assessment

Informal assessments do provide a picture of abilities across different formats; however, informal assessments may not measure specific retention and achievement. Informal assessments tend to be subjective and therefore are affected by the people involved. For example, if the teacher misses something in an observation or is in a bad mood when grading an essay, this may affect the outcome of the assessment. Although unprofessional, these tendencies can occur. Some informal assessments, such as reading through journals weekly, long essays, and large lab projects, are timely to score/assess.

CLASSROOM OBSERVATION

One of the most valuable and effective assessment tools available to any teacher is the classroom observation. As instructional decision makers, teachers must base their instructional strategies upon students' needs. An astute observer of student behaviors and performance is most capable of choosing instructional strategies that will best meet the needs of the learners. Classroom observations take place within the context of the learning environment thus allowing the observer the opportunity to notice natural behaviors and performances.

Classroom observations should be sensitive and systematic in order to permit a constant awareness of student progress. One of the shortcomings of classroom observations is that they are often performed randomly and frequently are focused on those students whose behaviors are less than desirable. If the teacher establishes a focused observation process then observations become more valuable. It has been suggested that a teacher focus his/her observations on five or six students at a time for a period of one to two weeks.

In order for observations to truly be useful, teachers must record the information obtained from observations. When doing a formal behavioral observation, the teacher will write what the child is doing for a designated time period. At times, the teacher will tally the occurrences of specific behaviors within a designated time period. When making focused observations that are ongoing, the teacher may simply use a blank piece of paper with only the student's name and date written on it and space for the teacher to write anecdotal notes. Other teachers might write on post-it notes and put the information in a student's file. If it is not possible to record the information as it occurs and is observed, it is critical that it be recorded as soon as possible in order to maintain accuracy.

Sometimes it is helpful to do an observation simply to watch for frequency of a specific behavior. An observation can answer questions such as: is the student on-task during independent work time? Is the student interacting appropriately with peers? Is the student using materials appropriately? These behaviors can be tallied on a piece of paper with the student's name and date of observation.

ALTERNATIVE ASSESSMENTS

Alternative assessment is an assessment where students create an answer or a response to a question or task, as opposed to traditional, inflexible assessments where students choose a prepared response from among a selection of responses, such as matching, multiple-choice or true/false. When implemented effectively, an alternative assessment approach will exhibit these characteristics, among others:

- Requires higher-order thinking and problem-solving
- Provides opportunities for student self-reflection and self-assessment
- Uses real world applications to connect students to the subject
- Provides opportunities for students to learn and examine subjects on their own, as well as to collaborate with their peers
- Encourages students to continuing learning beyond the assignment requirements
- Clearly defines objective and performance goals

Skill 9.3   Using knowledge of the different purposes (e.g., screening, diagnosing, comparing, monitoring) of various assessments and knowledge of assessment concepts (e.g., validity, reliability, bias) to select the most appropriate assessment instrument or technique for a given situation

SEE also Skill 9.1.

SCREENING, DIAGNOSIS, AND PLACEMENT

Intelligence tests have historically been considered relatively good predictors of school performance. These tests are standardized and norm referenced. Examples are the *Wechsler Intelligence Scale for Children-Fourth Edition (WISC-IV)*, Stanford-*Binet IV*, and *Kaufman Assessment Battery for Children-Second Edition (KACB-II)*.

Some intelligence tests are designed for use with groups, and are used for screening and identification purposes. The individual tests are used for classification and program placement. Since intelligence is a quality that is difficult to define precisely, results of intelligence tests should not be used to discriminate or define the person's potential. In recent years intelligence testing has evolved to include measures of multiple intelligences (Gardner, 1999) and these tests can further refine placement decisions for students with special needs. In many cases a significant discrepancy between scores on different intelligences helps to identify specific learning disabilities. Such measures also help show how a disability impacts performance in different areas of the curriculum.

There are many standardized achievement and educational skills tests, including state mandated testing, that are also used by school systems to help determine eligibility and placement.

VALIDITY, RELIABILITY, AND BIAS IN TESTING
Validity is how well a test measures what it is supposed to measure. Reliability is the consistency of the test. This is measured by whether the test indicates the same score for the child who takes it twice.

Bias in testing occurs when the information in the test or the information the student is required to respond to a multiple-choice question or constructed response (essay question) is not available to test takers who come from a different cultural, ethnic, linguistic, or socioeconomic background than the majority of the test takers.

Skill 9.4   Using rubrics, and interpreting and using information derived from a given assessment

SUBJECTIVE TESTS AND RUBRICS
Rubrics are the most effective tool for assessing items that can be considered subjective. They provide the students with a clearer picture of teacher expectations and provide the teacher with a more consistent method of comparing this type of assignment.

Sometimes, the rubric is as simple as a checklist, and other times, a maximum point value is awarded for each item on the rubric. Either way, rubrics provide a guideline of the teacher's expectations for the specifics of the assignment. The teacher usually discusses and models what is expected to fulfill each guideline, as well as provides a detailed outline of these expectations for reference.

For example, an elementary teacher may assign a total of 50 points for an entire paper. The rubric may award 10 points for note taking quality, 10 points for research skills, 20 points for content covered, 5 points for creative elements, and 5 points for organization and presentation. Then a certain number of points will be awarded in accordance with the students' performance. Rubrics allow students to be scored in multiple areas, rather than simply on a final product.

Teachers can also show students how to use scoring guides and rubrics to evaluate their own work, particularly before they turn it in. One particularly effective way of doing this is to have students examine models and samples of proficient work. Teachers should collect samples of good work, remove names and other identifying factors, and show these to students so that they understand what is expected of them. Often, when teachers do this, they're surprised to see how much students gain in terms of their ability to assess their own performance.

Skill 9.5   Recognizing strategies for planning, adjusting, or modifying lessons and activities based on assessment results

SEE also Skill 9.1.

USING ASSESSMENT INFORMATION TO MODIFY PLANS AND ADAPT INSTRUCTION

Assessment skills should be an integral part of teacher training. Teachers are able to use pre and post assessments of content areas to monitor student learning, analyze assessment data in terms of individualized support for students and instructional practice for teachers, and design lesson plans that have measurable outcomes and definitive learning standards. Assessment information should be used to provide performance-based criteria and academic expectations for all students in evaluating whether students have learned the expected skills and content of the subject area.

By making inferences on teaching methods and gathering clues for student performance, teachers can use assessment data to inform and have an impact on instructional practices. By analyzing the various types of assessments, teachers can gather more definitive information on projected student academic performance. Instructional strategies for teachers would provide learning targets for student behavior, cognitive thinking skills, and processing skills that can be employed to diversify student learning opportunities.

COMPETENCY 010   **UNDERSTAND INSTRUCTIONAL PLANNING AND APPLY KNOWLEDGE OF PLANNING PROCESSES TO DESIGN EFFECTIVE INSTRUCTION THAT PROMOTES THE LEARNING OF ALL STUDENTS**

Skill 10.1   **Recognizing key factors to consider in planning instruction (e.g., New York State Learning Standards for students, instructional goals and strategies, the nature of the content and/or skills to be taught, students' characteristics and prior experiences, students' current knowledge and skills as determined by assessment results, available time and other resources)**

LESSON PLANNING

Lesson plans are important in guiding instruction in the classroom. Incorporating the nuts and bolts of a teaching unit, the lesson plan outlines the steps of teacher implementation and assessment of teacher instructional capacity and student learning capacity. Teachers are able to objectify and quantify learning goals and targets in terms of incorporating effective performance-based assessments and projected criteria for identifying when a student has learned the material presented.

Critical Elements

The elements critical to the learning process include lesson content, quality materials, varied activities, specific goals, and consideration of learner needs. All components of a lesson plan including the unit description, learning targets, learning experiences, explanation of learning rationale and assessments must be present to provide both quantifiable and qualitative data to ascertain whether student learning has taken place and whether effective teaching has occurred for the students. A typical format would include the following items below:

1. Content of lesson plan: The plan contains guidelines for what is being taught and how the students will be able to access the information. Subsequent evaluations and assessments will determine whether students have learned or correctly processed the subject content being taught.
2. Materials: The plan provides a list of evaluated materials that will be used to implement the lesson content.
3. Unit Description: The plan provides description of the learning and classroom environment.
   a. Classroom Characteristics: The plan describes the physical arrangements of the classroom, along with the student grouping patterns for the lesson being taught. Classroom rules and consequences should be clearly posted and visible.
   b. Student Characteristics: The plan provides the demographics of the classroom that includes student number, gender, cultural and

ethnic backgrounds, along with Independent Education students with IEPs (Individualized Education Plans).

4. Learning Goals/Targets/Objectives: The plan defines the expectations of each lesson. Are the learning goals appropriate to the state learning standards and District academic goals? Are the objectives appropriate for the grade level and subject content area and inclusive of a multicultural perspective and global viewpoint?

5. Learning Experiences for students: The plan describes how student learning will be supported using the learning goals
   a. What prior knowledge or experiences will the students bring to the lesson? How will you check and verify that student knowledge?
   b. How will all students in the classroom be engaged? How will students who have been identified as marginalized in the classroom be engaged in the lesson unit?
   c. How will the lesson plan be modified for students with IEPs and how will Independent Education students be evaluated for learning and processing of the modified lesson targets?
   d. How will the multicultural aspect be incorporated into the lesson plan?
   e. What interdisciplinary linkages and connections will be used to incorporate across other subject areas?
   f. What types of assessments/evaluations will be used to test student understanding and processing of the lesson plan?
   g. How will students be cooperatively grouped to engage in the lesson?
   h. What Internet linkages are provided in the lesson plan?

6. Rationales for Learning Experiences: The plan provides data on how the lesson plan addresses student learning goals and objectives. Address whether the lesson provides accommodations for students with IEPs and provides support for marginalized students in the classroom.

7. Assessments: The plan describes pre- and post-assessments that evaluate student learning as it correlates to the learning goals and objectives. Do the assessments include a cultural integration that addresses the cultural needs and inclusion of students?

All components of a lesson plan (including the unit description, learning targets, learning experiences, explanation of learning rationale and assessments) must be present to provide both quantifiable and qualitative data to ascertain whether student learning has taken place and whether effective teaching has occurred for the students. National and state learning standards must be taken into account because not only will the teacher and his/her students be measured by the students' scores at the end of the year, the school will also. So, not only must the teacher be knowledgeable about state and local standards, s/he must structure his/her own classes in ways that will meet those frameworks.

Skill 10.2 **Analyzing and applying given information about specific planning factors (see above skill) to define lesson and unit objectives, select appropriate instructional approach(es) to use in a given lesson (e.g., discovery learning, explicit instruction), determine the appropriate sequence of instruction/learning for given content or learners within a lesson and unit, and develop specific lesson and unit plans**

GOALS AND OBJECTIVES

Teacher must be very knowledgeable about the writing of behavioral objectives that fall within the guidelines of the state and local expectations, and objectives must be measurable so that when the unit or semester is complete, teachers can know for sure whether accomplishments have been made. One might think that an objective would work well for a lesson and a goal might be better for a unit; that would definitely be correct. Each lesson should have at least one objective. That is, by the time the students finish the lesson, they should be able to demonstrate learning of SOMETHING that the teacher has decided to teach that day.

One of the major differences between a goal and an objective is that a goal is long-term and an objective is specific and observable. Once long-range goals have been identified and established, it is important to ensure that all goals and objectives are in conjunction with student ability and needs. Some objectives may be too basic for a higher level student, while others cannot be met with a student's current level of knowledge.

Evaluating Student Needs

There are many forms of evaluating student needs to ensure that all goals set are challenging yet achievable. Teachers should check a student's cumulative file, located in guidance, for reading level and prior subject area achievement. This provides a basis for goal setting but shouldn't be the only method used. Depending on the subject area, basic skills test, reading level evaluations, writing samples, and/or interest surveys can all be useful in determining if all goals are appropriate. Informal observation should always be used as well. Finally, it is important to take into consideration the student's level of motivation when addressing student needs.

When given objectives by the school or county, teachers may wish to adapt them so that they can meet the needs of their student population. For example, if a high level advanced class is given the objective, "*State five causes of World War II,*" a teacher may wish to adapt the objective to a higher level. "*State five causes of World War II and explain how they contributed to the start of the war.*" Subsequently, objectives can be modified for a lower level as well. "*From a list of causes, pick three that specifically caused World War II.*"

Setting Effective Goals and Objectives

First, goals and objectives must be clear. Clarity implies that the goal and objective must be clear for not only the teacher, but also the student and anyone else who might step into class on a particular day. If the objective is not clear in everyone's mind, it is probably not going to be clearly taught.

Here is a quick example: the teacher has a *goal* of teaching about nouns and verbs and an *objective* focusing on nouns, verbs, other parts of speech, and the uses of each one in a sentence. Given this goal and objective, most people would likely be confused as to what the teacher is really working on with students. In contrast, an objective such as this is much clearer: "Students will learn to contrast nouns and verbs in already-written sentences." Now there is an objective with clarity. The reader knows that the students should be able to get a sentence (age-appropriate length and complexity, by the way) and possibly circle the words that are nouns and underline the sentences that are verbs.

The goal and objective must also be significant and truly have purpose for both the standards and the life-long learning needs of students. Just because learning the parts of speech might be part of the state standards (such as the noun/verb example above), teachers might want to think twice about spending weeks upon weeks focusing on teaching this material. The significance is present, of course (all educated individuals SHOULD know the difference between the two parts of speech), but there are many other areas that students should focus on, as well.

Teachers must ensure that all goals and objectives are age-appropriate. This implies that the lessons teachers teach (and therefore the material the students are assessed on) should be appropriate to the developmental levels of the children in their classrooms. Typically, standards are defined very appropriately for each grade level. However, when a teacher takes a standard and translates it into a learning goal and an objective for a particular lesson, the teacher should remember that students will not learn the standard well if it is taught in a way that is completely too complex for their grade level and age.

Assessing Goals and Objectives

Teachers should judge all objectives on their ability to be assessed. This is, in many ways, the most important concept in evaluating the appropriateness of learning goals and objectives. Everything else can in many ways be judged on the assessment of how well students have learned the new information or skills. For example, say there is an objective that suggests that students will learn about the solar system. How is this assessed? There is so much to know about the solar system. Perhaps, the teacher will teach everything s/he knows about the solar system, but then s/he is teaching more about what s/he knows than about what students need to know. And when s/he assesses, s/he will assess them on what he taught, not what they should have learned. Therefore, an objective such as "Students will identify all the planets in the solar system" is much better because it can simply be assessed.

Here is another example to consider. If a teacher has the goal of teaching first graders advanced calculus, when the teacher thinks about assessing the students, s/he might realize that no matter how well a lesson was taught, the students did not have any context or background knowledge to make this an age-appropriate skill to learn about. In many ways, judging an objective on its ability to be assessed can highlight strengths and/or weaknesses in the other appropriateness criteria.

Addressing Standards

When an objective is responsive to students' current skills and knowledge, background, needs, and interests, this means there are multiple routes to learning a standard. Standards may seem very specific but when thought about closely, they can be approached from a variety of angles. While teachers may be more willing to teach the standards based on what they know about them or what they find to be interesting in them, teachers should remember that it would be more productive if they thought about their students' prior knowledge and personal interests. The learning will be more engaging and effective this way.

Finally, when objectives are aligned with campus and district goals, one can see that objectives can be tailored for various purposes but that they still can meet the learning needs of the standards. When a school has a mission, for example, of ensuring that students become aware of their communities and their environments (many charter and magnet schools have focus areas like this), the objectives can focus on these elements.

In general, teachers should realize that the higher the quality of the objective (if it is adhered to in the lesson), the higher the quality of instruction, and therefore, the higher the quality of learning.

Skill 10.3 **Identifying the background knowledge and prerequisite skills required by a given lesson, and applying strategies for determining students' readiness for learning (e.g., through teacher observation, student self-assessment, pretesting) and for ensuring students' success in learning (e.g., by planning sufficient time to preteach key concepts or vocabulary, by planning differentiated instruction)**

SEE Skills 2.4, 4.5, and 13.5.

Skill 10.4 **Using assessment information before, during, and after instruction to modify plans and to adapt instruction for individual learners**

SEE Skill 9.5.

Skill 10.5   Analyzing a given lesson or unit plan in terms of organization, completeness, feasibility, etc.

SEE Skills 10.1 and 10.2.

MANAGING INSTRUCTIONAL TIME

Time is a resource which must be provided for in planning, like any other resource. Poor allocation and management of time will result in poor instruction and the inability of students to properly comprehend and internalize the skills to be mastered.

When allocating classroom time, the teacher must assume there will be nonproductive events within and between learning activities. During daily lesson planning, the teacher should identify these events and account for the time necessary to complete each one. Failure to include this in the planning process may result in classroom instruction or activities being rushed or not completed, and lessons or assignments not fully understood by the students.

Conversely, if the teacher simply allocates an estimated amount of "down time" without identifying the probable events and quantifying the time, he or she may find that instructional activities are completed much sooner than expected. Some teachers will try to cover for this by "stretching" or repeating instruction, having a "spontaneous" question and answer session, using the time for "quiet study," or simply allowing the students to socialize until the end of the period. These are unproductive uses of time and may in fact prove to be counterproductive. Unplanned time is usually wasted time.

These nonproductive events are usually organizational and administrative tasks, such as:

- Taking and recording attendance
- Processing announcements
- Gathering or issuing homework assignments
- Distributing instructional materials
- Assembling members for group activities
- Responding to students questions regarding a new or revised process

Proper time management and allocation contribute to efficient classroom management and a positive learning environment. When things seem to go in fits and starts or there are frequent lulls in activity, students may respond as if the instruction or learning activity were dull and become bored, disinterested and uninvolved. If students feel uninvolved in a lesson, the teacher is probably wasting time teaching that lesson.

Strategies for Planning Time

In order to assess the time required for particular lessons and units, specific information about the content, materials, and activities involved must be known, at a detailed level, in order to allocate time appropriately. Within the specifications for most instructional materials provided by educational publishers, there are guidelines on using the material and recommendations for the allocation of time, by unit. Obviously, it is the teacher, not the textbook/media publisher, who determines what goes into a lesson plan and what is presented in the classroom—and how and when it will be presented.

Going beyond the guidelines, recommendations, and time approximations provided with such material, the teacher should decide what will and will not be used in the classroom. For each unit that will be used, the teacher should consider the component parts and ask the question, "What response do I want from the students at this point? Contemplation? Questions? Discussion or other activities? Writing or testing?" Based on his or her answers, the teacher should be able to approximate the effort involved and plan adequate time, accordingly. The same process would be used when the teacher designs and develops her or his own units or adopts them from another source.

REFLECTION

All of this is not to say that only activities conducted or directed by the teacher—with active teacher participation—have value. The needs of the students for personal review and reflection, self-assessment, to internalize ideas, information or skills, or to achieve a sense of completion should be recognized as valid, identified in the particular, and allocated appropriate time.

Purposes for allocating such time to students would include:

- After difficult or complex tasks or skills have been introduced
- After difficult or complex tasks or skills have been utilized
- After technically difficult or complex instructional materials have been introduced or utilized
- After independent research has been conducted by students
- After student reports or presentations to the class
- After returning graded examinations, assignments, or other evaluations to students
- After planned classroom activities and discussions
- After presentation or instruction on life skills, social skills, at-risk behaviors, etc.

The process of reflection needs to be planned for both during and after learning situations. Reflective thinking refers to the process of analyzing and making judgments about what has happened. It encourages students to continuously evaluate incoming information and be flexible, if appropriate, in their approach to a task. It also allows students to store information and transfer the learning experience to novel, future tasks.

Reflective thinking helps to hone higher-order thinking skills by relating new information to prior knowledge, thinking in the abstract, and using meta-cognitive skills to think about one's own thinking and learning. When allocating time for reflective thinking, the following tasks can be considered:

- Teacher modeling of metacognitive and self-explanation strategies
- Reviews of the learning task (e.g., KWL chart: What is Known, What we Want to Know, and What we have already Learned)
- Use of, and time for, reflective journaling for students to write their hypotheses/positions, reasons behind those ideas, and questions/weaknesses in their ideas
- Teacher posed questions that seek reasoning and evidence, specifically *why*, *how*, and *what*
- Collaborative activities that allow for learning about other points of view

SELF-ASSESSMENT
Self-assessment must also have time allocated to it in the course of designing a lesson or unit. Self-assessment is the process of students judging the quality of their work, based on given criteria, with the goal of improving performance in the future. The process of self-assessment itself is also helping to teach students to think critically, so that they do not need someone else to tell them how well they are doing. There is a solid body of evidence that supports the use of self-assessment for improving student performance, particularly in writing. And, equally as convincing, students often like to do it and are more motivated to persist on difficult tasks! Research also revealed that student attitudes toward evaluations were more positive when they were involved in the assessment.

The process of self-assessment is a learning experience. The process must first begin by involving students in defining the criteria on which they will be assessed. Teachers must then instruct students on how to apply that criterion to their own work. Teacher modeling, with examples, is crucial at this step. Students must then be given feedback on their self-evaluations so that they can learn how to most effectively use the process. Finally, students must be guided on how to use those self-evaluations to develop personal goals.

One popular method of self-assessment is using rubrics. Developing rubrics with students gives them the opportunity to participate in defining important criteria and also provides students with a tool to use during the learning task. Students can then systematically proceed through the assessment procedure, discuss specific areas of strength and/or weakness, and transition to goal setting in a more systematic and structured manner.

CLOSING A UNIT

Closure within a lesson or unit plan can often be overlooked; however it is a crucial time for students and teachers. Closure is the period of time when a lesson is wrapped up and the students are assisted in storing the new information into a meaningful context that can be applied in the future.

For students, closure often provides a brief overview, a reinforcement of key ideas, an affirmation of the material learned, or a time to clear up confusions or inconsistencies. For teachers, this is a time where learning can be solidified through reinforcement of key concepts and placed in the larger context of a unit or idea. It can also provide insight into which students have a clear understanding of the task and which ones need more clarification.

Sample Closure Activities

Some sample closure activities include:

- A KWL chart, with a focus on the "L" section (What has been Learned)
- 3-2-1: 3 Things learned, 2 Questions, 1 Thing liked/Strategy I used
- Circle, Square, Triangle (for higher-level students): Things/ideas that are still circling in my mind (still thinking about), things/ideas that square with what I know/believe (confirmation of known information), three points I've learned
- 3 Whats: *What* Did I learn? So *what*? (Why is it important?) *What* now? (How does this relate to what we have learned/will learn?)

Skill 10.6 Applying strategies for collaborating with others to plan and implement instruction

Depending on the educational situation, team-teaching, or the use of aides or assistants in the classroom, often serves to modify the behavior of students, positively. It is not just the presence of more authority figures but a more diverse environment, more opportunity for individual attention, and a perceived sense of increased security, which engenders a positive attitude among the students.

PARAPROFESSIONALS

A paraprofessional is often brought into a classroom for the benefit of the special needs student. The role of the paraprofessional or any teaching assistant or aide in the classroom must be clearly defined to promote the learning experience for all children and avoid an unnecessary hindrance (or worse, conflict of wills) in the classroom. It is the responsibility of the teacher—often in concert with a team of special education personnel and parents—to clearly define this role.

People skills and management skills are necessary for the teacher to work effectively with assistants in the classroom. These are not unlike the skills necessary to manage a classroom, but the individuals involved will quite likely consider themselves as peers to the teacher. Perceived attitudes and actual interactions will be on a different level than between teacher and student, but there is ultimately one authority in the classroom, and that must be the teacher.

Defining Responsibilities

The primary objective is to determine and define what activities the individual should undertake to support the teacher's mission to provide the highest standards of education for each student and the class as a whole. By appropriate planning and continual monitoring, the teacher can *avoid* the following situations which have been experienced by other teachers:

- Teacher neglect (or "surrender" of responsibility) for a student under the direct care of a paraprofessional
- Allowing an assistant to separate students with disabilities from classmates during a classroom activity although the students' needs and abilities were compatible with classmates regarding the activity
- Allowing an assistant to distract students through activities or discussions which are not related to the current lesson activity
- Allowing a paraprofessional to provide a barrier (intentional or not) between students under the assistant's care and interaction with other classmates
- Allowing an assistant to question or comment upon the teacher's lesson plan, presentation, evaluation methods, etc., in front of the students
- Allowing an assistant to intervene in a matter of classroom discipline
- Allowing an assistant to initiate and conduct conversations with parents without authority or prior approval

VOLUNTEERS

Having volunteers in the classroom can be beneficial in the classroom. Volunteers can provide extra individualized attention to students while the rest of the class is engaged in other work, or they can offer additional assistance in small group activities. However, as a teacher begins to use the aid of volunteers in their classroom, they will need to devise a plan on how they will be used. Teachers will need to designate time either before or after class to discuss the plans with the volunteers. As the classroom volunteers become acquainted with the needs of the students and the teacher's style of teaching, they will, as a rule, need less clarification of daily activities.

Volunteers are normally required to check in and out at the front office before they enter the classroom. Make sure the name of the volunteer is prominently displayed on the front of the name tag that the volunteer wears. The majority of school districts are now requiring a criminal background check on all volunteers that spend time in the classroom. Be sure that all classroom volunteers are familiar with fire drill procedures and are acquainted with the safety exits in the building.

MONITORING HELP IN THE CLASSROOM

Paraprofessionals and volunteers can be a real help in the classroom, especially since schools now have limited budgets and can rarely afford classroom aides. Setting forth strategies to monitor the help in the classroom may take an effort and once they are in place the results can be positive. However, these plans need to be specific to the paraprofessional or volunteer in the class.

STRATEGIES

- Volunteers should be aware of particular skills students need to practice
- Discuss student and grade confidentiality with the volunteer
- Teacher and volunteer agree upon a daily schedule of events
- Disciplinary measures should be discussed and enforced thoroughly
- Provide encouraging and helpful feedback to volunteers

The effective monitoring of help in the classroom can be a positive experience for the teacher. Teachers can then provide a more enriching experience for their students by using parents, volunteers, and paraprofessionals in their classrooms.

COMPETENCY 011   UNDERSTAND VARIOUS INSTRUCTIONAL APPROACHES, AND USE THIS KNOWLEDGE TO FACILITATE STUDENT LEARNING

Skill 11.1   **Analyzing the uses, benefits, or limitations of a specific instructional approach (e.g., direct instruction, cooperative learning, interdisciplinary instruction, exploration, discovery learning, independent study, lectures, hands-on activities, peer tutoring, technology-based approach, various discussion methods such as guided discussion, various questioning methods) in relation to given purposes and learners**

SEE Skill 2.4 for information on differentiated instruction and cooperative learning.

SEE Skill 8.4 for information on interdisciplinary learning.

SEE Skill 12.2 for information on different types of learners.

SEE Skill 13.8 for information on peer and group learning.

SEE Skill 14.2 for information on cooperative learning.

SEE Skill 14.4 for information on discussion and questioning.

DIRECT INSTRUCTION
Siegfried Engelmann and Dr. Wesley Becker, and several other researchers proposed the direct instruction method. Direct Instruction (DI) is a teaching method that emphasizes well-developed and carefully-planned lessons with small learning increments. DI assumes that the use of clear instruction eliminates misinterpretations and therefore improves outcomes. Their approach is being used by thousands of schools. It recommends that the popular valuing of teacher creativity and autonomy be replaced by a willingness to follow certain carefully prescribed instructional practices. At the same time, it encourages the retention of hard work, dedication, and commitment to students. It demands that teachers adopt and internalize the belief that all students, if properly taught, can and will learn.

DISCOVERY LEARNING
Beginning at birth, discovery learning is a normal part of the growing-up experience. This naturally occurring phenomenon can be used to improve the outcomes within classrooms. Discovery learning, in the classroom, is based upon inquiry, and it has been a factor in many of the advances mankind has made through the years. For example, Rousseau constantly questioned his world, particularly the philosophies and theories that were commonly accepted. Dewey, himself a great discoverer, wrote, "There is an intimate and necessary relation

between the processes of actual experience and education." Piaget, Bruner, and Papert have all recommended this teaching method as well. In discovery learning, students solve problems by using their own experiences and their prior knowledge to determine what truths can be learned. Bruner wrote "Emphasis on discovery in learning has precisely the effect on the learner of leading him to a constructionist, to organize what he is encountering in a manner not only designed to discover regularity and relatedness, but also to avoid the kind of information drift that fails to keep account of the uses to which information might have to be put."

WHOLE GROUP DISCUSSION
Whole group discussion can be used in a variety of settings, but the most common is in the discussion of an assignment. Since learning is peer-based with this strategy, students gain a different perspective on the topic, as well as learn to respect the ideas of others. One obstacle that can occur with this teaching method is that the same students tend to participate over and over while the same students also do not participate time after time. However, with proper teacher guidance during this activity, whole group discussions are highly valuable.

CASE METHOD LEARNING
Providing students an opportunity to apply what they learn in the classroom to real-life experiences has proven to be an effective way of both disseminating and integrating knowledge. The case method is an instructional strategy that engages students in active discussion about issues and the problems inherent in practical application. It can highlight fundamental dilemmas or critical issues and provide a format for role playing ambiguous or controversial scenarios. Obviously, a successful class discussion involves planning on the part of the instructor and preparation on the part of the students.

ACTIVE LEARNING
Does not all instruction encourage students to think? Well, hopefully, but research tells us that students learn greater amounts when they are engaged in active learning. Active learning derives from the assumptions that (1) learning is by nature an active endeavor and (2) that different people learn in different ways (Meyers and Jones, 1993). Students need to discover, to process, apply, and judge information in order to truly learn. This is achieved through planning a lesson that allows students to talk, listen, read, write, and reflect.

A great in-class activity that promotes active learning is "Think-Pair-Share". Students are given a question or problem to solve. They then "think" independently for a few minutes, discuss their ideas in a "pair" to encourage processing of different perspectives and evaluation of each others' ideas, and then "share" their ideas with the whole class, encouraging synthesis, and further processing and evaluation. Students can incorporate information from text they have read or may be asked to write about the given activity at a later point. Such an activity can be used with classes of all ages and sizes.

INQUIRY-BASED LEARNING

The central theme to inquiry-based learning is that learning is driven more so by student questions and elaboration than it is by teacher lessons. Does this sound counter-intuitive? Inquiry-based learning still requires a teacher to have solid goals, objectives, and lesson plans. However, it also relies heavily on creating an environment where students must solve problems, discuss, and analyze. It also requires flexibility and collaborative learning, and most importantly, solid questioning techniques.

Open-ended questions require complex thinking and give opportunities for different ways of thinking. The teacher has a responsibility to model good listening and questioning so that the students can utilize the same techniques.

Think about the following "rules for questioning":

- Ask questions that require substantive answers. Avoid yes/no questions.
  - "What do we know about making webpages?" vs. "Has anyone ever made a webpage before?"
- Avoid questions where the answer is a simple fact or a one-word answer.
  - "What year was President Kennedy killed? vs. "What factors played into President Kennedy's assassination?"
- Try to pose contradictions or use phrases such as, "Tell me more about that." or "What will happen as a result of that?" "Explain." "Expand."
- Apply questions that apply to current and real-life situations
  - "What would happen if this situation took place today? How would people react?"

Keeping in mind how to facilitate students' higher-order thinking skills by using the above techniques and instructional methods will make for a dynamic and engaging classroom environment.

Skill 11.2   Recognizing appropriate strategies for varying the role of the teacher (e.g., working with students as instructor, facilitator, observer; working with other adults in the classroom) in relation to the situation and the instructional approach used

SEE Skill 2.5.

Skill 11.3   Applying procedures for promoting positive and productive small-group interactions (e.g., establishing rules for working with other students in cooperative learning situations)

SEE Skills 2.4 and 14.2 for information on cooperative learning.

Skill 11.4 **Comparing instructional approaches in terms of teacher and student responsibilities, expected student outcomes, usefulness for achieving instructional purposes, etc.**

SEE Skill 2.4 for information on differentiated instruction and cooperative learning.

SEE Skill 8.4 for information on interdisciplinary learning.

SEE Skill 11.1 for information on direct instruction, discovery learning, and inquiry-based learning.

SEE Skill 12.2 for information on different types of learners.

SEE Skill 13.8 for information on peer and group learning.

SEE Skill 14.2 for information on cooperative learning.

SEE Skill 14.4 for information on discussion and questioning.

COMPETENCY 012   **UNDERSTAND PRINCIPLES AND PROCEDURES FOR ORGANIZING AND IMPLEMENTING LESSONS, AND USE THIS KNOWLEDGE TO PROMOTE STUDENT LEARNING AND ACHIEVEMENT**

Skill 12.1   **Evaluating strengths and weaknesses of various strategies for organizing and implementing a given lesson (e.g., in relation to introducing and closing a lesson, using inductive and deductive instruction, building on students' prior knowledge and experiences)**

STRUCTURING LESSONS

When organizing and sequencing objectives the teacher needs to remember that skills are building blocks. Because most goals are building blocks, all necessary underlying skills should be determined and a teacher must evaluate if the student has demonstrated these abilities. For example, to do mathematical word problems, students must have a sufficiently high enough level of reading to understand the problem.

Many teachers adhere to Bloom's Taxonomy of thinking skills. Bloom identified six levels of thinking within the cognitive domain (from low to high):

- Knowledge (define, list, organize, recall, label)
- Understanding (classify, explain, identify, review, discuss)
- Application (illustrate, apply, practice, solve, write)
- Analysis (categorize, compare, criticize, examine, question)
- Synthesis (arrange, collect, compose, create, propose, design, develop)
- Evaluation (argue, assess, defend, estimate, predict, support)

Bloom's research showed that 95 percent of how students were required to think was at the lowest level, knowledge, with tasks such as recall and memorizing used the most. Today, teachers are encouraged to develop instruction that requires thinking at the higher levels.

Ordering Thinking Skills

Educational objectives can be helpful to construct and organize objectives. Knowledge of material, such as memorizing definitions or famous quotes, is low on the taxonomy of learning and should be worked with early in the sequence of teaching. Eventually, objectives should be developed to include higher-level thinking such as comprehension (i.e., being able to use a definition); application (i.e., being able to apply the definition to other situations); synthesis (i.e., being able to add other information); and evaluation (i.e., being able to judge the value of something).

As a teacher, it is important to be aware of the skills and information that are pertinent to the subject area being taught. Teachers need to determine what information a student should carry with them at the end of a term. The teacher should also be aware of skills needed to complete any objective for that subject area and determine how skilled their students are at using them.

Long-Range vs. Short-Range Objectives
Once the desired knowledge, skills, and attitudes have been established, a teacher must develop short-range objectives designed to help in the achievement of these outcomes. An objective is a specific learning outcome that is used to achieve long-range goals. Objectives should be stated in observable terms such as: to state, to demonstrate, to list, to complete or to solve. Objectives should be clear and concise (i.e., students will be able to state five causes of World War II). It should also be stated in the lesson plan which curriculum objectives are met with each lesson and how it relates to course goals.

A list of the materials needed for the lesson is needed which should be followed by the specific methodologies and/or activities for the lesson. Effective teachers always include a unique activity or anticipatory set to kick off the lesson—something that hooks the students to ensure their engagement. Then the lesson is introduced and the activity(ies) begin. Since most classrooms have varied learning abilities, the teacher should prepare some activities in this list that allow for differentiated instruction.

Closing a Lesson
Lessons should close with a closing activity, review, recap, or summarizing activity. The teacher should also include how the students are to be or were assessed during the activities, as well as how the teacher assesses his/her own instruction and what can be added or changed for next time. Finally, enrichment extensions should be listed for any student who is looking for more.

Pacing Lessons
How, when, and the pace at which lessons are presented is also important. A teacher should be flexible and diverse in how they arrange and present lessons. Teachers should be sure to provide information through a variety of contexts, in a myriad of ways, and in a logical sequence. When an assortment of material is diverse and connected to the world around the students, the material has more impact and meaning to the students.

Focusing on the needs evident in almost any classroom population, the teacher will want to use textbooks that include some of the activities and selections to challenge the most advanced students as well as those who have difficulty in mastering the material at a moderate pace. Some of the exercises may be eliminated altogether for faster learners, while students who have difficulty may need to have material arranged into brief steps or sections.

Skill 12.2 **Recognizing the importance of organizing instruction to include multiple strategies for teaching the same content so as to provide the kind and amount of instruction/practice needed by each student in the class**

APPROACHING DIFFERENT LEARNING STYLES

Multiple Intelligence theory supports that there are many different approaches to learning and that students learn in many different ways. It is important for teachers to consider these different learning styles so that s/he may vary activities and instruction so as to touch on all learning styles.

Auditory learners learn by hearing. They like to read to themselves out loud and like to speak in class. These students tend to like music, languages, oral reports, participate in study groups, and follow directions well. To augment instruction for auditory learners, use videos, lecture, group discussion, audiotapes, oral exams, and even recordings of material.

Visual learners learn by seeing, and optimal learning is experienced when they see charts, maps, videos, graphs, pictures, etc. For example, visual learners may struggle with an essay exam because it is challenging to recall test material that they heard rather than saw. Visual learners tend to be good at spelling, fashion, math (especially with charts), and sign language to start. For visual learners, it is good for them to draw out maps or charts, make outlines, copy the board, diagram sentences, use color coded notes and highlighters, draw, illustrate, use flashcards, utilize educational videos and have quiet study time.

Kinesthetic learners learn by doing and experiencing. These students like sports, labs, research projects, role playing, adventure stories, model building, music, field trips, and dance. These students also tend to take breaks often, be a bit fidgety, and have poorer handwriting than others. Some useful strategies to help a kinesthetic learner are for them to study with others, study in short blocks of time, take lab classes, role play, and use games (such as matching games) and manipulatives that tie in to learning.

Multicultural Learning and Perspectives

When planning instruction for a diverse group (or teaching about diversity, for that matter) incorporate teaching through the use of perspective. There is always more than one way to "see" or approach a problem, an example, a process, fact or event, or any learning situation. Varying approaches for instruction helps to maintain the students' interest in the material and enables the teacher to address the diverse needs of individuals to comprehend the material. Meeting the requirement to enable students within a diverse classroom to acquire the same academic skills (at the same levels) can be aided considerably by incorporating teaching through the use of perspective into the unit plan.

Curriculum objectives and instructional strategies may be inappropriate and unsuccessful when presented in a single format which relies on the student's understanding and acceptance of the values and common attributes of a specific culture which is not his or her own. Planning, devising, and presenting material from a multicultural perspective can enable the teacher in a culturally diverse classroom to ensure that all the students achieve the stated, academic objective.

Even when the student population is largely culturally homogeneous, teaching with cultural perspective is always an asset to student comprehension and learning. History, as a subject, would be just one obvious example. The study of history includes the interactions of people from different cultures or subcultures. The point of view of, and impact on, each culture must be presented during instruction to ensure a comprehensive understanding of issues and events by the students. And in order to understand these points of view and impacts, it will be necessary to study the backgrounds of the cultures involved.

Teaching from multiple perspectives opens the door to a world of ideas teachers can use to make education an interesting, fun, and effective learning experience where every student can be included in the process and be successful in attaining the objectives. The possibilities may only be limited by the teacher's imagination. Should that limit actually be reached, the teacher has only to look to his or her colleagues to expand the horizon of teaching possibilities.

Skill 12.3   **Evaluating various instructional resources (e.g., textbooks and other print resources, primary documents or artifacts, guest speakers, films and other audiovisual materials, computers and other technological resources) in relation to given content, learners (including those with special needs), and goals**

CHOOSING CLASSROOM MATERIALS

In considering suitable learning materials for the classroom, the teacher must have a thorough understanding of the state-mandated curriculum. According to state requirements, certain objectives must be met in each subject taught at every designated level of instruction. Keeping in mind the state requirements concerning the objectives and materials, the teacher must determine the abilities of the incoming students assigned to his/her class or supervision. It is essential to be aware of their entry behavior—that is, their current level of achievement in the relevant areas.

Teachers should have a toolkit of instructional strategies, materials, and technologies to encourage and teach students how to problem-solve and think critically about subject content. With each curriculum chosen by a district for school implementation comes an expectation that students must master benchmarks and standards of learning skills.

Studies have shown that students learn best when what is taught in lecture and textbook reading is presented more than once in various formats. In some instances, students themselves may be asked to reinforce what they have learned by completing some original production—for example, by drawing pictures to explain some scientific process, by writing a monologue or dialogue to express what some historical figure might have said on some occasion, by devising a board game to challenge the players' mathematical skills, or by acting out (and perhaps filming) episodes from a classroom reading selection. Students usually enjoy having their work displayed or presented to an audience of peers. Thus, their productions may supplement and personalize the learning experiences that the teacher has planned for them.

Textbooks

Most teachers choose to use textbooks, which are suitable to the age and developmental level of specific student populations. Textbooks reflect the values and assumptions of the society that produces them, while they also represent the knowledge and skills considered to be essential in becoming an educated adult. Finally, textbooks are useful to the school bureaucracy and the community, for they make public and accessible the private world of the classroom. Teachers should ensure that the textbooks used are current, thorough, representative of multiple perspectives, and free of cultural stereotypes.

Other Materials

Aside from textbooks, there is a wide variety of materials available to today's teachers. Computers are now commonplace in schools. Hand-held calculators support problem solving as they eliminate the need for students to be automatic with math facts in order to learn math concepts. Videocassettes (VCR's) and DVDs are common and permit the use of home-produced or commercially produced tapes. Textbook publishers often provide films, recordings, and software to accompany the text, as well as maps, graphics, and colorful posters to help students visualize what is being taught. Teachers can usually scan the educational publishers' brochures that arrive at their principal's or department head's office on a frequent basis.

Libraries and Media Centers

Yesterday's libraries are today's media centers. Teachers can usually have projectors delivered to the classroom to project print or pictorial images (including student work) onto a screen for classroom viewing. Some teachers have chosen to replace chalkboards or whiteboards with projectors that reproduce the print or images present on the plastic sheets known as transparencies, which the teacher can write on during a presentation or have machine-printed in advance. In either case, the transparency can easily be stored for later use.

Technology

Newer technologies such as wireless projectors make student access to teacher information even easier as they allow teachers to write and/or type onto a computer and that information is automatically projected onto the classroom screen (or even wall). Another higher-tech option that is replacing transparencies, projectors, and chalkboards is digital whiteboards, such as SMART boards. These digital screens allow teachers to project images from their computer, write on the boards, and use their hands or other implements to edit, erase, and move items on the screen. Such technology provides for a truly multi-sensory experience for students who are able to physically work with the information they are learning at the board.

This is an age where technology continues to expand at an ever increasing pace. Most students have a cursory understanding of different technologies and some are quite advanced, maybe even more so than their teachers. In order to engage students, it is important that teachers learn how to utilize everyday tools such as the internet, blogs, wikis, podcasts, and other new digital technologies.

In an art or photography class, or any class in which it is helpful to display visual materials, slides can easily be projected onto a wall or a screen. Cameras are inexpensive enough to enable students to photograph and display their own work, as well as keep a record of their achievements in teacher files or student portfolios. Teaching students how to do this type of work digitally is also of value. Many high school courses, in particular, now allow students to access digital media and editing. Additionally, students can create their own blog to track achievements or portfolios.

Assistive Technology
In order to enhance student learning for all students, it is also crucial to have an understanding of assistive technology. Assistive technology "offers a bridge between a student's needs and his or her abilities. It connects a student's abilities with an educational opportunity that would otherwise be blocked by a disability." (Hecker, L., & Engstrom, E.U., 2005.) Familiarity with general categories of assistive technology, such as screen readers, speech-to-text software, word prediction tools, book on tape/CD, personal computers, or digital assistants for typing and even calculators, gives a teacher the means to ask questions and access resources for students that will enable a student to succeed.

Skill 12.4   Demonstrating understanding of the developmental characteristics of students (e.g., with regard to attention and focus, writing or reading for extended periods of time) when organizing and implementing lessons

SEE Skills 1.1, 1.2, 1.3, 1.4, 1.5, and 1.6.

Skill 12.5   Applying strategies for adjusting lessons in response to student performance and student feedback (e.g., responding to student comments regarding relevant personal experiences, changing the pace of a lesson as appropriate)

SEE also Skills 9.5 and 17.1.

TEACHER OBSERVATIONS

The value of teacher observations cannot be underestimated. It is through the use of observations that the teacher is able to informally assess the needs of the students during instruction. These observations will drive the lesson and determine the direction that the lesson will take based on student activity and behavior. After a lesson is carefully planned, teacher observation is the single most important component of an instructional presentation. If the teacher observes that a particular student is not on-task, s/he will change the method of instruction accordingly. S/he may change from a teacher-directed approach to a more interactive approach. Questioning will increase in order to increase the participation of the students. If appropriate, the teacher will introduce manipulative materials to the lesson. In addition, teachers may switch to a cooperative group activity, thereby removing the responsibility of instruction from the teacher and putting it on the students.

COMPETENCY 013   UNDERSTAND THE RELATIONSHIP BETWEEN STUDENT MOTIVATION AND ACHIEVEMENT AND HOW MOTIVATIONAL PRINCIPLES AND PRACTICES CAN BE USED TO PROMOTE AND SUSTAIN STUDENT COOPERATION IN LEARNING

Skill 13.1   **Distinguishing between motivational strategies that use intrinsic and extrinsic rewards, and identifying the likely benefits and limitations of each approach**

SEE also Skill 13.2.

INTRINSIC AND EXTRINSIC MOTIVATION

Extrinsic motivation is motivation that comes from the expectation of rewards or punishments. The rewards and punishments can be varied. For example, in social situations, most human beings are extrinsically motivated to behave in common, socially-accepted ways. The punishment for NOT doing so might be embarrassment or ridicule. The reward for doing so might be the acceptance of peers. In the classroom, rewards might be grades, candy, or special privileges. Punishments might be phone calls to parents, detention, suspension, or poor grades.

Intrinsic motivation is motivation that comes from within. For example, while some children only read if given extrinsic rewards (e.g., winning an award for the most pages read), other children read because they enjoy it.

There are benefits and drawbacks of both methods of motivation. In reality, it should be noted that in an ideal world, all motivation would be intrinsic. But this is not the case. Consider having to clean an apartment, dorm room, or house. The "reward" of a clean living space at the end of the activity is appreciated, but most people do not particularly enjoy the process of cleaning and only put up with it for the end result.

Those who work in education of course want all students to be intrinsically motivated. They want students to not care about grades or prizes as much as they might want them to do their work, listen attentively, and read just because they want to learn. And while all teachers should work tirelessly to ensure that they develop intrinsic motivation as much as possible within their students, everyone knows that for certain students and subjects, extrinsic motivators must be used.

Skill 13.2 Analyzing the effects of using various intrinsic and extrinsic motivational strategies in given situations

SEE also Skill 13.1.

EXTRINSIC MOTIVATORS IN THE CLASSROOM

What extrinsic motivators are useful in the classroom? Well, to start, if things like candy and prizes are always used to get students to pay attention in class, soon, they will expect these things and possibly not pay attention in their absence. Specific praise is another good motivator. Instead of simply stating, "Nice painting, Mary" for an art class, one could say "Excellent job, Mary. Your use of color emphasizes a happy mood." Specific praise highlights exactly what the student is doing well and clearly emphasizes what the student did well that met expectations.

Likewise, if punishment is always used as a motivator, students may be more consumed with fear than with the frame of mind that is most conducive to learning. So, while grades can consume many students, having benchmarks and standards are indeed useful for many teachers. Punishments, if they are reasonable and if students know what to expect (with consistent application), can be useful in making sure students behave appropriately. The best punishments, though, are ones which a whole school has decided will be consistently used from classroom to classroom and grade level to grade level.

Skill 13.3 Recognizing factors (e.g., expectations, methods of providing specific feedback) and situations that tend to promote or diminish student motivation

FACTORS THAT AFFECT MOTIVATION

Motivation is an internal state that activates, guides, and sustains behavior. Educational psychology research on motivation is concerned with the volition or will that students bring to a task, their level of interest and intrinsic motivation, the personally held goals that guide their behavior, and their belief about the causes of their success or failure.

Some factors that affect students' motivation include:

- High expectations set by the instructor
- Clear objectives about how to succeed in the class
- Varied instructional strategies are utilized
- The value of learning is emphasized rather than just grades
- Assignments are given in a timely manner with respect/consideration for outside commitments like jobs, sports, or other extracurricular activities
- Teacher cares genuinely for student success
- Desire to boost self-confidence

- Teachers who are easy to understand, fair, experienced, organized, interested, and passionate

Skill 13.4 Recognizing the relationship between direct engagement in learning and students' interest in lessons/activities

SEE also Skill 13.5.

STRATEGIES FOR INCREASING MOTIVATION

Effective teachers encourage students to develop small practices that they can utilize each day to increase motivation. There are many techniques teachers can implement in their class and/or with individual students to help increase their motivation. First off, teachers can enhance student motivation by planning and directing interactive, "hands-on" learning experiences. Research substantiates that teamwork and/or cooperative group projects decrease student behavior problems and increase student on-task behavior. Students who are directly involved with learning activities are more motivated to complete a task to the best of their ability.

Another strategy is to have students create daily and unit lists or goals for learning. Students could also create "dream boards"—poster boards that are collages of pictures that depict what successes they will find with their learning.

A third strategy is to break larger tasks into more manageable steps. In higher-ordered learning atmospheres, sometimes the projects can appear too challenging. Sometimes students are overwhelmed and prematurely give up on a project when it is presented as a huge, looming assignment. If the teacher helps the students see the smaller steps ("baby steps"), they can take to handle it one piece at a time their confidence will increase, as well as their motivation to do a good job. Students will also find more confidence and maintain motivation if they check off the items they have accomplished; this allows students to visually see their progress. Be sure to give positive feedback on work, participation, behaviors that are found to be satisfying and do this early in the project and frequently, so that students start off strong and with the correct expectations.

A fourth strategy is to have students identify their connections with the assignments. Make it personal. When a student feels the connection to the work, he or she can relate to the material better, they become personally invested and are more motivated to do good work when they see the learning as valuable. Therefore, personal meaning and connection can be a positive motivational strategy.

A fifth strategy is to give students control. This especially will help with students becoming more self-motivated. When the student or student groups sense they are leading the assignment, that sense of control empowers them to take hold of their own learning.

With students who are especially difficult to motivate, the sixth strategy of using incentives and rewards programs can be effective, but be sure to be sparing with such rewards and make sure rewards are given out only for successful completion—not just for participating.

A seventh strategy is to create a positive learning environment where the teacher genuinely cares about each participant. Teachers should ensure that all students feel like a valued member of this authentic learning community.

Motivation is one of the most important factors that affects student learning, and it is imperative that today's teacher focus on ensuring all of their students are properly motivated and set up for successful learning.

Skill 13.5   Applying procedures for enhancing student interest and helping students find their own motivation (e.g., relating concepts presented in the classroom to students' everyday experiences; encouraging students to ask questions, initiate activities, and pursue problems that are meaningful to them; highlighting connections between academic learning and the workplace)

SEE also Skill 13.4.

LINKING PRIOR KNOWLEDGE WITH CURRENT LESSONS

Most young students come to school ready and eager to learn, but as the grades pass, many students become bored and uninterested in school. By middle school, many students simply complete assignments for the sake of doing so, rather than with an understanding as to why that particular learning was important. Most teachers would agree that in order to truly engage students, the students must be genuinely motivated to learn. In many classrooms, it can be quite a challenge to present subjects in a way that motivates everyone at one time. This challenge is greater when the students feel that what they are learning has no connection or use in their own lives. As a result, their attention decreases, resulting in lower student achievement. Educators are finding, however, that if students are motivated to learn, they will invest more effort in participation and classroom assignments if they feel there is a purpose to the work.

Strategies for Classroom Motivation

Motivational researchers have found several strategies that help increase classroom motivation. First off, it is recommended that teachers stimulate student curiosity by asking thought-provoking questions. When there is a gap between what students know and what they want to know, teachers will be able to utilize the natural curiosity which arises as a result of that gap by having students explore this discrepancy. With young children, this need to explore is inherent, and so these students can use manipulatives, games, and play to explore their topics.

A common tool used to activate and record prior knowledge for the class is a KWL chart. KWL charts consist of three columns, each with a letter heading, K, W, and L. These charts help organize what students know (K), what they want to know (W), and (later) what they have learned (L).

Secondly, connections to what they are learning should be made to both the students' prior experience (if possible) as well as to their emotions. When links to memory and emotion are provoked in learning, the brain can relate, retain, and store the information more effectively than if it was presented in isolation. When connected to something the student remembers, likes, enjoys, is curious about, etc., the student is better able to make connections between the old and new material, therefore making better sense of the world around them and the new information they are receiving.

For example, teachers could ask young students, "What is wrong with our playground?" This question will provoke emotion for a place the students typically like, pinpoint a discrepancy with what is there and what they might want, and pose a problem they could problem solve. Depending on responses and teacher direction, lessons in economics, language, environmental, physics, citizenship, and more could evolve as a result. Not only are these topics now interrelated, they are also relevant to the students.

VARYING INSTRUCTIONAL STRATEGIES
Classrooms have begun to drift away from being entirely composed of lectures (or direct instruction). By varying presentation of material, teachers increase learning in their classrooms. There are literally hundreds of instructional techniques that can be used at many levels from early childhood through advanced high school courses. A good glossary of these strategies can be viewed at http://glossary.plasmalink.com/glossary.html.

Discussions
One excellent, and common, strategy is classroom discussion. This strategy encourages respect, open thinking, and an atmosphere of a community when used effectively in a classroom. Typically, teachers begin a discussion by stating or suggesting a goal for the group(s). This can be done by posing a question, asking an opinion about a topic, quoting a statistic or current research, or having the students come up with their own topic. Nowadays, discussions can take the form of small group, large group, online via web boards, cross classroom, debate, and more.

For discussions to be effective, teachers must set clear expectations for discussion sessions, as well as inform students on how they will be evaluated on their participation. Teachers must also control and use their classroom space strategically, as well as to be sure to actively monitor student groups when they are working together. If the teacher is leading a large group discussion, he or she must ask good, direct questions, as well as call on individual students.

Inquiry

Inquiry is another common instructional strategy. This technique encourages students to ask questions in order to form a possible answer or hypothesis to solve a problem. Through their questioning, students are typically expected to collect and/or analyze data to support their solution, which is derived from their inquiries. This strategy is especially useful in providing feedback to both teachers and students. It also provides direct connections between the teachers and students, as well as between students as a group.

Problem Solving

Inquiry is related to another strong instructional strategy—problem solving. Whether individually, in pairs, or in groups, students are given problems for which they are to present solutions. In the best scenarios, teachers will present real-world problems to students who will utilize inquiry and other critical-thinking skills to arrive at possible solutions. Another variation is for teachers to ask students to develop one or multiple problem scenarios to perhaps present to other students or groups.

Bringing It All Together

Many types of instructional strategies, including discussions, inquiry, and problem solving can be incorporated or implemented with cooperative learning strategies. Some, but certainly not all, other ways to vary instruction are listed below:

- Activating prior knowledge
- Brainstorming
- Analogies
- Evaluating cause and effect
- Venn diagrams or other visuals
- Chronological sequencing
- Circles or centers
- Journaling
- Dramatization
- Write, pair, share

Skill 13.6 Recognizing the importance of utilizing play to benefit young children's learning

THE IMPORTANCE OF PLAY

Too often, recess and play is considered peripheral or unimportant to a child's development. It is sometimes regarded as a way for kids to just get physical energy out or a "tradition" of childhood. The truth is, though, that play is very important to human development. In this country, even though most people are very industrious, they also believe strongly that all individuals deserve time to relax and enjoy the "fruits of our labors." But even more importantly, for the full development of children (who will soon be active citizens of our democracy, parents, spouses, friends, colleagues, and neighbors), play is an activity that helps teach basic values such as sharing and cooperation. It also teaches that taking care of oneself (as opposed to constantly working) is good for human beings and creates a more enjoyable society.

The stages of play development move from solitary (particularly in infancy stages) to cooperative (in early childhood), but even in early childhood children should be able to play on their own and entertain themselves from time to time. Children who do not know what to do with themselves when they are bored should be encouraged to think about particular activities that might be of interest. It is also extremely important that children play with peers. While the emerging stages of cooperative play may be awkward (as children will at first not want to share toys, for example), with some guidance and experience children will learn how to be good peers and friends.

Contributions to Development
Playing with objects helps children to develop motor skills. The objects that children play with should be varied and age appropriate. For example, playing with a doll can actually help to develop hand-eye coordination. Sports, for both boys and girls, can be equally valuable. Parents and teachers need to remember that sports at young ages should only be for the purpose of development of interests and motor skills—not competition. Many children will learn that they do not enjoy sports, and parents and teachers should be respectful of these decisions.

In general, play is an appropriate way for children to learn many things about themselves, their world, and their interests. Children should be encouraged to participate in different types of play and they should be watched over as they encounter new types of play.

Skill 13.7 Recognizing the importance of encouragement in sustaining students' interest and cooperation in learning

SEE also Skills 13.1, 13.2, and 13.3.

ENCOURAGING STUDENTS
Children learn best when they feel they are a vital part of the shared classroom experience. All students want to learn and they prefer to be partners in discovery. As Robert L. Fried has said, "education is about relationships (Robert L. Fried, *The Passionate Learner*, 2001)". Encouraging a student is placing importance on what that student has to offer to the classroom dynamic. Teachers can use quite a variety of methods to create a respectful and safe classroom that motivates all students to reach their potential.

Classroom Ideas

In order to celebrate student accomplishments and exemplary behavior towards others, teachers might allow students to design their own rewards or ceremonies to commemorate these achievements. Highlighting a student's out-of-school accomplishments will allow others to see a different, positive side rather than just an in-school personality. Designing a lesson for the classroom utilizing Gardner's concept of multiple intelligences will allow, depending upon the activity, the talented readers, artists, actors, and athletes in the room to each enjoy the spotlight.

A safe classroom is vital in encouraging students to succeed. Allowing student participation in making and upholding the rules, discussing proper ways to behave, and making decisions on what is "fair" or "unfair," will help students become better listeners, more emotionally intelligent, and better at limiting classroom disruptions through positive peer pressure. Music, games, and role-playing scenarios are ways to get students of all ages thinking about proper social conduct. Increasing the ratio of adults in the room will also provide role models for students. With careful thought and preparation, a teacher can invite parents and grandparents into the classroom to participate in lessons and activities. This will also increase the senses of pride and belonging for those students with visiting family.

The family and neighborhood community are vital catalysts in encouraging students to be at their best. A classroom can be the initial connection to the surrounding community for students, especially for those who have recently arrived from other cities or even other nations. Opening up the classroom to guest speakers from small businesses, law-enforcement, representatives of various ethnic groups, artist co-ops, and volunteer organizations can show students the positive possibilities of life outside their own paradigms. Encountering positive role-models in the immediate community can be quite empowering for a child, encouraging goal-setting and self-actualization.

Skill 13.8 Recognizing the importance of utilizing peers (e.g., as peer mentors, in group activities) to benefit students' learning and to sustain their interest and cooperation

THE ROLE OF PEERS

The ability to work and relate effectively with peers contributes greatly to the child's sense of competence. In order to develop this sense of competence, students need to successfully acquire the information base and social skill sets that promote cooperative effort in achieving academic and social objectives.

Middle-level students develop a deep social and emotional association with their peers. While young people are often self-conscious and perceive deficits in their intelligence, physical makeup, and personalities when compared to their peers, they also want to be accepted by their peers. Usually, they establish productive, positive social and working relationships with one another. Often, they are inclined to consider the perceptions and reactions of peers and value their opinions, above all else.

Some students not only perceive themselves as outsiders, but are, in fact, treated as such by their peers. While many schools provide training in social skills for students who experience peer rejection, the success of these programs is often limited by the lack of social context in the exercises. A recent study in the *Journal of Primary Prevention* evaluated and documented the effectiveness of classroom-level rather than individual-oriented approaches. Team-led groups consisting of "accepted" and "rejected" students in 24 middle-school classrooms met weekly to participate in non-academic, cooperative activities and cooperative academic work. The study found that, after the experiment, there was a significant increase in the number of students who reported that "almost all" or "all" of their peers respected them and their opinions.

Acceptance by, and interaction with, one's peers is an overwhelming priority in the life of most middle-level students. And pursuit of this social necessity is not restricted to school-time; it permeates their entire lives. But it is within the classroom setting where the positive and negative aspects of peer relations can be monitored, evaluated, and focused through planning and instruction into constructive, enabling relationships.

USING GROUPS

Young children should be developing social skills coincidentally with other life skills and academic skills. The most logical and practical venue for this development is the classroom. Not only does this afford most children their only, daily opportunity to interact socially with a diverse grouping of peers and adults, it also enables the teacher of young students to ensure that this development is planned, directed, monitored, and evaluated.

All activities the teacher plans for groups of students or the entire class should be age/grade appropriate and provide for the introduction, utilization, and development of social skills as well as academic skills. Each such exercise must have stated and measurable objectives. There are a variety of resources available to the classroom teacher planning such activities. There is a tremendous variety of single medium and multimedia, modular planning and instruction packages available through educational publishers. Not to be overlooked are the programs and activities developed by colleagues within the school system and beyond (via the Internet, for example).

It is beneficial for the teacher to remain current with the studies and findings published in numerous journals related to child and educational psychology and physical and intellectual development in early childhood. For example, several studies—past and present—have shown that girls tend to be more communicative, one with the other, while boys are more prone to be physically active, together, but less responsive to verbal interaction, one with the other. While this is a generalization, it still predicts that an effective grouping will include an approximately equal mix of girls and boys, with the teacher monitoring and encouraging the participation of all in each aspect of the planned activity.

As in this example, awareness of research and findings in the study of childhood development will inform the teacher's application of appropriate groupings and goals for developing teamwork among younger students.

Example Group Activities
The following is a small sampling of teacher-created, team building group activities for elementary school children, available for sharing with colleagues, via the Internet. There are thousands of similar lesson plans and activities available to address the development of social and academic skills through teamwork, among young children in the classroom setting.

- **Arthur: Group Stories**: An activity where students can create stories as a group. There are several variations available.
- **Spider Web**: In this team building activity, students can get to know each other while creating a unique design.
- **Trading Cards**: Children can share information about themselves by creating personalized trading cards. This could be used as an "ice-breaker" activity.
- **Can You Build It?**: Students can work together toward a common goal in this team activity. It can also be used as an "ice-breaker."
- **Who Am I?**: Children can use this activity to get to know each other by sharing about themselves and working together.
- **Mad Minute Relay**: Students can learn math in a team environment with this timed activity.
- **All of Me**: This activity can help students get to know each other by drawing pictures that show some of the different aspects of their lives, and sharing the pictures with classmates.
- **We're Different/We're Alike**: Students can learn more about each other with this lesson by using Venn diagrams to describe the ways in which they are similar and different.
- **Make a Class Pictogram**: Children can use this activity to help them understand the nature of social groups and their roles as members of various groups.
- **It's Too Loud in Here!**: This lesson plan gives students the opportunity to work as a team and participate in decision-making processes in the classroom.
- **A-Z Teacher's Stuff: Teamwork**: What does it mean to be a team? In this lesson plan, students can learn to define teamwork and work together in groups.

COMPETENCY 014   UNDERSTAND COMMUNICATION PRACTICES THAT ARE EFFECTIVE IN PROMOTING STUDENT LEARNING AND CREATING A CLIMATE OF TRUST AND SUPPORT IN THE CLASSROOM, AND HOW TO USE A VARIETY OF COMMUNICATION MODES TO SUPPORT INSTRUCTION

Skill 14.1   Analyzing how cultural, gender, and age differences affect communication in the classroom (e.g., eye contact, use of colloquialisms, interpretation of body language), and recognizing effective methods for enhancing communication with all students, including being a thoughtful and responsive listener

AGE-APPROPRIATE COMMUNICATION

It is vital for a teacher to communicate to children in an age-appropriate manner. Not only will the teacher better implement educational goals and objectives with proper communication but respect between students and teacher begins with this understanding and all levels of success follow. The most important idea is to truly listen to students, no matter what their age. Respect and cooperation begins when the child feels the adult cares. With that in mind, the teacher who effectively studies how various age-groups encode and decode language and non-verbal cues has much to gain.

Pre-School Communication

Preschoolers, from 3-6 years of age, normally speak in complete sentences. They can tell stories, sometimes out of order; but as they enter kindergarten, the order of their explanations becomes more linear. Preschoolers enjoy fantasy and play and relish learning through acting as imaginary characters. Children from 3-6 years of age are also beginning to recognize the connection between the written and spoken word. Whole language opportunities abound. Traffic signs and basic safety symbols can be taught. Puzzles and visual games create conversational and vocabulary enriching opportunities. Allowing children of this age to write thank-you notes or create birthday cards for others places their earnest efforts in front of an appreciative audience.

Primary Communication

Primary school children between the ages of 6-12 speak like adults. They are full of questions and this is the key to encouraging their learning. Children of this age become increasingly concerned with peer acceptance and love to solve problems within groups. The use of conversation is, in fact, the best way to discuss goals and problem-solving with a primary school student. Talking to children of this age about likes and dislikes and how they are getting along with others plugs a teacher into the culture of the classroom and can help resolve conflict before it starts. It's also important to calmly explain the reasons for an appropriate behavior when correcting a child of this age. Discussing the implications of inappropriate behavior can help the child visualize scenarios and consequences. This age group also has a great sense of humor and it is extremely advantageous for the instructor of these classrooms to allow for this.

SEE also Skill 4.4.

CLASSROOM COMMUNICATION AND GENDER

Most teachers will say that they consciously attempt to treat all students the same regardless of gender. However, a teacher might make eye contact with males more than females. Teachers may ask higher order questions of males rather than of females or pay more attention to the responses of males. Females may receive less attention in the classroom in general, or receive lower scores on average. A teacher may even speak primarily of male characters or read mostly from books by male authors.

Dealing with Gender Bias

Our society creates gender bias within the realms of home, advertising, and cultural touchstones like the internet, radio, television, and literature. It is imperative that educators become aware of possible gender bias in their own classrooms and work to overcome it in order to create a more equitable environment. The best way to do this is through third-party feedback.

A teacher must be open-minded and open-hearted to accept feedback concerning gender bias. This is because most bias is unconscious. One method of feedback is to allow an administrator or another teacher to sit in the room with a classroom seating chart. The observer then marks where the teacher stands when interacting with the class, and can identify which students receive interaction. During this observation general posture, eye contact, non-verbal cues, and student/teacher reactions can also be monitored.

A second method of feedback is to develop a typed-response, anonymous questionnaire for the students, to be completed in the presence of an objective third-party like an administrator or guidance counselor. The questionnaire would ask the student how often they have contributed to class discussions or, how often they have raised their hand in class. Another question asks how the teacher most often recognizes the student: by name, nodding, or pointing. When there is a technical skill to be mastered, even a video to be set up, is it a boy that is most often asked to complete the task?

Student questionnaires to determine the level of gender bias in a classroom can be eye-opening and possibly awkward for the teacher; yet this information, along with careful reflection and discussion with administrators and peers can also lead to increased student trust and respect, and certainly greater student achievement.

CLASSROOM COMMUNICATION AND CULTURE

There are two types of communication found in every culture: *direct* communication and *indirect* communication. Direct communication is explicit, usually involves words, and the speaker wants to be clearly understood ("I am hungry; I want to go to lunch"). Indirect communication involves not only the words someone says, but the context of what is said. There are often non-verbal cues and it is up to the listener to create the speaker's full meaning ("I'd love to try that new deli on Main Street," and the speaker rubs her tummy).

Different cultures use varying degrees of direct and indirect communication when they interact within their own culture. Some cultures are generally reserved in nature and allow time to pass to show respect for a question. Other cultures have a more frenetic personality, answer passionately and immediately, and might not have concepts like "lining up quietly" for recess, or for anything. In addition, all cultures have their own specific folkways when it comes to interacting with authority figures, like teachers.

Some cultures train their youngsters to never look an authority in the eye. Some cultures consider it disrespectful to look away. A youngster from a particular culture might hide a wide smile in his hand while you attempt to correct him. Yet, in his culture, he's displaying that he's very embarrassed to be singled out. A child might be from a culture that has experienced endless war, or has recently lived in a refugee camp. She may be terrified of authority, or of missing lunch due to a short meeting with a teacher or an educational assistant. A recent immigrant might ask herself: "Why aren't these children sitting properly at their desks? Why is the teacher allowing them to slouch?" Another might think: "Why are these students asking all these questions? Why aren't they silently and studiously writing down the teacher's words?"

The Cultural Mosaic

In this cultural mosaic we call the United States of America it is up to our school systems, and specifically our classroom educators, to learn about and engage with each individual student so that the best possible chance for success can be reached for that child. It is important for the instructor to visit appropriate resources and invite cultural leaders to the classroom, both in order to provide insight into a student's educational experience.

A responsible educator must learn how to best respect and interact with *all* students. It is true that people do assimilate to the predominant culture over time and that extra time must be taken to accommodate English Language Learners (ELL). However, diverse cultural mores and folkways, ethnic histories, and unique personal experiences, can be celebrated and commemorated within the classroom in order to create a rich experience for all students. In this environment, the children of the predominant culture soon come to realize how each student in the classroom is unique, interesting, and worthy of respect.

SEE also Skills 3.5, 5.1, 5.2, 5.3, and 5.4.

Skill 14.2 **Applying strategies to promote effective classroom interactions that support learning, including teacher-student and student-student interactions**

SEE also Skills 2.4 and 5.4.

COOPERATIVE LEARNING

Cooperative learning is one of the best researched and useful teaching strategies in which students are grouped in various ways to engage in learning activities designed to increase their understanding of a subject. Teachers often vary the design of the groups, and the core principle with cooperative learning is that each member of the group is responsible for a specific role. This role entrusts each member to be responsible for their own learning, as well as the other members' learning. When the group is cohesive and each member participates, the idea is that all the students will have a solid understanding of the topic, as well as a sense of worth to the group's success.

Five Elements of Cooperative Learning

Cooperative learning is not just small group work. There are certain elements that must be expected from students in order to obtain the optimum learning results from a cooperative effort. These five elements are:

1. **Positive Interdependence**: All members' efforts are required for success. The group cannot succeed without the each individual's unique contribution. Each member is indispensable for success.
2. **Face-to-Face Interaction**: Members must all orally participate and explain their "part" and ensure that the other member's understand and inter-connect their information with the rest of the information.
3. **Individual + Group Accountability**: Some ways to assess this include:
    a. Groups must remain small to ensure all students participate and are accountable for a portion of the work
    b. Incorporate some form of individual assessment after each activity or project
    c. Frequent observation of groups to monitor participation and learning
    d. Have students re-teach the concepts learned in the group to another group
4. **Interpersonal & Small-Group Skills**: Cooperative learning encourages students to practice their leadership, trust-building, communication, decision-making, and conflict-management skills.
5. **Group Processing**: Groups should periodically self-assess how their learning is going, how the members are contributing, how their relationships are working, what is working and what is not, and decide

what modifications, if any, are needed and ways to implement those changes.

Research supports that cooperative techniques enhance student learning and achievement and retention, increase oral and social skills, and boost social relations, self-esteem, and student involvement. Some examples of cooperative learning include:

- Centers
- Writer's Workshops
- Three-Step Interview
- Think-Pair-Share
- Literature Circles
- Round Robin

Skill 14.3   Analyzing teacher-student interactions with regard to communication issues (e.g., those related to communicating expectations, providing feedback, building student self-esteem, modeling appropriate communication techniques for specific situations)

HIGH EXPECTATIONS

In a document prepared for the Southern Regional Education Board, titled *Strategies for Creating a Classroom Culture of High Expectations*, Myra Cloer Reynolds summarized the process necessary to meet the stated objective when she wrote, "Motivation and classroom management skills are essential to creating and sustaining an environment of high expectations and improvement in today's schools."

In some school systems, there are very high expectations placed on certain students and little expectation placed on others. Often, the result is predictable: you get exactly what you expect to get and you seldom get more out of a situation or person than you are willing to put in. A teacher is expected to provide the same standards of excellence in education for all students. This standard cannot be upheld or met unless the teacher has (and conveys) high expectations for all students.

Considerable research has been done, over several decades, regarding student performance. Time and again, a direct correlation has been demonstrated between the teacher's expectations for a particular student and that student's academic performance. This may be unintended and subtle, but the effects are manifest and measurable. For example, a teacher may not provide the fullest effort on behalf of the student when there are low expectations of success. And the student may "buy into" this evaluation of his or her potential, possibly becoming further scholastically burdened by low self-esteem. Other students, with more self-confidence in their own abilities, might still go along with this "free ride," willing to do only what is expected of them and unwittingly allowing this disservice to hamper their academic progress.

Conveying High Expectations

There are a variety of ways in which a teacher can convey high expectations to students. Much has to do with the attitude of the teacher and positive interactions with the students—clearly stating expectations and reinforcing this at every opportunity.

- Notify the class of your high expectations for their academic success. Let them know that they will be able to acquire all the skills in which you will be instructing them, and you take personal responsibility and pride in their success.
- Speak to the class about the opportunity to support your goals for their success. Let them know that you appreciate having a student approach you with questions, problems, or doubts about her or his performance, understanding of class work, or ability to succeed. That sort of help enables you to help them and helps you succeed as a teacher.
- Never lower standards or "dilute" instruction for certain students. It is the teacher's responsibility to ascertain the means to bring the student's academic performance up to standards.
- Use all forms of teacher communication with students to reinforce your high expectations for them—as a class, and especially as individuals. What we internalize as individuals, we utilize in group settings.

An example of an opportunity to communicate expectations would be when writing comments on exams and papers being returned to individual students. Positive reinforcement should be provided regarding the progress that the student is making regarding the high expectations for his or her academic achievement. If the work itself is below expectations—perhaps even substandard—provide positive, constructive comments about what should be done to meet the expectations. Express confidence in the student's ability to do so. A negative comment, like a negative attitude, is unacceptable on the part of the teacher. The teacher may deem it necessary to speak one-on-one with the student regarding his or her performance. Remember, however, that no student ever feels motivated when reading the words "see me" on an exam or assignment.

Barriers to Communication

While teachers should never consider that all student learning is based on teachers communicating to students, much valuable information does occur in the transmission of words between teacher and student. The problem, however, is in dealing with the various types of learning difficulties that students have, as well as all the other environmental factors and learning preferences.

First, various disabilities, including hearing loss, Language-Based Learning Disabilities, Attention Deficit Hyperactivity Disorder, Central Auditory Processing Disorder, and others, can severely impact a student's ability to successfully listen and comprehend what a teacher says. In such cases, teachers should communicate with Special Education and other resource teachers about procedures and practices to follow. But teachers can also place these students in specific classroom locations, give them "partners" who can assist, and periodically check in with them to find out how they are doing. Environmental factors can either aid or inhibit a teacher's communication to students. Often, air conditioners and other room and building noises can impact students' understanding of course content.

Students also have various preferences in how they best understand; some need a lot of teacher explanation and assistance, and others need very little. It is important for the teacher to be very receptive to student comprehension levels and the potential need for further communication (verbal or nonverbal). While one can never judge how much students know from just looking at their expressions, for example, it is possible to get a pretty good idea if a change of communication style or activity is needed—or if they simply need further review.

Skill 14.4   Recognizing purposes for questioning (e.g., encouraging risk taking and problem solving, maintaining student engagement, facilitating factual recall, assessing student understanding), and selecting appropriate questioning techniques

DISCUSSION AND QUESTIONING
Beginning-teacher training explains that the focus of the classroom discussion should be on the subject matter and controlled by teacher-posed questions. When a student response is correct, it is not difficult to maintain academic focus. However, when the student response is incorrect, this task is a little more difficult. The teacher must redirect the discussion to the task at hand, and at the same time not devalue the student response. It is more difficult for the teacher to avoid digression when a student poses a non-academic question.

For example, during the classroom discussion of *Romeo and Juliet*, the teacher asks "Who told Romeo Juliet's identity?" A student raises his or her hand and asks, "May I go to the rest room?" The teacher could respond in one of two ways. If the teacher did not feel this was a genuine need, he or she could simply shake his or her head no while repeating the question, "Who told Romeo Juliet's identity?" If the teacher felt this was a genuine need and could not have waited until a more appropriate time, he or she may hold up the index finger indicating "just a minute" and illicit a response to the academic question from another student. Then, during the next academic question's pause time, the teacher could hand the student the bathroom pass.

Encouraging Participation

It is risky for students to respond to questions in a classroom. If a student is ridiculed or embarrassed by an incorrect response, the student may shut down and not participate thereafter in classroom discussion. One way to respond to an incorrect answer is to ask the child, "Show me from your book why you think that." This gives the student a chance to correct the answer and redeem him or herself.

Another possible response from the teacher is to use the answer as a non-example. For example, after discussing the characteristics of warm-blooded and cold-blooded animals, the teacher asks for some examples of warm-blooded animals. A student raises his or her hand and responds, "A snake." The teacher could then say, "Remember, snakes lay eggs; they do not have live birth. However, a snake is a good non-example of a mammal." The teacher then draws a line down the board and under a heading of "non-example" writes "snake." This action conveys to the child that even though the answer was wrong, it still contributed positively to the class discussion. Notice how the teacher did not digress from the task of listing warm-blooded animals, which in other words is maintaining academic focus and at the same time allowed the student to maintain dignity.

Learning is increased when the teacher acknowledges and amplifies the student responses. Additionally, this can be even more effective if the teacher takes one student's response and directs it to another student for further comment. When this occurs, the students acquire greater subject matter knowledge. This is due to a number of factors. One is that the student feels that he or she is a valuable contributor to the lesson. Another is that all students are forced to pay attention because they never know when they will be called on, which is known as group alert.

Group Alert and Wait-Time

The teacher achieves group alert by stating the question, allowing for a pause time for the students to process the question and formulate an answer, and then calling on someone to answer. If the teacher calls on someone before stating the question, the rest of the students tune-out because they know they are not responsible for the answer. Teachers are advised to also alert the non-performers to pay attention because they may be called on to elaborate on the answer. Non-performers are defined as all the students not chosen to answer.

One part of the questioning process is wait-time, the time between the question and either the student response or teacher follow-up. Many teachers vaguely recommend some general amount of wait-time (approximately five seconds or until the student starts to get uncomfortable or is clearly perplexed), but the focus here is on wait-time as a specific and powerful communicative tool that speaks through its structured silences. Embedded in wait-time are subtle clues about the judgments of a student's abilities and the expectations of individuals and groups.

For example, the more time that a student is allowed to mull through a question, the more the teacher trusts his or her ability to answer that question without getting flustered. As a rule, the practice of prompting is not a problem. Giving support and helping students reason through difficult conundrums is part of being an effective teacher.

Incorporating Student Responses
The idea of directing the student comment to another student is a valuable tool for engaging the lower achieving student. If the teacher can illicit even part of an answer from a lower-achieving student and then move the spotlight off of that student onto another student, the lower achieving student will be more likely to engage in the class discussion the next time. This is because they were not put "on the spot" for very long, and they successfully contributed to the class discussion.

Additionally, the teacher shows more acceptance and value to student responses, not by correcting, but by acknowledging, amplifying, discussing, or restating the comment or question. If student responses are allowed, even if it is blurted out, the response must be acknowledged, and the student should be told the quality of the response.

For example, the teacher asks, "Is chalk a noun?" During the pause time a student says, "Oh, so my bike is a noun." Without breaking the concentration of the class, the teacher looks to the student, nods and then places his or her index finger to the lips as a signal for the student not to speak out of turn and then calls on someone to respond to the original question. If the blurted-out response is incorrect or needs further elaboration, the teacher may just hold up his or her index finger as an indication to the student that the class will address that in a minute when the class is finished with the current question.

A teacher acknowledges a student response by commenting on it. For example, the teacher states the definition of a noun and then asks for examples of nouns in the classroom. A student responds, "My pencil is a noun." The teacher answers, "Okay, let us list that on the board." By this response and the action of writing "pencil" on the board, the teacher has just incorporated the student's response into the lesson. A teacher may also amplify the student response through another question directed to either the original student or to another student. For example, the teacher may probe the response by saying, "Okay," giving the student feedback on the quality of the answer, and then adding, "What do you mean by 'run' when you say the battery runs the radio?"

Another way of showing acceptance and value of student response is to discuss the student response. For example, after a student responds, the teacher would say, "Class, let us think along that line. What is some evidence that proves what Susie just stated?" And finally, the teacher may restate the response. For example, the teacher might say, "So you are saying, the seasons are caused by the tilt of the earth. Is this what you said?"

Therefore, a teacher keeps students involved by utilization of group alert. Additionally, the teacher shows acceptance and value of student responses by acknowledging, amplifying, discussing, or restating the response. This contributes to maintaining academic focus.

Skill 14.5   Applying strategies for adjusting communication to enhance student understanding (e.g., by providing examples, simplifying a complex problem, using verbal and nonverbal modes of communication, using audiovisual and technological tools of communication)

ENHANCING STUDENT UNDERSTANDING

Generally speaking, complex concepts can be taught in two manners: deductively or inductively. In a deductive manner, the teacher gives a definition along with one or two examples and one or two non-examples. As a means of checking understanding, the teacher will ask the students to give additional examples or non-examples and perhaps to repeat the definition. In an inductive manner, the students will derive the definition from examples and non-examples provided by the teacher. The students will test these examples and non-examples to ascertain if they possess the attributes that meet the criteria of the definition.

Using Definitions

It cannot be assumed that students are gaining meaning through definitions. It is quite possible that some students are able to memorize definitions without actually understanding the concept. If students understand concepts and gain meaning from definitions, they will be able to apply this information by giving both examples and non-examples. Students will further be able to list attributes and recognize related concepts. Research indicates that when students gain knowledge through instruction that includes a combination of giving definitions, examples, non-examples, and by identifying attributes, they are more likely to grasp complicated concepts than by other instructional methods.

Using Examples and Non-Examples

To help simplify complex ideas, the teacher can help define the concept more clearly for students by providing both examples of the concept, as well as non-examples. Several studies have been carried out to determine the effectiveness of giving examples as well as the difference in effectiveness of various types of examples. It was found conclusively that the most effective method of concept presentation included giving a definition along with examples and non-examples and also providing an explanation of the examples and non-examples. These same studies indicate that boring examples were just as effective as interesting examples in promoting learning.

Additional studies have been conducted to determine the most effective number of examples that will result in maximum student learning. These studies concluded that a few thoughtfully selected examples are just as effective as several examples. It was determined that the actual number of examples necessary to promote student learning was relative to the learning characteristics of the learners. It was again ascertained that learning is facilitated when examples are provided along with the definition.

Using Critical Attributes

Learning is further enhanced when critical attributes are listed along with a definition, examples, and non-examples. Classifying attributes is an effective strategy for both very young students and older students. According to Piaget's pre-operational phase of development, children learn concepts informally through experiences with objects just as they naturally acquire language. It is during this stage that students' language develops, as well as an ability to understand symbols and classifications. One of the most effective learning experiences with objects is learning to classify objects by a single obvious feature or attribute. Children classify objects typically, often without any prompting or directions. This natural inclination to classify objects carries over to classifying attributes of a particular concept and contributes to the student's understanding of concepts.

In order to scaffold students to learn at increasingly higher levels, it is crucial to initially simplify complex ideas. This is important for all students and especially important for students with learning disabilities, for whom research reinforces the need for simplifying ideas and concepts. Strategies to simplify complex ideas include utilizing visual and/or tactile aids to help students make connections, breaking ideas into smaller manageable parts (potentially over several days) and relating new ideas to background knowledge and a central, unifying idea.

Effective teachers are well versed in the areas of cognitive development, which is crucial to presenting ideas and or materials to students at a level appropriate to their developmental maturity. Effective teachers have the ability to use non-verbal and verbal patterns of communications that focus on age-appropriate instructions and materials.

NON-VERBAL COMMUNICATION

The effective teacher communicates non-verbally with students by using positive body language and expressing warmth, concern, acceptance, and enthusiasm. Effective teachers augment their instructional presentations by using positive non-verbal communication such as smiles, open body posture, movement, and eye contact with students. The energy and enthusiasm of the effective teacher can be amplified through positive body language.

A teacher's body language has an even greater effect on student achievement and ability to set and focus on goals. Teacher smiles provide support and give feedback about the teacher's affective state. A deadpan expression can actually be a detriment to the student's progress. Teacher frowns are perceived by students to mean displeasure, disapproval, and even anger. Studies also show that teacher posture and movement are indicators of the teacher's enthusiasm and energy, which emphatically influence student learning, attitudes, motivation, and focus on goals. Teachers have a greater efficacy on student motivation than any person other than parents and therefore it is crucial to be a reflective practitioner, be open to constructive feedback, and be cognizant of the outstanding impact that communication style can have on students.

VERBAL COMMUNICATION

Consistent with Piagean theory of cognitive development, younger children (below age eight) have poor language competencies that result in a poor ability to solve complicated problems. Educational instructions and information should be saturated with simplified language to compensate for the limited language competencies of younger children. Older children (age eight and older) have developed a greater ability to understand language and therefore are capable of solving complex problems. Older children are capable of understanding more advanced instructions and materials that require more advanced language skills.

As the classroom environment increasingly becomes a milieu saturated with cognitive, social, and emotional developmental levels and cultural diversity, the effective teacher must rise to the challenge of presenting ideas and materials appropriate for varying levels of students. Additionally, materials and ideas must be organized, sequenced, and presented to students in a manner consistent with the basic principles of English in a manner relevant to students as a whole.

Using Communication Tools

Often the ability to simplify and effectively communicate information is related to the communication tools that a teacher is using to instruct on the targeted lesson. Research reinforces the need for multi-sensory instruction for learning. Providing a visual or tactile learning experience, in addition to a verbal definition or an example, can often be the key in helping a student make connections. Appropriate visuals can include pictures, graphs, videos, or demonstrations. Tactile experiences can be as simple as touching an object or as complex as building a model or completing an experiment. Taking into account the multiple intelligences that are present in a classroom means that a teacher must consider communicating in a variety of modalities.

Extensive research highlights the fact that new learning occurs when novel information is integrated with that which the learner already knows. The act of activating background knowledge to enhance student understanding often relates back to providing and obtaining examples from students. The process of relating those examples and background knowledge to a central unifying idea is what helps students make the cognitive leap to learning new, and complex, information.

Skill 14.6   **Demonstrating knowledge of the limits of verbal understanding of students at various ages and with different linguistic backgrounds and strategies for ensuring that these limitations do not become barriers to learning (e.g., by linking to known language; by saying things in more than one way; by supporting verbalization with gestures, physical demonstrations, dramatizations, and/or media and manipulatives)**

SEE Skills 4.1, 4.2, 4.3, and 4.4.

COMPETENCY 015 UNDERSTAND USES OF TECHNOLOGY, INCLUDING INSTRUCTIONAL AND ASSISTIVE TECHNOLOGY, IN TEACHING AND LEARNING; AND APPLY THIS KNOWLEDGE TO USE TECHNOLOGY EFFECTIVELY AND TO TEACH STUDENTS HOW TO USE TECHNOLOGY TO ENHANCE THEIR LEARNING

Skill 15.1 Demonstrating knowledge of educational uses of various technology tools, such as calculators, software applications, input devices (e.g., keyboard, mouse, scanner, modem, CD-ROM), and the Internet

The computer system can be divided into two main parts—the hardware and the software. Hardware can be defined as all the physical components that make up the machine. Software includes the programs (sets of instructions) that enable that machine to do a particular job.

HARDWARE

Input devices are those parts of the computer that accept information from the user. The most common input devices are the keyboard and the mouse. Other more specialized input devices might include joysticks, light pens, touch pads, graphic tablets, voice recognition devices, and optical scanners.

Output devices are the parts of the computer that display the results of processing for the user. These commonly include the monitor and printers, but a computer might also output information to plotters and speech synthesizers. Monitors and printers can vary greatly in the quality of the output displayed. Monitors are classified according to their resolution (dpi = dots per square inch).

Printers

Printers vary in the way they produce "hard copy" as well as in the quality of the resultant product. With market prices coming down, they are becoming much more affordable. The best hard copies are produced by laser printers, but laser printers are also the most expensive. They are usually found in offices where volume is not high but the best quality is desired.

Hard Drives

Storage devices enable computers to save documents and other important files for future editing. Hard drives are built into most computers for the storage of the large programs used today. As programs increase in size and complexity to make use of the enhanced graphic and sound capabilities of today's computers, the amount of storage space on a hard drive has become increasingly important. An option that adds portability for students to move small files from one computer to another is a flash drive. For example, this device allows students to bring in a paper from home to print up in the school's computer lab.

CDs and DVDs

Many schools avoid the limitations imposed by the hard drive's storage space by using networks to deliver programs to the individual systems. The CD-ROM drives of multimedia computers that can access CD-ROM disks containing large amounts of information and usually including sound, graphics, and even video clips. For even larger files, a Digital Video Disk/Rewriteable (DVD R/W) can be used for storing of data, music, movies and other large files. They can be used repeatedly to be updated and store the information that is needed at the time. Another option is for students to use an external hard drive which adds portability to move around stored data, as well as to use as a backup system.

One way to take advantage of the computer's ability to store vast amounts of data is to utilize them in the classroom as a research tool. Entire encyclopedias, whole classical libraries, specialized databases in history, science, and the arts can be obtained on CD-ROM disks to allow students to complete their research from the classroom computer. With the "Search" feature of these programs, students can type in a one or two word description of the desired topic and the computer will actually locate all articles that deal with that topic. The student can either read the articles on the computer monitor or print them out.

CPU and Motherboard

The last hardware component of a computer system is the Central Processing Unit, or CPU, along with all the memory chips on the motherboard. This "brain" of the computer is responsible for receiving input from the input or storage devices, placing it in temporary storage (RAM or Random Access Memory), performing any processing functions required by the program (like mathematical equations or sorting) and eventually retrieving the information from storage and displaying it by means of an output device.

SOFTWARE

Software consists of all the programs containing instructions for the computer and is stored on the hard drive, CD-ROM disks, or can be downloaded with proper permissions. Programs fall into two major groups: operating systems and application programs. Operating system programs contain instructions that allow the computer to function. Applications are all the jobs that a user might wish to perform on the computer. These might include word processors, databases, spreadsheets, educational and financial programs, games, and telecommunications programs.

Educational Software

With a surplus of educational software on the market, it is important for an educator to be able to evaluate a program before purchasing it. There are three general steps to follow when evaluating a software program. First, one must read the instructions thoroughly to familiarize oneself with the program, its hardware requirements, and its installation. Once the program is installed and ready to run, the evaluator should first run the program as it would be run by a successful student, without deliberate errors but making use of all the possibilities available to the student. Thirdly, the program should be run making deliberate mistakes to test the handling of errors. One should try to make as many different kinds of mistakes as possible, including those for incorrect keyboard usage and the validity of user directions.

Many school districts have addressed the overwhelming number of educational software products by publishing a list of approved software titles for each grade level in much the same way that they publish lists of approved text books and other classroom materials. In addition, most districts have developed a software evaluation form to be used by any instructor involved in the purchase of software that is not already on the "approved" list.

NETWORKS
A network is composed of two or more computers, linked together. More specifically, a computer network is a data communications system made up of hardware and software that transmits data from one computer to another. In part, a computer network includes physical infrastructure like wires, cables, fiber optic lines, undersea cables, and satellites. The other part of a network is the software to keep it running. Computer networks can connect to other computer networks to create a vast computer network.

There are numerous configurations for computer networks, including:

- Local-area networks (LANS)—the computers are all contained within the same building
- Wide-area networks (WANS)—the computers are at a distance and are connected through telephone lines or radio waves
- Campus-area networks (CANs)—the computers are within a specific, geographic area, such as a school campus or military base
- Metropolitan-area networks (MANs)—a data network developed for a specific town or city
- Home-area networks (HANs)—a network contained within a private home which connects all the digital devices
- Internet—the communicating and sharing of data via shared routers and servers using common protocols

Depending on the type of network access, the teacher has productivity and instructional information and communications capabilities available from the next office or around the world.

Skill 15.2   Recognizing purposes and uses of common types of assistive technology (e.g., amplification devices, communication boards)

IDEA provides the following definition of an assistive technology device:

"Any item, piece of equipment, or product system, whether acquired commercially off the shelf, modified, or customized, that is used to increase, maintain or improve functional capabilities of children with disabilities."

AT devices can increase the following for a person with a disability:
- Level of independence
- Quality of life
- Productivity
- Performance
- Educational/vocational options
- Success in regular education settings

A variety of AT devices are available to address the functional capabilities of students with disabilities. Zabala (2000) identified AT devices in fourteen major areas.

ACADEMIC AND LEARNING AIDS
Electronic and non-electronic aids such as calculators, spell checkers, portable word processors, and computer-based software solutions that assist the student in academic areas.

Reading
AT solutions that address difficulty with reading may include:
- *Colored overlays:* Overlays that alter the contrast between the text and background are helpful for students with perceptual difficulties. It may be necessary to experiment to determine the best color or combination of colors for a student.
- *Reading Window:* A simple, no-tech solution for students who have difficulty with tracking. A "frame" is constructed from tag board or cardboard, allowing the student to see one line of text at a time as he/she moves down the page.
- *Spell Checker or Talking Dictionary:* Students type in words they are having difficulty reading and the device will say the word for them.
- *Auditory Textbooks:* Students who have difficulty reading traditional print texts may use audio-taped texts or texts on CDs to follow along as the text is read aloud. Textbooks on tape or CD are available to students with disabilities through Recordings for the Blind and Dyslexic, as are specialized CD players that allow the student to key in pages, headings or chapters to access specific text quickly. Some even allow the student to insert electronic bookmarks.

- *Talking Word Processing Programs:* Low cost software applications that provide speech output of text displayed on the computer monitor. Some programs highlight the text as it is read.

Spelling

AT is available to support spelling in handwritten and computer generated text.

- *Personal Word List or Dictionary:* Students maintain a list of commonly misspelled words for personal reference; can be handwritten or computer generated.
- *Hand-Held Spell Checker:* Students type in words and a list of correctly spelled words that closely approximate the misspelled word is provided. Some models offer speech feedback.
- *Word Processing Program with Spell Check:* Most word processing programs offer a spell check feature in which misspelled words are underlined.
- *Talking Word Processing Program with Spell Check:* These programs are helpful for students who cannot visually identify the correct word on a traditional spell check program. The talking feature allows the student to "listen" for the correct spelling of the word.

Writing

AT to support writing includes a number of low and high tech options.

- *Alternative Paper:* For students with fine motor difficulties, modifying the writing paper may be appropriate. One solution is to provide paper with bold lines. Another solution is to use a tactile paper that has a raised line that the student can actually feel. Some students benefit from using graph paper, placing one letter in each box, to improve legibility. Graph paper can also be used for math problems, to assure that the numbers are in alignment.
- *Pencil Grips:* This is an inexpensive alternative that gives the student with fine motor difficulties a larger and more supportive means of grasping a pencil.
- *Adapted Tape Recorder:* Students who have difficulty with writing may be allowed to tape record some of their assignments. Adapted tape recorders can also be used to record class lectures for students who have difficulty taking notes. Tape recorders with an index feature allow the student to mark key points on a tape for later reference
- *Portable Word Processor:* For students with significant writing difficulties, a portable word processor can provide an alternative to using pencil and paper. These devices use a full size keyboard and allow the student to type in texts. Files can be stored in the device to be uploaded to a computer at a later time. Advantages over a traditional computer or laptop are the economical price, portability, and long battery life.
- *Talking Word Processor Software:* These programs provide feedback by reading aloud what the student has typed in, allowing the student to hear

what he has written. This type of multisensory feedback assists the student in identifying and correcting errors.

- *Word Prediction Software:* This type of software is beneficial for students who have difficulty with spelling and grammar. As the first letter or letters of a word are typed in, the computer predicts the word the student is typing. This type of technology is of benefit to students who type slowly as it reduces the number of keystrokes needed to complete a word.
- *Outlining and Webbing Software:* This type of software assists students who have difficulty organizing thoughts and planning. Webbing programs allow for graphic diagrams to give the student a visual representation of what is needed to complete the writing task.
- *Voice Recognition Software:* This type of software has gained in popularity in recent years due to its wide commercial applications. Voice recognition allows the student to "speak" into the computer and the spoken word is translated into written text on the computer screen.

Math
To support students with difficulties in math, both low tech and high tech options are available.

- *Calculators*: Students who have difficulty performing math calculations can benefit from the use of a calculator. Adapted calculators may have larger buttons or larger display screens that are useful for students with physical disabilities. Talking calculators are available for students with visual impairments.
- *On-Screen Electronic Worksheets:* For student with physical disabilities who have difficulty with writing, worksheets can be produced in an on-screen format, allowing the student to use a computer screen to answer the questions.
- *Manipulatives of all types:* Students who have difficulty acquiring or retaining math concepts often benefit from objects designed to provide a kinesthetic or visual illustration of the concept. These low tech aids include such things as place value blocks, fraction strips, geared clocks, play money, etc.

ASSISTIVE LISTENING DEVICES AND ENVIRONMENTAL AIDS
Electronic and non-electronic aids such as amplification devices, closed captioning systems, and environmental alert systems that assist a student with a hearing impairment to access information that is typically presented through an auditory modality.

- *Assistive Listening Devices:* These devices amplify sound and speech and are appropriate for a student with a hearing impairment. Personal amplification systems are portable and can be used in different environments. These systems consist of a transmitter that transmits the sound to the student's receiving unit. Personal sound field systems consist of a transmitter and a receiver, along with a portable speaker. Sound field systems can also be installed in entire rooms.

- *Text Telephones (TTY):* Students with hearing impairments may use the TTY keyboard to type messages over the telephone. Some TTYs have answering machines and some models offer a print out of the text.
- *Closed Captioning Devices:* Modern televisions are equipped with closed captioning options that present the text on the television screen.
- *Environmental Aids:* These can include adapted clocks, notification systems, pagers, and warning devices. Visual alert systems may be configured to alert the student of a doorbell, telephone ringing, or smoke detector sounding. Personal pagers may have vibrating and text messaging options.
- *Real Time Captioning:* This may be used to caption speech, such as class lectures and presentations to a text display. A computer with specialized software and a projection system are needed for this type of software.

AUGMENTATIVE COMMUNICATION
Electronic and non-electronic devices and software solutions that provide a means for expressive and receptive communication for students with speech and language impairments.

- *Object-Based Communication Displays:* Low tech solutions that use actual objects to represent daily activities. The student selects or touches the object to communicate a want or need.
- *Picture Communication Boards and Books:* Low tech solutions that use pictures to represent messages. The pictures are organized according to categories or activities in the student's day.
- *Alphabet Boards:* Students who are able to spell, but have limited language can use an alphabet board to communicate. The student touches the letters to spell out words, phrases, or sentences.
- *Talking Switches:* these devices allow for recording of one or two messages. The student activates the switch to "say" the message. A picture may be used in conjunction with the device.
- *Voice Output Devices (Low Tech):* Multiple messages can be recorded on these devices. Messages are recorded and accessed by the student to communicate wants and needs. The low tech models can range in capacity from one to up to sixty-four messages. Pictures are used on the device as a representative of each message.
- *Voice Output Devices (Middle Tech):* On these devices, the messages are represented by picture symbols. These devices have the capacity to store multiple messages on multiple levels.
- *Voice Output Devices (High Tech):* High tech voice output devices are very sophisticated pieces of technology that allow the student to use a computer generated voice to speak for him/her. Some devices uses paper

based displays, while others are computer generated (dynamic) displays. Some offer a keyboard to allow the student to type in messages as well.

- *Integrated Communication Solutions:* Several software-based applications are available that use a laptop computer in conjunction with a voice output system.

VISUAL AIDS

Aids such as magnifiers, talking calculators, Braille writers, adapted tape players, screen reading software applications, and Braille note-taking devices that assist a student with a visual impairment to access and produce information in a print format.

- *Braille Writer:* A portable device for producing Braille. Students type in text on the keyboard, using the six key entry method. A copy of the text in Braille is embossed on the paper inserted into the Braille writer.
- *Electronic Braille Writer:* An updated version of the Braille writer, the electronic Braille writer is lightweight and offers the option of the text being read aloud to the student. A Braille copy of the text can also be printed out.
- *Closed Circuit Television (CCTV):* Assists students with visual impairments by enlarging text and graphics. The page to be read is placed on the base under the camera. The image is displayed on a monitor, with an appropriate level of magnification for the student. Foreground and background colors can be altered for the individual student.
- *Text Enlargement Software:* Software is available to increase the size of the text and graphics displayed on the computer monitor.
- *Screen Reading Software*: Screen reading software may also be of benefit to students with visual impairments. These applications allow the computer to read the text aloud.

The IEP committee determines the need for AT devices and services. Most school districts have policies/procedures regarding AT assessments and have teams of professionals that conduct the evaluation. Often the assessment team will include physical or occupational therapists and speech therapists, to address communication and physical needs. The student's teacher(s) and parents are often included in the AT evaluation. Once it has been determined that an AT device or service is needed, the student's IEP team should document the required device(s) in the IEP.

Skill 15.3 **Recognizing issues related to the appropriate use of technology (e.g., privacy issues, security issues, copyright laws and issues, ethical issues regarding the acquisition and use of information from technology resources), and identifying procedures that ensure the legal and ethical use of technology resources**

LEGAL RESPONSIBILITIES AND TECHNOLOGY

In this technological age, it is important that teachers be aware of their legal responsibilities when using computers in the classroom. As public employees, teachers are particularly vulnerable to public scrutiny. It is also the responsibility of educators to model as well as teach ethical computer behaviors.

Recent Changes

In 1980, P. L.96-517, Section 117 of the copyright act was amended to cover the use of computers. The following changes were made:

1. The definition of a "computer program" was inserted and is defined now as "a set of statements or instructions to be used directly in a computer in order to bring about a certain result."

2. The owner of a copy of a computer program is not infringing on the copyright by making or authorizing the making of or adaptation of that program if the following criteria are met:

    o The new copy or adaptation must be created in order to be able to use the program in conjunction with the machine and is used in no other manner.

    o The new copy or adaptation must be for archival purposes only and all archival copies must be destroyed in the event that continued possession of the computer program should cease to be rightful.

    o Any copies prepared or adapted may not be leased, sold, or otherwise transferred without the authorization of the copyright owner.

Multiple Copies of a Program

The intent of this amendment to the copyright act is to allow an individual or institutional owner of a program to make "backup" copies to avoid destruction of the original program disk, while restricting the owner from making copies in order to use the program on more than one machine at a time or to share with other teachers. Under the Software Copyright Act of 1980, once a program is loaded into the memory of a computer, a temporary copy of that program is made. *Multiple machine loading* (moving from machine to machine and loading a single program into several computers for simultaneous use) constitutes making multiple copies, which is not permitted under the law.

Since the same is true of a networked program, it is necessary to obtain permission from the owner of the copyright or purchase a license agreement before multiple uses of a program in a school setting.

Risks of Ignoring the Law

Infringement of copyright laws is a serious offense and can result in significant penalties if a teacher chooses to ignore the law. Not only does the teacher risk losing all personal computer equipment but he or she is also placing their job as an educator in jeopardy.

APPROPRIATE USE OF TECHNOLOGY

Students must exercise responsibility and accountability in adhering to technology usage during the school day. Internet usage agreements define a number of criteria of technology use that a students must agree to in order to have access to school computers. Students who violate any parts of the computer usage agreement are subject to have all access to school computers or other educational technology denied or blocked.

District and school policies are developed to provide a consistent language of expectation for students using school technology with an acceptable use policy. Districts are liable for the actions of students and teachers in school communities who use publicly funded and legislatively funded technology. The standards of usage for school computers are created to maximize student use for educational purposes and to minimize student surfing for non-educational sites that minimize learning during class times.

QUESTIONS FOR ANALYZING SOURCES

To determine the authenticity or credibility of your sources, consider these questions:

- Who created the source, and why? Was it created through a spur-of-the-moment act, a routine transaction, or a thoughtful, deliberate process?
- Did the recorder have firsthand knowledge of the event? Or, did the recorder report what others saw and heard?
- Was the recorder a neutral party, or did the recorder have opinions or interests that might have influenced what was recorded?
- Did the recorder produce the source for personal use, for one or more individuals, or for a large audience?
- Was the source meant to be public or private?
- Did the recorder wish to inform or persuade others? Did the recorder have reasons to be honest or dishonest?
- Was the information recorded during the event, immediately after the event, or after some lapse of time? How large a lapse of time?

DOCUMENTATION

Documentation is an important skill when incorporating outside information into a piece of writing. Students must learn that research involves more than cutting and pasting from the Internet and that plagiarism is a serious academic offense.

Students must recognize that stealing intellectual property is an academic and, in some cases, a legal crime; thus students need to learn how to give credit where credit is due.

Students should be aware of the rules that apply to borrowing ideas from various sources. Increasingly, the consequences for violating these rules are becoming more severe. Pleading ignorance is less and less of a defense. Such consequences include failing an assignment, losing credit for an entire course, expulsion from a learning environment, and civil penalties. Software exists that enables teachers and other interested individuals to determine quickly whether a given paper includes plagiarized material. As members of society in the information age, students are expected to recognize the basic justice of intellectual honesty and to conform to the systems meant to ensure it.

There are several style guides for documenting sources. Each guide has its own particular ways of signaling that information has been directly borrowed or paraphrased, and familiarity with the relevant details of the major style guides is essential for students. Many libraries publish overviews of the major style guides, and most bookstores will carry full guides for the major systems. Relevant information is readily available on the web as well.

Documentation of sources takes two main forms. The first form applies when citing sources in the text of the document or as footnotes or endnotes. In-text documentation is sometimes called *parenthetical documentation* and requires specific information within parentheses placed immediately after borrowed material. Footnotes or endnotes are placed either at the bottom of relevant pages or at the end of the document.

In addition to citing sources within the text, style guides also require a bibliography, a references section, or a works cited section at the end of the document. Sources for any borrowed material are to be listed according to the rules of the particular guide. In some cases, a "works consulted" listing may be required even though no material is directly cited or paraphrased to the extent that an in-text citation is required.

The major style guides include the *Modern Language Association Handbook (MLA)*, the *Manual of the American Psychological Association (APA), and the Chicago Manuel of Style, Turabian, and Scientific Style and Format: the CBE Manual.*

Documentation of sources from the Internet is particularly involved and continues to evolve at a rapid pace. The best bet is to consult the most recent online update for a particular style guide.

Skill 15.4   Identifying and addressing equity issues related to the use of technology in the classroom (e.g., equal access to technology for all students)

TECHNOLOGICAL BACKGROUND

Teachers need to understand that their students will have a variety of ability levels and experience with technology. It is also important to know that a lack of technological proficiency may actually be a source of embarrassment to students. When students come to school with a wide variety of skills, teachers need to find unique ways to provide students who have fewer skills with more opportunities to learn. The extra challenge is to do this in a way that does not compromise the ability of other students to grow in their understanding of technology. Often, group-based work can be very helpful.

Unfortunately, students who have access to computers outside of school often feel like they know everything already and are reluctant to listen to instruction on lab etiquette or program usage. The teacher must be constantly on guard to prevent physical damage to the machines from foreign objects finding their way into disk drives, key caps from disappearing from keyboards (or being rearranged), or stray pencil or pen marks from appearing on computer systems.

Highly experienced students might be tempted to engage in technological activities that affect the productivity of the computers, causing the district's technology team time and energy (for example, saving games on hard drives, moving files into new directories or eliminating them altogether, creating passwords to prevent others from using machines, etc.). At the same time, the other students need a lot of assistance to prevent accidents caused by their inexperience. It is possible to pair inexperienced students with more capable ones to alleviate some of the problems. Teachers must constantly rotate around the room and students must be prepared before their arrival in the lab so that they know exactly what to do when they get there to prevent them from exercising their creativity.

ENSURING FAIR OPPORTUNITY FOR TECHNOLOGY USE

Teachers must ensure that all students have similar opportunities to use technology, particularly as the students with the least home exposure will need more time. If the number of computers available for student use is limited, the students can be rotated singly or in small groups to the computer centers as long as they are well oriented in advance to the task to be accomplished and the rules to be observed. Rules for using the computer should be emphasized with the whole class prior to individual computer usage and then prominently posted.

If a computer lab is available for use by the curriculum teacher, the problem of how to give each student the opportunity to use the computer as an educational tool might be alleviated, but a whole new set of problems must be dealt with. Again the rules to be observed in the computer lab should be discussed before the class ever enters the lab and students should have a thorough understanding of the assignment. When a large group of students is visiting a computer lab, it is very easy for the expensive hardware to suffer from accidental or deliberate harm if the teacher is not aware of what is going on at all times. Students need to be aware of the consequences for not following the rules because it is so tempting to experiment and show off to their peers.

Skill 15.5 Identifying effective instructional uses of current technology in relation to communication (e.g., audio and visual recording and display devices)

INSTRUCTIONAL TECHNOLOGY

The tools teachers have available to them to present information to students are growing. Where just 10 years ago teachers needed to only know how to use word processing programs, grading programs, and overhead projectors, today, electronic slideshows and white boards are becoming the new "norm," and other methods of information distribution are expected from teachers by principals, parents, and students alike.

Technological tools are varied, and to ensure that the ones selected for use in the classroom are effective at providing students with good instruction, teachers will want to think about the relationship between instructional objectives and the technological tools. Instructional technology tools can be divided into three primary categories: (a) instruction/practice/assessment, (b) creation, and (c) research.

Instruction/Practice/Assessment Tools

The first category, broadly labeled instruction/practice/assessment, refers to instructional or assessment programs that students typically work on individually, sometimes in relationship to wider class activities, but often as "extra" work. This might include reading programs where all students would spend a certain amount of time per week on a particular reading practice program that may have short formative assessments. Or it could be an accelerated program or a program that is meant for students who finish assignments early. While these types of programs can have multiple benefits, they do not necessarily teach students *about* technology, as the programs are very user-friendly and straightforward.

Creation Tools

The second category, creation, refers to activities where students use word processing tools, spreadsheet tools, graphic tools, or multi-media tools to either demonstrate proficiency with the technology, or more likely, to demonstrate (or practice) proficiency with a skill that can be evidenced through technology. This sounds confusing, but think of it this way: typing an essay on a word processing program is seemingly all about the task of writing (composition, grammar, etc.), but in reality, students would need to know how the technology works and how it can assist in the production of the writing. Often, graphic and multi-media programs are used in ways that allow students to demonstrate proficiency in certain subjects in alternative or unconventional ways.

Research Tools
The final category would be research. This is where students use the Internet, databases, or software programs to find new information. While many students are proficient with the Internet, teachers should not assume that students know how to properly research a topic online. In fact, one of the most important technological *and* literacy skills is the evaluation of written material. For example, students need to be taught how to decide whether a website on the topic they are researching is valid information or not.

Skill 15.6 **Applying strategies for helping students acquire, analyze, and evaluate electronic information (e.g., locating specific information on the Internet and verifying its accuracy and validity)**

ACCURACY AND VALIDITY
The Internet contains a tremendously wide variety of information that ranges in accuracy and validity. Unlike newspapers and books that undergo a fact check or are reviewed by an editor, the Internet is an open forum for websites, blogs, posts, opinions and information. Students must first be made aware of this fact alone (that material posted on the Internet may or may not have been approved for content before it was available to all). For example, the teacher should make students aware that Wikipedia can be a good source of information, but that it is not edited or approved prior to publication. Then, students will need to evaluate the material for accuracy, validity, and if it suits his or her needs.

Before the lesson is introduced, information should be screened. At younger levels, students should be directed and contained to pre-selected sites, and then at older levels, students should be given possible options for sites to help in the assignment. Not only does this help save the students time from wasted searches (as they hone this skill) it keeps them on track to safe sites. Of course, even though districts typically have filters in line to keep students on safe sites, students should be closely monitored at all times when browsing the Internet.

Students should take part in the discussion of what types of sites would be considered reliable before they begin searching. Are they looking for surveys, opinions, text, or media? Then students should consider what sites are likely to be credible? In a research project on the colonization of America, would a student rather view a site from the New World Encyclopedia, PBS, and/or Joe Smith, Age 8, third grade project?

Once browsing, students should find the author's credentials (job, institution, training, etc.) of each site as a first step in determining credibility. Another factor to consider is when it was written. For certain research, time will be sensitive. A third factor would be to consider for whom it was written. Knowing an author's audience will provide insight into the material that is provided. The students should also consider how comprehensive the information is, as well as how reasonable the information is when considering accuracy. Finally, students should consider utilizing multiple good quality sites to "cross check" and merge information when appropriate.

Skill 15.7 Evaluating students' technologically produced products using established criteria related to content, delivery, and the objective(s) of the assignment

EVALUATING STUDENT PERFORMANCE WITH TECHNOLOGY

When teachers ask students to produce something with technology, typically to practice—and then prove proficiency—with a particular content-based skill or area of knowledge, they are giving students the opportunity to be creative with new learning. Furthermore, they are giving students the chance to utilize knowledge in authentic situations.

As with any "open-ended" assignment, teachers will be more objective in their evaluations, as well as be more specific about expectations to students, if they develop scoring criteria, rubrics, or other evaluation guides. The following elements should be considered:

Design

This is the format that the product takes. Teachers can (considering developmental level) expect that students will present information in a way that is organized, clear, and straightforward. However, with design, non-language elements, such as graphics, pictures, sounds, video, etc., students can demonstrate an added element of creativity. Furthermore, it can help to add a symbolic touch that conveys more than words can. While clarity is important, even in this regard, the use of non-linguistic material must not confuse the viewer.

Content Delivery

This refers to the method of technology used. The teacher should make it clear to students what program an assignment should be completed in. For example, an essay would be better completed in a word processing program. A more creative piece could be done in a multi-media program format. Teachers can evaluate the ways in which the tool is used. For example, if the teacher asks students to produce something in a multi-media program, content must be taught (say for a history lesson). But the teacher would also have to teach students how to use the program, itself. Students will end up demonstrating knowledge of the content (history), as well as the method of content delivery (the computer program).

Audience

When students focus on audience, they consider what the audience will need to comprehend. So, while a very creative student may have fun with a program and use it to do very unusual things, the student would not be evaluated highly if the work did not focus on presenting information in a clear manner to the anticipated audience. Teachers do not always have to be the "audience," though. Either teachers can ask students to produce something for hypothetical situations, or they can suggest to students that their audience is the rest of the class.

Relevance

This could actually be the most important element. Students may demonstrate incredible proficiency with the technological tool, but if they do not demonstrate how it was used to prove proficiency on the content, then the activity was done for the sake of the technological tool only. Teachers want to encourage students to view technology as a tool for learning, research, and presentation.

DOMAIN III   **THE PROFESSIONAL ENVIRONMENT**

COMPETENCY 016   **UNDERSTAND THE HISTORY, PHILOSOPHY, AND ROLE OF EDUCATION IN NEW YORK STATE AND THE BROADER SOCIETY**

Skill 16.1   **Analyzing relationships between education and society (e.g., schools reflecting and affecting social values, historical dimensions of the school-society relationship, the role of education in a democratic society, the role of education in promoting equity in society)**

SEE also Skill 16.2.

BEYOND ACADEMICS
Public education should be concerned with more than academic standards. School is a place where children can learn skills of good citizenship, time management, goal setting, and decision-making. But teachers must be deliberate about teaching these skills. Like most good teaching, students will have much more success learning these things if they get the opportunity to practice them. That is why a classroom should be like a little "community" where children get opportunities to help with chores and maintain responsibility for certain things. Some of the ways teachers can do this include setting up stations and centers throughout the classroom. With a classroom that contains various centers, student desks consist of only one physical component of the classroom. Teachers can set up student mailboxes to store certain materials. They can also arrange manipulatives and other classroom objects in various places that students are required to maintain and keep clean.

Time Management and Organization
A technique that many teachers use is rotating various chores each week. One student might be responsible for ensuring that materials get distributed to students. Another student might supervise clean-up time. Another student might assist with preparation of manipulatives. Not only does this type of activity improve time management and organizational skills in students, it creates a type of classroom community that is motivating to students. In a way, it causes students to feel safer and more included in their classroom environment.

In addition to physical classroom arrangement and student responsibility, teachers should focus on teaching children skills for time management and goal setting. Teachers can use a variety of materials and expectations to do this. For example, many teachers have students write down class-time agendas each morning and then set personal goals for the school-day. Then, they might have their students reflect on whether or not they met these goals and whether or not they successfully completed all agenda items.

Long Term Goals and Responsibility

Finally, learning centers, although usually used for the purpose of teaching content-area skills, can be great tools for teaching responsibility and independence. Teachers can use this time to work independently with students. While they do so, students in small groups travel from one center to another, completing various learning activities. For example, one center might ask students to read a story together and answer a few questions. Another center might have computers and require students to complete various computer-based learning activities. Doing this promotes independent and group learning skills and gives students opportunities to set and monitor short-term goals.

In addressing the needs of middle-level students to acquire decision making, organizational, and goal-setting skills, the teacher is establishing a foundation which will contribute to each student's success in education and beyond. As young people mature and are put in a position of making more choices, independent of adult advice or supervision, their abilities at decision-making and goal setting become vital.

Skill 16.2   Demonstrating knowledge of the historical foundations of education in the United States and of past and current philosophical issues in education (e.g., teacher-directed versus child-centered instruction)

SEE also Skill 16.1.

HISTORICAL FOUNDATIONS OF EDUCATION

The relationship between education and society is ever evolving. Originally, schools were primarily only accessible to the wealthy. In poorer and more rural families, the children were needed to help the family either by working and bringing home a wage, or by helping to tend the house or farm. Large families might have older children watch the younger children—none of these children were typically able to get schooling, or if they did, it was intermittent and spotty. Thus, the schools reflected the social value of having a large, uneducated work force.

Integration of Poor Students

Around the time of the Great Depression, Franklin Roosevelt's New Deal increasingly helped keep young people in school while adults were given the menial tasks that children had once performed. While the primary reason for fuller schools was not education so much as a reorganization of workers—making room in the workforce for the out-of-work adults—the result was that poorer children began to be more evenly and regularly educated and would eventually set the foundations for a middle class.

Integration of Racially Diverse Students

After *Plessy v. Ferguson* in 1896 (but before *Brown v. The Board of Education* in 1954), "separate but equal" school facilities segregated the African-American children from the Caucasians. However, it was clear that African-American schools generally received less funding than schools for white children. *Brown v. Board of Education of Topeka* struck down segregation after the Supreme Court ruled that a separate but equal form of education would never truly give African-American children an equal foundation in learning. Society would begin to follow suit, albeit slowly, as segregated facilities began to fall away.

FEDERAL, STATE, AND LOCAL INVOLVEMENT IN EDUCATION

Generally, schools and education are considered the great equalizer—giving each child a level start in life, the same tools to work with so that each might chisel out his or her future, regardless of class, color, religion, or other factors. However, because schools depend largely on local funding from city and state budgets, not all schools are created equal. The tax money in poorer towns does not stretch as far as the money in wealthier neighborhoods, and schools and their facilities often suffer for it.

Recently, the federal government has begun to step in and attempt to make schools throughout the nation more equal in standards, so that every child gets a solid grounding in learning. In 2001, the federal government implemented the **No Child Left Behind Act**, which aims to improve schools by increasing educational standards and holding schools, school districts, and states accountable for performance and progress of students.

Another proposal for equalizing educational opportunity has been for school vouchers, which would allow parents to choose which school their children attend. This idea is based on the principle that if the local school does not have desirable facilities, then children could attend one that does. Contesters of this plan say that vouchers would only cause poor schools to become even less desirable as students flee and less tax money comes in.

TYPES OF SCHOOLS

Another issue in governance has been the debate between local, neighborhood, and choice schools. Neighborhood schools are those in which students attend based on their home address. For the past few decades, some school districts have provided students with the option of attending **magnet schools**, or schools that are available for any student within the district. Usually, these schools have themes, such as business academies or college preparatory curricula. In addition to magnet schools, money now is available for **charter schools**, which do not have to abide by the same policies as regular public schools. Magnet schools do not have to be run by school districts, but they take money from the districts in which their students originate. So, for example, if the local public school gets $5,000 per student per school year from local property taxes and the state (or however the state finances schools), that $5,000 would instead go to the charter school if one student opted to go there.

Finally, in some states and cities, **voucher money** is available for students attending private schools; in this plan, the government gives parents part or all of the money that would have been put into the local public district(s) so that they can use it to send their children to private schools. None of these options is without controversy in this country.

Skill 16.3 **Applying procedures for working collaboratively and cooperatively with various members of the New York State educational system to accomplish a variety of educational goals**

SEE Skill 16.4 for a description of how educational policy in New York State is created.

SEE Skill 16.5 for a description of the duties of various organizations within the New York State educational system.

WORKING WITHIN ACTIVIST EDUCATIONAL ORGANIZATIONS
There are two activist organizations that will greatly affect an educator's career. The local teachers union helps educate and protect the rights of school employees, and the school's parent/teacher organization (PTO) advocates and fundraises for its students and their activities. It is important for a newly hired educator to attend meetings of these organizations in order to decide whether or not to join them. A union meeting provides a professional atmosphere outside of the workplace where a new employee can speak to fellow workers about the advantages and challenges within a school district. The PTO is a great place to meet motivated parents who are willing to do the "leg work" often needed to plan and finance field trips, guest speakers, extracurricular clubs and sports, and special awards. As well, if unpopular or counter-productive school-related legislation is in danger of being enacted, or if there is an increasing social problem in the school's neighborhood, PTOs usually contain willing and able activists with excellent networking and mobilizing abilities. Both unions and PTOs, when positive and effective, help to build strong educational communities and support systems for families, their children, and school employees.

INTERACTING WITH THE LOCAL SCHOOL BOARD
Teachers usually have their hiring reviewed and confirmed, or not, by the district school board. Members of the board finance the local schools, inspect these schools, and hire administrative personnel to run them. These hired administrators include the principals of the schools and the district's chief administrative officer, the superintendent. Since the local school board creates educational policy for the students and teachers in its district, parents, teachers, and even students will often ask to be placed on the agenda during the board's

public meetings in order to present an issue of importance. There is also usually a segment of the meeting reserved for public comment and members of the community are invited to voice their opinions and concerns. In this way, all of New York State's communities exercise their most basic democratic rights as they hash out each month, often passionately, the best ways to educate their children.

Skill 16.4 Analyzing differences between school-based and centralized models of decision making

DECISION-MAKING MODELS

Centralized Decision Making
Centralized decision making is when a large entity (the federal government or even the state government) makes the decisions that will affect all the smaller groups (local schools). Centralized decision making helps set one standard, everyone shares the same objectives, and the same content is used by everyone. The idea is that everything becomes equal and so the results should also be equal across the board—all the students should do equally well and because the teachers use the same content they can discuss it with one another at length and be on the same page.

Centralized decision making also helps reduce paperwork and administrative costs since everyone is doing the same thing, reporting should be streamlined and fewer administrators are needed. With centralized decision making, standardization is key, and it becomes easy to spot problems with a student, teacher, or district that is struggling or failing to meet those standards.

School-Based Decision Making
School-based decision making is more costly because it requires more administration to handle the many different programs that might be occurring within each individual school. Also, the reporting system becomes more complicated as each school may be doing something different, and so the central administration (state or federal) requires more time and more manpower to sift through the increased information from each school. It takes longer to spot problems.

However, school-based decision making has several benefits, including the school's ability to make changes when students or teachers are having difficulty. Schools can make their own decisions about what content to teach, which textbooks to use, and adjust as needed when something isn't working. School-based decision making also gives parents more ability to effect changes because their voices can be heard more immediately by the local school board, rather than having to fight the state or federal governments for changes to curriculum.

Skill 16.5 **Applying knowledge of the roles and responsibilities of different components of the education system in New York (e.g., local school boards, Board of Regents, district superintendents, school principals, Boards of Cooperative Educational Services [BOCES], higher education, unions, professional organizations, parent organizations)**

LOCAL SCHOOL BOARDS

Local school boards are often charged with spending the public money on schools. They have the fiscal responsibility to manage the local schools' money in such a way that the schools are able to meet their educational goals and requirements (such as the standards set by No Child Left Behind). Local school boards are generally made up of locally elected officials.

THE NEW YORK STATE BOARD OF REGENTS

The New York State Board of Regents is made of 16 members elected by the State Legislature. There is a member for each of the 12 judicial districts and 4 members who serve at large. Each member serves a five-year term. The board of regents is responsible for the general supervision of all educational activities in the state and presides over the New York State Education Department. Various committees within the board handle such topics as:

- Developing guidelines for cultural education
- Creating and monitoring aid programs to cultural institutions
- Developing policy for standards of professional conduct and competence and disciplinary processes

SUPERINTENDENTS AND PRINCIPALS

A district superintendent is the chief officer of the school district over which he or she supervises. The superintendent's job is to implement the policies set by the board of regents and to advocate for his/her district when necessary.

A school principal is head of the individual school. He or she is under the supervision of the superintendent. The principal handles disciplinary actions for students in the school and may also discipline teachers for minor infractions. For major violations, the principal will consult with the superintendent, who may in turn go to the board of regents.

BOARDS OF COOPERATIVE EDUCATIONAL SERVICES

Boards of Cooperative Educational Services (BOCES) were created under the Intermediate School District Act in 1948. BOCES allow small school districts to combine their financial power to share costs of services and programs that no one small district would be able to afford on its own. BOCES are voluntary. A district is free to buy their own services separate from others if it feels it can better service its students in that manner.

UNIONS

Unions such as the New York State United Teachers and other professional organizations allow teachers to work together and develop professionally. These organizations also help keep teachers up-to-date on current educational standards and developments. Unions in particular often work to make sure teachers receive fair wages and that when a teacher is facing charges for an alleged crime, he or she receives adequate legal counsel. Unions tend to be active in lobbying the legislature on behalf of the teaching community.

PARENT ORGANIZATIONS

Parent organizations, such as the PTO or PTA, allow parents to have access to their children's schools, and it also provides them a voice in school-based decisions. These organizations also allow parents and teachers to work together on behalf of the students.

COMPETENCY 017   **UNDERSTAND HOW TO REFLECT PRODUCTIVELY ON ONE'S OWN TEACHING PRACTICE AND HOW TO UPDATE ONE'S PROFESSIONAL KNOWLEDGE, SKILLS, AND EFFECTIVENESS**

Skill 17.1   Assessing one's own teaching strengths and weaknesses

EVALUATING TEACHER EFFECTIVENESS

It is important for teachers to involve themselves in constant periods of reflection and self-reflection to ensure they are meeting the needs of the students. There are several avenues a teacher might take in order to assess his or her own teaching strengths and weaknesses. Early indicators that a self-evaluation might be necessary include having several students that do not understand a concept. In such a case, a teacher might want to go over his or her lesson plans to make sure the topic is being covered thoroughly and in a clear fashion. Brainstorming other ways to tackle the content might also help. Speaking to other teachers, asking how they teach a certain skill, might give new insight to one's own teaching tactics.

The very nature of the teaching profession—the yearly cycle of doing the same thing over and over again—creates the tendency to fossilize, to quit growing, and to become complacent. The teachers who are truly successful are those who have built into their own approach to their jobs and to their lives safeguards against that. They see themselves as constant learners, and believe that learning never ends. They are careful never to teach their classes the same as they did the last time. They build in a tendency to reflect on what is happening to their students under their care or what happened this year as compared to last year. What worked the best? What did not work so well? What can be changed to improve success rates? What about continuing education? Should they go for another degree or should they enroll in more classes?

Teachers will encounter situations daily where students have difficulty with a fact, task, concept, or idea or when the student does not get it, does not acquire the skill, or cannot internalize the information. As the teacher, what can be done? Repeat the instruction, verbatim, until it sinks in? Chastise or cajole the student into acknowledging an understanding? Since the teacher is genuinely concerned about the student's acquisition of skills and academic success, they will immediately realize that the dilemma is theirs, not the student's, and they will seek different ways to communicate an understanding of the information so that the student will completely comprehend and acquire a meaningful skill. After all, if the student does not succeed, it is the teacher who has failed.

Determining a Better Approach

In determining a better approach for providing an understanding to the student, teachers should consider many options and define the more probable ones to be used for instruction. The process for identifying viable options would include a teacher asking the following questions of themselves and answering them:

- What different words or phrasing might be used to say the same thing?
- How would I explain an opposite condition or fact, and would a negative example provide an understanding through contrast?
- If I imagined that the problem/fact/skill which I want to teach was an object which I could move around in any direction, would I be able to identify the "object's" component parts? Could I revise my explanation to provide a better understanding by starting from a different component part, reordering the component parts or redefining the component parts?
- Is there something preexisting in the student's acquired knowledge/skills which I can use to redirect or reinforce my explanation by making reference or demonstrating a link?
- Is there something specific to the student's culture or life experience which could inform my explanation/instruction?

In a student-centered learning environment, the goal is to provide the best education and opportunity for academic success for all students. Integrating the developmental patterns of physical, social, and academic norms for students will provide individual learners with student learning plans that are individualized and specific to their skill levels and needs. Teachers who effectively develop and maximize a student's potential will use pre- and post-assessments to gain comprehensive data on the existing skill level of the student in order to plan and adapt curriculum to address and grow student skills. Maintaining communication with the student and parents will provide a community approach to learning where all stakeholders are included to maximize student-learning growth.

Any good teacher will understand that he or she needs to self-evaluate and adjust his or her lessons periodically. Signing up for professional courses or workshops can also help a teacher assess his or her abilities by opening one's eyes to new ways of teaching.

Skill 17.2   Using different types of resources and opportunities (e.g., journals, inservice programs, continuing education, higher education, professional organizations, other educators) to enhance one's teaching effectiveness

PROFESSIONAL DEVELOPMENT OPPORTUNITIES
Professional development opportunities for teacher performance improvement or enhancement in instructional practices are essential for creating comprehensive learning communities. In order to promote the vision, mission, and action plans of school communities, teachers must be given the toolkits to maximize instructional performances. The development of student-centered learning communities that foster the academic capacities and learning synthesis for all students should be the fundamental goal of professional development for teachers.

The level of professional development may include traditional district workshops that enhance instructional expectations for teachers or the more complicated multiple day workshops given by national and state educational organizations to enhance the federal accountability of skill and professional development for teachers. Most workshops on the national and state level provide clock hours that can be used to renew certifications for teachers every five years. Typically, 150 clock hours is the standard certification number needed to provide a five-year certification renewal, so teachers must attend and complete paperwork for a diversity of workshops that range from 1–50 clock hours according to the timeframe of the workshops.

Most districts and schools provide in-service professional development opportunities for teachers during the school year dealing with district objectives/expectations and relevant workshops or classes that can enhance the teaching practices for teachers. Clock hours are provided with each class or workshop, and the type of professional development being offered to teachers determines clock hours. Each year, schools are required to report the number of workshops, along with the participants attending the workshops to the superintendent's office for filing. Teachers collecting clock hour forms are required to file the forms to maintain certification eligibility and job eligibility.

When a teacher is involved in the process of self-reflection and self-assessment, one of the common outcomes is that the teacher comes to identify areas of skill or knowledge that require more research or improvement on his/her part. S/he may become interested in overcoming a particular weakness in performance or may decide to attend a workshop or consult with a mentor to learn more about a particular area of concern.

Skill 17.3   Applying strategies for working effectively with members of the immediate school community (e.g., colleagues, mentor, supervisor, special needs professionals, principal, building staff) to increase one's knowledge or skills in a given situation

PROFESSIONAL GROWTH
Part of being an effective teacher is to not only get students to grow educationally but to allow oneself to continue to grow. Working with other members of the school community—peers, supervisors, and other staff—will provide the grounding needed to increase skills and knowledge sets. Identifying possible mentors, such as respected teachers and ones that should be emulated, is one step. Search out other teachers who have had an amount of success in the desired areas. Ask them questions and for advice on brushing up lesson plans. Talk to a supervisor or the principal when experiencing difficulties or when there is more to be learned. They may know of development training seminars, books, journals, or other resources that might help.

Vertical Teaming

Many school districts have implemented teaming systems that encourage teachers working interactively with each other and the other professional in the schools. One example of this is vertical teaming where groups of educators of the same discipline but from different grade levels work cooperatively to plan curriculum, units, and lessons across multiple grade levels to ensure an effective flow of instruction. For example, a team of middle school science teachers would team together, at least one from each grade level, to develop, plan, organize, and implement the science curriculum for students' entire "stay" at that school building. This planning eliminates repeat of material and encourages all teachers to utilize higher-ordered and critical thinking skills throughout each year of the curriculum.

Horizontal Teaming

Another teaming example is horizontal teaming. In this system, teachers in one grade level work to integrate all of the subjects taught across the grade. For example, in a team of four fifth grade teachers, teachers may collaborate to find the connections between language arts, science, math, and social studies to present interdisciplinary instruction across the entire fifth grade level. Then, each teacher implements instruction by teaching one of the subjects to all four sections of fifth grade. This system cuts down on planning for each teacher and encourages solid educational connections between subjects and material, therefore enhancing the real-life applications of the material, as well as student interest.

Team Teaching

Team teaching is another teaming option. Team teaching consists of two or more teachers involved in the classroom instruction. In this system, teachers share the roles of instructor, monitor, and additional supporter, etc., to share the instructional workload and increase individual student achievement. In this model, teachers must be clear with one another regarding objectives, roles, and assessment so each teacher can conduct his or her role most effectively.

Mentoring Systems

Mentoring systems are another important element in schools. New teachers tend to be overwhelmed with the start of their first few school years and having guidance from an experienced teacher can help them navigate their new responsibilities. Mentors can offer guidance in all areas including classroom setup, materials, organization, classroom management, curriculum implementation, planning, and events such as "Back to School" night, staff responsibilities, and emotional support. Research supports that implementing strong and effective mentoring programs benefits the new teachers, as well as the student achievement in the new teacher's classroom.

Teachers should remember that they are part of a team of professionals, and that their personal success is part of a greater success that everyone hopes to achieve.

The teacher is the manager of his classroom. If teachers are sharing the same student, they can, together, develop a strategy for dealing with that student. The same is true of parents. That relationship must not be adversarial unless there is no other way to handle the student and the situation. In communications with other teachers, administration, and parents, respectful, reciprocal communication solves many problems.

COLLABORATION

Collaboration is a powerful tool to build a professional learning community. When teachers work together on lesson and unit planning, they learn new techniques, test ideas on each other, and develop stronger instructional methods. Many researchers say that collaborating can be more powerful in instructional practice than attending professional development. This is because people learn in a more natural setting and can get assistance from those who give them the new ideas.

While teachers often find that they spend considerable time in their classrooms with children, schools are organized in such a way that many groups of people have important and powerful roles. Some people are specialists and are meant to assist teachers in their work. Specialists are certified teachers who specialize in certain learning needs. Others are administrators (or various levels of administrators) that run the school programs. And others are board members or district officials that oversee all schools in the district. This section will look at each group in particular.

Special Education & Child Study Teams

Special education teachers are specialists with students who may have learning or physical disabilities. Reading specialists focus on students who need additional assistance in reading. Special education teachers work with regular education teachers, as well as other school staff, to develop, implement, and evaluate students with special needs. Special education teachers play an important role in the development and implementation of each student's 504 plan or Individualized Education Plan (IEP). These plans are legal documents stating the educational, behavioral, objectives, and goals for each student.

Gifted and talented teachers are included in this group, as they oversee the individual needs of students with specific, advanced abilities.

Many schools have Child Study Teams made up of additional professionals who aid students with various needs. These often include the students' teachers, parents, and the inclusion of necessary professionals which could include occupational therapists, special education teachers, speech therapists, guidance counselors, and school psychologists.

Curriculum Coordinator

Curriculum coordinators serve as the leader in the development and implementation of a subject. These professionals work with teachers who are involved in instruction of a particular subject. For example, the Language Arts Curriculum Coordinator would ensure that all the teachers who teach language arts understand the curriculum, have the materials to implement the curriculum, plan and conduct professional development, update curriculum, and so on.

Technology Coordinator

Technology coordinators either work entirely at one school, or they work for a variety of schools within a district. These people develop programs and assist teachers in the use of technology or curricular programs.

Parent-Teacher Organizations

Most schools have some form of a parent-teacher organization (PTO, PTA, etc) where active parents volunteer for various events and needs at the school and are dedicated to promoting the well-being of the students at the school. Typically, PTO members organize fundraising, school events, and social events for students, educational speakers, book fairs, and more. These volunteers are often organized to help volunteer in the library, office, classrooms or where they are needed.

Skill 17.4 Analyzing ways of evaluating and responding to feedback (e.g., from supervisors, students, parents, colleagues)

TEACHER EVALUATIONS

Often, teachers are fearful about being evaluated by their principals. However, most principals are not out to criticize teachers or find fault with their methods. They simply want to help all teachers be successful in their jobs. A teacher appraisal is merely a method of "assessing" a teacher and providing them with feedback to help them improve practice.

Usually, the process begins with principals working on particular goals and objectives that teachers will work to attain throughout the year. These goals and objectives typically are the things that principals will look to see improvement on within the school year.

Teachers should consider areas that the principal can be of assistance in. For example, if a teacher feels uncomfortable with something that the principal will observe, the teacher may see an appraisal as a perfect opportunity to ask to attend professional development activities. Principals will most likely see such a request as a good thing. It shows initiative and desire to improve.

Finally, teachers should be proactive about getting support from other teachers, mentors, and instructional coaches when they feel they have areas in which they need significant work.

COMPETENCY 018   **UNDERSTAND THE IMPORTANCE OF AND APPLY STRATEGIES FOR PROMOTING PRODUCTIVE RELATIONSHIPS AND INTERACTIONS AMONG THE SCHOOL, HOME, AND COMMUNITY TO ENHANCE STUDENT LEARNING**

Skill 18.1   **Identifying strategies for initiating and maintaining effective communication between the teacher and parents or other caregivers, and recognizing factors that may facilitate or impede communication in given situations (including parent-teacher conferences)**

COMMUNICATING WITH STUDENT FAMILIES

Teachers possess a variety of methods to communicate with families. Many early childhood and elementary teachers choose to start off the year (or end the summer) with a friendly letter welcoming the students to the classroom, in addition to introducing him/herself to the students and their families. Many teachers choose to include their school phone number, as well as email, so parents can reach out at their earliest desire or need. In the higher grades, teachers typically provide at least a handout with their course content and contact information as a reference for parents and students. This communication sets an open and positive tone with the families so they know how to reach the teacher and that s/he is willing to communicate.

Another good form of communication is to set up a weekly avenue of communication. Advances in technology have made communication with parents even easier. Email can be a source of quick and effective communication (and eliminates the "I lost the note" response from students). Some teachers maintain classroom websites that list a class calendar, and sometimes even test dates, project due dates and other helpful information. Other teachers utilize online classroom management systems where attendance, grades, notes, assignments, class calendars, and more are all available in one place through a login.

PARENT-TEACHER CONFERENCES

When a conference is scheduled, whether at the request of the teacher or parent, the teacher should allow sufficient time to prepare thoroughly. Collect all relevant information, samples of student work, records of behavior, and other items needed to help the parent understand the circumstances. It is also a good idea to compile a list of questions or concerns you wish to address. Arrange the time and location of the conference to provide privacy and to avoid interruptions.

Begin the conference by putting the parents as ease. Take the time to establish a comfortable mood, but do not waste time with unnecessary small talk. Begin the discussion with positive comments about the student. Identify strengths and desirable attributes but do not exaggerate.

As issues or areas of concern are addressed, be sure to focus on observable behaviors and concrete results or information. Do not make judgmental statements about parent or child. Share specific work samples, anecdotal records of behavior, etc., which demonstrate clearly the concerns you have about the student. Be a good listener and hear the parent's comments and explanations. Such background information can be invaluable in understanding the needs and motivations of the child.

Finally, end the conference with an agreed plan of action between parents and teacher (and, when appropriate, the student). Bring the conference to a close politely but firmly, and thank the parents for their involvement.

A day or two after the conference, it is a good idea to send a follow-up note to the parents. In this note, briefly and concisely reiterate the plan or step agreed to in the conference. Be polite and professional; avoid the temptation to be too informal or chatty. If the issue is a long-term one, such as the behavior or on-going work performance of the student, make periodic follow-up contacts to keep the parents informed of the progress.

Skill 18.2   Identifying a variety of strategies for working with parents, caregivers, and others to help students from diverse backgrounds reinforce in-school learning outside the school environment

Teachers today will deal with an increasingly diverse group of cultures in their classrooms. And while this is an exciting prospect for most teachers, it creates new challenges in dealing with a variety of family expectations for school and teachers. First, teachers must show respect to all parents and families. They need to set the tone that suggests that their mission is to develop students into the best people they can be. And then they need to realize that various cultures have different views of how children should be educated.

Second, teachers will have better success when they talk personally about each student. Even though teachers may have many students, when they share personal things about each student, parents will feel more confident that their child will be "in the right hands." Third, it is very important that teachers act like they are partners in the children's education and development. Parents know their children best, and it is important to get feedback, information, and advice from them.

Finally, teachers will need to be patient with difficult families, realizing that certain methods of criticism (including verbal attacks, etc.) are unacceptable. Such circumstances would require the teacher to get assistance from an administrator. This situation, however, is very unusual, and most teachers will find that when they really attempt to be friendly and personal with parents, the parents will reciprocate and assist in the educational program.

THE IMPORTANCE OF REGULAR COMMUNICATION

The support of the parents is an invaluable aid in the educational process. It is in the best interests of child, parent, and teacher for there to be cooperation and mutual support between parent and teacher. One of the teacher's professional responsibilities is to establish and maintain effective communication with parents. A few basic techniques to pursue are oral communication (phone calls), written communication in the form of general information classroom newsletters, notes to the parent of a particular child, and parent-teacher conferences.

When it is necessary to communicate (whether by phone, letter, or in person) with a parent regarding a concern about a student, allow a "cooling off" period before making contact with the parent. It is important to remain professional and objective. The purpose for contacting the parent is to elicit support and additional information that may have a bearing on the student's behavior or performance. Be careful to not demean the child and do not appear antagonistic or confrontational. It is also a nice courtesy to notify parents of positive occurrences with their children. The teacher's communication with parents should not be limited to negative items.

When parents contact the teacher with concerns, the teacher should respond professionally and promptly. Be sure to keep a copy of, print up, or save all correspondence with parents in the event it is needed for future reference.

ENGAGING STUDENT FAMILIES

Research proves that the more a family is involved in a child's educational experience, the more that child will succeed academically. The problem is that often teachers assume that involvement in education simply means that the parents show up to help at school events or participate in parental activities on campus. With this belief, many teachers devise clever strategies to increase parental involvement at school. Parents are invited in to assist with workshops, attend class trips, participate as a room parents, organize special events, read to the class, speak of an occupation, help with classroom housekeeping, and more. Parents can also be involved by volunteering for the PTO/A, library help, office help, and other tasks. Some teachers plan a few events a year in the classroom for special parties, presentations and events.

However, just because a parent shows up to school and assists with an activity does not mean that the child will learn more. Also, many parents work all day long and cannot assist in the school. Teachers, therefore, have to think of different ways to encourage parental and family involvement in the educational process. Quite often, teachers have great success within involving families by just informing families of what is going on in the classroom. Newsletters are particularly effective at this. Parents love to know what is going on in the classroom, and this way, they will feel included. In newsletters, for example, teachers can provide suggestions on how parents can help with the educational goals of the school. For example, teachers can recommend that parents read with their children for 20 minutes per day. To add effectiveness to that, teachers can also provide suggestions on what to do when their children come across difficult words or when they ask a question about comprehension. This gives parents practical strategies.

Teachers can also provide very specific suggestions to individual parents. For example, say a student needs additional assistance in a particular subject. The teacher can provide tips to parents to encourage and increase deeper understandings in the subject outside of class.

Skill 18.3 Applying strategies for using community resources to enrich learning experiences

THE COMMUNITY AS A RESOURCE

The community is a vital link to increasing learning experiences for students. Community resources can supplement the minimized and marginal educational resources of school communities. With state and federal educational funding becoming increasingly subject to legislative budget cuts, school communities welcome the financial support that community resources can provide in terms of discounted prices on high end supplies (e.g. computers, printers, and technology supplies), along with providing free notebooks, backpacks, and student supplies for low-income students who may have difficulty obtaining the basic supplies for school.

Community stores can provide cash rebates and teacher discounts for educators in struggling school districts and compromised school communities. Both professionally and personally, communities can enrich the student learning experiences by including the following support strategies:

- Provide programs that support student learning outcomes and future educational goals
- Create mentoring opportunities that provide adult role models in various industries to students interested in studying in that industry
- Provide financial support for school communities to help low-income or homeless students begin the school year with the basic supplies
- Develop paid internships with local university students to provide tutorial services for identified students in school communities who are having academic and social difficulties processing various subject areas
- Provide parent-teen-community forums to create public voice of change in communities
- Offer parents without computer or Internet connection stipends to purchase technology to create equitable opportunities for students to do research and complete word.doc paper requirements
- Stop in classrooms and ask teachers and students what's needed to promote academic progress and growth

Community resources are vital in providing that additional support to students, school communities, and families, particularly those struggling to remain engaged or in declining educational institutions competing for federal funding and limited district funding. The commitment that a community shows to its educational communities is a valuable investment in the future. Community resources that are able to provide additional funding for tutors in marginalized classrooms or help schools reduce classrooms of students needing additional remedial instruction directly impact educational equity and facilitation of teaching and learning for both teachers and students.

Skill 18.4 **Recognizing various ways in which school personnel, local citizens, and community institutions (e.g., businesses, cultural institutions, colleges and universities, social agencies) can work together to promote a sense of neighborhood and community**

SEE also Skill 18.3.

MENTORING
Mentoring has become an instrumental tool in addressing student achievement and access to learning. Adult mentors work individually with identified students on specific subject areas to reinforce the learning through tutorial instruction and application of knowledge. Providing students with adult role models to reinforce the learning has become a crucial instructional strategy for teachers seeking to maximize student learning beyond the classroom. Students who work with adult mentors from culturally diverse backgrounds are given a multicultural aspect of learning that is cooperative and multi-modal in personalized instruction.

Connecting with community resources will also provide viable avenues of support in helping students who need additional academic remediation access learning. There are diverse programs that are offered through the local universities and community agencies that connect college students or working adults with subject areas and classrooms in need of additional student interns/adult volunteers to support the academic programs in school communities.

COMPETENCY 019   UNDERSTAND RECIPROCAL RIGHTS AND RESPONSIBILITIES IN SITUATIONS INVOLVING INTERACTIONS BETWEEN TEACHERS AND STUDENTS, PARENTS/GUARDIANS, COMMUNITY MEMBERS, COLLEAGUES, SCHOOL ADMINISTRATORS, AND OTHER SCHOOL PERSONNEL

Skill 19.1   Applying knowledge of laws related to students' rights in various situations (e.g., in relation to due process, discrimination, harassment, confidentiality, discipline, privacy)

SEE also Skill 19.3.

DUE PROCESS

The due process clause of the Constitution of the United Sates indicates that no state can deprive any person of life, liberty, or property without due process of law. Liberty interest has been defined to encompass a wide range of personal freedoms. The courts have described liberty as consisting of fundamental rights that are "essential to the orderly pursuit of happiness by free men."

This clause has major implications for educators for several reasons. Prior to the Fourteenth Amendment, the earlier amendments applied to the federal government only. Another important factor lies in the nature of public education: It is a state governmental function. When educators are acting in their professional capacities, they are "the state." Therefore, when educators interact with parents and students, they must be sure that they are functioning in a way that does not deprive any individual of his or her substantive rights.

For example, before a student can be suspended for a significant period of time, that student must be accorded procedural due process, because the right to an education accrues to the student as a property interest through the state constitution. The sources of substantive rights are multiple and varied, but regardless of the source, the due process clause of the Fourteenth Amendment will protect them. The major elements of procedural due process are notice, a hearing, and an impartial tribunal.

EQUAL PROTECTION

The Fourteenth Amendment includes the equal protection clause, which guarantees that laws will provide equal treatment and will be nondiscriminatory. The Fourteenth Amendment required the federal government and states to pass legislation that would implement equal protection. Federal law protects people from discrimination on the basis of race, color, national origin, religion, gender, age, and disability.

Teachers and administrators are employed by public schools, which are paid for in large part by taxes. Public schools involve compulsory requirements for student attendance, standards and state certifications for teachers, and testing and assessment requirements of the state. Thus the teachers and administrators employed by public schools are state actors, meaning they are acting on behalf of a governmental body and must ensure that students' rights are not infringed upon.

Race, Color, and National Origin
The term "race" is used to describe the categorization of people into various groups based on heritable characteristics. Some students identify as being of one race, and others identify as belonging to multiple racial groups. Race is a social construct that has changed over time in response to cultural and political influences. Educators must not show favoritism toward any specific group of students, nor may they demonstrate indifference toward any students on the basis of race, color, or national origin. Such actions are illegal.

Religion
Schools must make accommodations to address the religious needs of students. There are many ways in which schools can both accommodate students' religious needs and also create policies that are regularly reviewed to ensure that as new religions and belief systems emerge, students' beliefs and values are not being hindered. For example, a student who is absent for a religious holiday or reason should be excused and should have a reasonable time to make up the work missed. Dress code polices must be reviewed to ensure that they do not have a discriminatory effect. For example, even if school policy forbids the wearing of baseball caps and hats, it mustn't disallow the wearing of turbans or other religious garments. Schools also must ensure that they are not ignoring bullying based on religious clothing or practice and that they set, in policy and practice, a tone that accommodates students' religious beliefs.

Sex, Marital Status, and Sexual Orientation
Gender and marital status are protected classes throughout the United States. Favoritism or gender-biased policy making in schools is prohibited. Similarly, educators should avoid favoring students of a particular gender. In New York, sexual orientation is also a protected class, and schools must not discriminate against students on the basis of their sexual preference or gender identity. This includes students who are transgender (that is, students who are physically one gender but associate strongly with the other gender).

Disability
There are multiple definitions of disability, depending on the law that is being applied. The broad definition of disability under the Americans with Disabilities Act (ADA) is any mental or physical impairment that significantly limits major life activity. Someone whom others perceive as having such an impairment is also defined as having a disability. The Individuals with Disabilities Education Act

(IDEA) specifically lists disability conditions that fall under the law. These categories are:

- Autism
- Deaf-blindness
- Emotional disturbance
- Hearing impairment
- Mental retardation
- Multiple disabilities
- Orthopedic impairment
- Other health impairment
- Specific learning disability
- Speech or language impairment
- Traumatic brain injury
- Visual impairment

Age

Age is a protected class in terms of government employment. As long as a person is 18 years of age or older, he or she is eligible for employment in state or federal government. The government cannot discriminate, on the basis of age in hiring, retaining, or compensating employees.

The Invisible Student

The invisible student is a phenomenon that occurs when an educator fails to recognize or pay attention to students of a particular race, gender, or the like. Ignoring a group of students constitutes unequal treatment and is discriminatory. Not calling on students of a particular group or barring them from participation in class discussion is discriminatory. Even if an educator has good intentions or believes she or he is shielding the student(s) from ridicule by classmates, this unequal treatment is discriminatory. "Invisible student" discrimination often happens when students are not native English speakers and teachers find them difficult to understand. By ignoring these students, educators send a message to the general student body that particular students are not worthy of consideration.

The Very Visible Student

When a teacher praises or compliments a student on the basis of his or her race, national origin, gender, or the like, the teacher is drawing attention to that student that could lead other students to stereotype students of a particular protected class. For example, say a teacher is passing back math tests to her class and remarks, "As always, Ronnie and Kim got 100 percent!" referring to the only students of Asian origin in her class. This makes these students particularly visible to the other students and could lead to stereotyping of Asian students as superior in math to students of other ethnicities. The educator has singled out students and differentiated expectations for them on the basis of their ethnic group. Similarly, when a teacher praises female students for keeping the classroom tidy and praises male students for academic excellence, students may begin to feel that women are not able to achieve high academic scores and that male students should not help with classroom cleaning duties. Making students of a particular protected class visible for certain behaviors or tasks is a form of illegal discrimination.

FEDERAL LEGISLATION

The **Individuals with Disabilities Education Act** (IDEA) was originally enacted by Congress in 1975 to make sure that, like other children, children with disabilities had the opportunity to receive a free appropriate public education. The most recent amendments were passed by Congress in December 2004, with final regulations published in August 2006. In some senses, the law is very new, even though it has a long, detailed, and powerful history. IDEA guides how states and school districts provide special education and related services to more than six million eligible children with disabilities.

The **Family Educational Rights and Privacy Act** (FERPA) (20 U.S.C. § 1232g; 34 CFR Part 99) is a federal law that protects the privacy of student education records. The law applies to all schools that receive funds under an applicable program of the U.S. Department of Education. FERPA gives parents certain rights with respect to their children's education records. These rights transfer to the student when she or he reaches the age of 18 or attends a school beyond the high school level. Students to whom these rights have transferred are "eligible students."

Title IX of the Educational Amendments of 1972 states that no individual shall, on the basis of sex, be excluded from participation in, be denied the benefits of, or be subjected to discrimination under any educational program or activity that receives or benefits from federal assistance. This statute covers the areas of admission, educational programs and activities, access to course offerings, counseling, the use of appraisal and counseling materials, and athletics.

Title VI of the Civil Rights Act of 1964 extends protection from discrimination on the basis of race, color, or national origin to any program or activity receiving federal financial assistance.

Title VII of the Civil Rights Act of 1964 states that it is unlawful for an employer to discriminate against any individual with respect to compensation, terms, conditions, or privileges of employment because of that individual's race, color, religion, sex, or national origin. Some exceptions are noted in this statute. It does not apply to a religious organization that seeks individuals of a particular religion to perform the work of the organization. Where suspect classifications (those classifications having no basis in rationality) represent bona fide occupational qualifications, they are permitted. Classifications based on merit and seniority is also acceptable under this statute.

Title III of No Child Left Behind (NCLB) mandates the provision of funding and support to help school districts meet the needs of students with limited proficiency in the English language and promotes best practices in doing so. Because children without English language skills cannot demonstrate proficiency on assessments designed for students whose first language is English, it is critical to ensure that language support is provided and that the school fosters an atmosphere that does not discriminate against any students on the basis of language skills or accent. Title III created the Office of English Language Acquisition (OELA) to oversee the budget and use it to "close the achievement gap between limited English proficiency students and their native-English speaking counterparts."

Skill 19.2   Applying knowledge of a teacher's rights and responsibilities in various situations (e.g., in relation to students with disabilities, potential abuse, safety issues)

SEE also Skills 3.6, 6.3, and 7.6.

ABUSE SITUATIONS

The child who is undergoing abuse is the one whose needs must be served first. A suspected case gone unreported may destroy a child's life, and their subsequent life as a functional adult. It is the duty of any citizen who suspects abuse and neglect to make a report to their administrator/child protective services (an organization which identifies and handles cases of abuse), and it is especially important and required for state licensed and certified persons to make a report. All reports can be kept confidential if required, but it is best to disclose one's identity in case more information is required. This is a personal matter that has no impact on qualifications for license or certification. Failure to make a report when abuse or neglect is suspected is punishable by revocation of certification and license, a fine, and criminal charges.

It is the right of any accused individual to have counsel and make a defense, as in any matter of law. The procedure for reporting makes clear the rights of the accused, who stands before the court innocent until proven guilty, with the right to representation, redress and appeal, as in all matters of United States law. The state is cautious about receiving spurious reports but investigates any that seem real enough. Some breaches of standards of decency are not reportable offenses, such as possession of pornography that is not hidden from children. But teachers should make the report, and let the counselor make the decision. In this case, a teacher's conscience is clear, and they will have followed all procedures that keep them from liability. The obligation to report is immediate when abuse is suspected.

There is no time given as an acceptable or safe period of time to wait before reporting, so hesitation to report may be a cause for action. One should not wait once suspicion is firm. Reasonable suspicion is all that is needed, not actual proof, which is the job for the investigators.

EMOTIONAL DISTURBANCES

Many safe and helpful interventions are available to the classroom teacher when dealing with a student who is suffering serious emotional disturbances. First, and foremost, the teacher must maintain open communication with the parents and other professionals who are involved with the student whenever overt behavior characteristics are exhibited. Students with behavior disorders need constant behavior modification, which may involve two-way communication between the home and school on a daily basis.

The teacher should also initiate a behavior modification program for any student that might show emotional or behavioral disorders. Such behavior modification plans can be effective means of preventing deviant behavior. If deviant behavior does occur, the teacher should have arranged a safe and secure time-out place where the student can go for a respite and an opportunity to regain self-control. Often when a behavior disorder is more severe, the student must be involved in a more concentrated program aimed at alleviating deviant behavior such as psychotherapy. In such instances, the school psychologist, guidance counselor, or behavior specialist is directly involved with the student and provides counseling and therapy on a regular basis.

As a last resort, many families are turning to drug therapy. Once viewed as a radical step, administering drugs to children to balance their emotions or control their behavior has become a widely used form of therapy. Of course, only a medical doctor can prescribe such drugs. Great care must be exercised when giving pills to children in order to change their behavior, especially since so many medicines have undesirable side effects. It is important to know that these drugs relieve only the symptoms of behavior and do not get at the underlying causes. Parents and teachers need to be educated as to the side effects of these medications.

SCHOOL SAFETY AND SECURITY

School leaders are charged with providing students a safe, efficient, comfortable school building. While school districts and funding levels play significant parts in the aesthetics of a school building, basic safety and comfort issues are the responsibility of a school's administrative team. Various strategies can be put into place in order to promote satisfactory levels of building safety and efficiency.

A principal—or designee, such as an assistant principal—should be responsible on a <u>daily</u> basis to make rounds on a campus in order to verify a checklist of items. Such items might include visiting restrooms to ensure that everything is working properly and that students have clean, well operating facilities to use. A checklist might also include examining blacktop in the athletic areas to ensure that students would be safe running or playing on outside surfaces.

The school building must be in an operable condition. Any broken item that could pose a safety risk should be dealt with. Furniture that gets in the way of door areas must be moved. All doors should be completely operable and able to be opened quickly in an emergency. Windows should be able to be opened. Air conditioners, heaters, gas systems, plumbing, and electricity should all be able to be turned off easily and quickly if the need arises. This last point is a particular concern for many schools. If a specific custodian knows how to complete all those procedures, other individuals also need to learn how to operate such equipment in the case of that custodian's absence.

Skill 19.3   **Applying knowledge if parents' rights and responsibilities in various situations (e.g., in relation to student records, school attendance)**

STUDENT RECORDS

The student permanent record is a file of the student's cumulative educational history. It contains a profile of the student's academic background as well as the student's behavioral and medical background. The purpose of the permanent record is to provide applicable information about the student so that the student's individual educational needs can be met. If any specialized testing has been administered, the results are noted in the permanent record. Any special requirements that the student may have are indicated in the permanent record. Highly personal information, including court orders regarding custody, is filed in the permanent record as is appropriate. The importance and value of the permanent record cannot be underestimated. It offers a comprehensive knowledge of the student.

Other pertinent individual information contained in the permanent record includes the student's attendance, grade averages, and schools attended. Personal information such as parents' names and addresses, immunization records, child's height and weight, and narrative information about the child's progress and physical and mental well being is an important aspect of the permanent record. All information contained within the permanent record is strictly confidential and is only to be discussed with the student's parents or other involved school personnel.

Maintaining the Student Record

The current teacher is responsible for maintaining the student's permanent record. All substantive information in regard to testing, academic performance, the student's medical condition, and personal events are placed in the permanent record file. Updated information in regard to the student's grades, attendance, and behavior is added annually. These files are kept in a locked fireproof room or file cabinet and cannot be removed from this room unless the person removing them signs a form acknowledging full responsibility for the safe return of the complete file. Again, only the student's parents (or legal guardians), the teacher or other concerned school personnel may view the contents of the permanent record file.

The permanent record file follows the student as he/she moves through the school system with information being updated along the way. Anytime the student leaves a school, the permanent record is transferred with the student. The permanent record is regarded as legal documentation of a student's educational experience.

The contents of any student records should be indicative of the student's academic aptitude and/or achievement. The information contained should never be in any way derogatory or potentially damaging. It is important to keep in mind that others who view the contents of the records may form an opinion of the student based on the information in the student's record or file. Anyone who places information in a student's record must make every effort to give an accurate reflection of the student's performance while maintaining a neutral position as to the student's potential for future success or failure.

Confidentiality
The most essential fact to remember in regard to students' records is that the information within is confidential. Although specific policies may vary from one school or district to another, confidentiality remains constant and universal. Teachers never discuss any student or his/her progress with anyone other than the student's parents or essential school personnel. Confidentiality applies to all student information whether it is a student's spelling test, portfolio, standardized test information, report card, or the contents of the permanent record file.

The significance of the student's records is not to be taken lightly. In many instances, teachers have access to a student's records before actually meeting the student. It is important for the teacher to have helpful information about the student without developing any preconceived biases about the student.

Careful regard must be given to all information that is added to a student's file without diluting the potential effectiveness of that information. It is also important to be cognizant of the fact that the primary function of student records is that they are intended to be used as a means of developing a better understanding of the students' needs and to generate a more effective plan for meeting these needs.

Skill 19.4   Analyzing the appropriateness of a teacher's response to a parent, a community member, another educator, or a student in various situations (e.g., when dealing with differences of opinion in regard to current or emerging policy)

SEE Skills 18.1 and 18.2.

DOMAIN IV   **INSTRUCTION AND ASSESSMENT: CONSTRUCTED-RESPONSE ITEM**

Content addressed by the constructed-response assignment is described in Domain II, competencies 007 – 015

Sample Written Assignment

Instructions: Write an answer of 300–600 words that addresses the topic described below.

- You need to identify the grade level involved, and provide information about the purpose of your approach, the strategies you would employ, and the rationale or reasoning behind your plan of action.
- Imagine the intended reader of this essay to be another educator.
- Take your time and think through what you want to write before you start.
- You may want to outline the essay before you actually start writing.

Your school district is barely meeting the AYP standards of No Child Left Behind in several areas. Although there are no official external goals that must be met, the faculty, administration and parents want to improve student achievement across the board and prevent any difficulties with AYP scores. A joint task force has been formed to identify methods to help all students improve their performance. To this end, they have asked teachers to submit ideas for consideration. **Describe a plan that you believe would positively impact student achievement in multiple subject areas.**

A good response by an elementary teacher:

This plan is designed for third graders.

Student achievement is affected by many factors. These include the teacher's style and attitude, the curriculum and instructional methods, the atmosphere of the classroom and the school, the home environment from which students come, students' unique learning styles, individual student needs and/or limitations, cultural and linguistic diversity, and prior learning experiences. In spite of individual differences and needs, all students can be supported to learn and grow in the academic environment with the right attention and approach. A commitment to an inclusive classroom, where students of all achievement levels work together and diversity is honored and supported, goes a long way to ensuring student success. Attending to students' individual academic and psychosocial needs and working collaboratively with parents and community supports are also essential in helping to ameliorate or remove obstacles to student achievement.

Another major element in student achievement is student motivation. My plan is to implement instructional approaches that will increase student motivation, thereby raising student achievement. I would recommend focusing on two areas: child-centered learning methodologies and an integrated curriculum. The advantages of the integrated curriculum is that it mirrors the real world, where learning crosses "subject" lines such as reading, science, the arts, math, social studies, and language arts. This is especially effective for young children as their worldview is not broken down into discrete "subjects." An integrated curriculum feels familiar to them and engages their natural curiosity, enhancing their motivation to learn.

(continued on next page)

Using child-centered instructional techniques increase the likelihood that students will enjoy learning. When they enjoy the process of learning, they are more highly motivated to complete tasks, to take risks to learn new things, and to consider new ideas. By capitalizing on young children's innate urge to discover and explore, as well as their use of play to attain mastery, child-centered approaches for young children can yield a high level of engagement and motivation to learn.

Specific child-centered learning methodologies could include the following:

- Generating a list of questions that students want to answer on a specific topic; these questions can be posted in the classroom with space for the answers to be added as the class learns about the topic. The teacher will develop activities across subjects to help student address these questions.

- Using integrated subject learning stations that the students can choose from, as long as they complete three out of five within a given time frame.

- Incorporating play activities into the classroom that access content-related material across subject areas. An example might be to put on a play about the animals that live in the forests and the fields.

- Being attuned to and utilizing teachable moments as they occur in classroom activities as well as on the playground.

- Creating small group activities where the students have the chance to make choices as a group about what and how they are going to study. For example, in groups of three or four, students have a worksheet with five key words related to the topic under study. The task is to learn three things about each of the key words. They can ask their parents/guardians for information, go to the library and ask for help, look in books in the classroom, or share information they already know. They may use the Internet, draw a picture of the key word, or create a pantomime. Each group can then share or post their information for the entire class.

A good response by a secondary teacher:

This plan is designed for eleventh graders.

Student achievement is affected by many factors. These include the teacher's style and attitude, the curriculum and instructional methods, the atmosphere of the classroom and the school, the home environment from which students come, students' unique learning styles, individual student needs and/or limitations, cultural and linguistic diversity, and prior learning experiences. In spite of individual differences and needs, all students can be supported to learn and grow in the academic environment with the right attention and approach. A commitment to an inclusive classroom, where students of all achievement levels work together and diversity is honored and supported, goes a long way to ensuring student success. Attending to students' individual academic and psychosocial needs and working collaboratively with parents and community supports are also essential in helping to ameliorate or remove obstacles to student achievement.

Another major element in student achievement is student motivation. My plan is to implement instructional approaches that will increase student motivation by engaging them in self-chosen topics, thereby raising student achievement. I would use two strategies to improve student achievement with eleventh graders: using self-directed study and informational interviewing. These could be incorporated in various subject courses, such as English, social studies, science, and the arts. The intent behind both of these strategies is to engage students in active exploration of topics relevant to them, and to help them to take responsibility for their learning process in and out of the classroom.

In both of these strategies, I would provide some guidelines and a rubric for assessment. The specific goals to be evaluated by the rubric would be part of the student's process of determining their topic and the learning approaches they will employ.

(continued on next page)

Self-directed study involves students picking a topic among those included in a specific curriculum and determining what they want to learn about that topic. They establish goals, learning strategies, and intended outcomes. There are checkpoints built in so they can receive feedback as they work on their project to ensure that they have crafted a workable plan and benefit from the teacher's input. They can utilize a wide range of methods (such as using the arts to describe scientific ideas or concepts) and sources (creative non-fiction, the Internet, professionals in the field as well as textbooks). Outcomes can be equally varied.

Informational interviewing can be incorporated into a self-directed study project or can stand on its own as a strategy to engage students. The key is to generate interest in students to find a topic or profession about which they are curious. It can be a particular job, a scientific theory, a method of manufacture, or a form of artistic expression. The goal is for students to identify key questions that need to be asked in order to answer their general inquiry, identify informants (e.g., someone who performs a certain job or someone who works in the field of study), conduct the interview(s), and then create a report about the topic. The report must meet certain criteria per the teacher-derived rubric, but students have a lot of freedom in how the report is created (e.g., written text, artistic expression, power-point presentation).

Both of these approaches can be part of a larger strategy to engage students in learning by drawing on interactions with real-world information and to take learning beyond the classroom. This learning can be brought back into the classroom through "poster sessions" (as is used at professional conferences) or in discussion groups or public speaking activities. All of these activities provide opportunities for the student to develop self-responsibility and a positive self-concept, also factors in increasing student motivation and achievement.

Sample Test

Directions: Read each item and select the best response.

1. **What developmental patterns should a professional teacher assess to meet the needs of the student?**
(Average) (Skill 1.1)

   A. Academic, regional, and family background
   B. Social, physical, and cognitive
   C. Academic, physical, and family background
   D. Physical, family, and ethnic background

2. **How many stages of intellectual development does Piaget define?**
(Average) (Skill 1.1)

   A. Two
   B. Four
   C. Six
   D. Eight

3. **According to Piaget, what stage is characterized by the ability to think abstractly and to use logic?**
(Easy) (Skill 1.1)

   A. Concrete operations
   B. Pre-operational
   C. Formal operations
   D. Conservative operational

4. **At approximately what age is the average child able to define abstract terms such as honesty and justice?**
(Rigorous) (Skill 1.1)

   A. 10–12 years old
   B. 4–6 years old
   C. 14–16 years old
   D. 6–8 years old

5. **Students who can solve problems mentally have...**
(Average) (Skill 1.1)

   A. Reached maturity
   B. Physically developed
   C. Reached the pre-operational stage of thought
   D. Achieved the ability to manipulate objects symbolically

6. **What is the most significant development emerging in children at age two?**
(Easy) (Skill 1.2)

   A. Immune system develops
   B. Socialization occurs
   C. Language develops
   D. Perception develops

7. **What strategy can teachers incorporate in their classrooms that will allow students to acquire the same academic skills even though the students are at various learning levels?** *(Rigorous) (Skill 1.3)*

   A. Create learning modules
   B. Apply concrete rules to abstract theories
   C. Incorporate social learning skills
   D. Follow cognitive development progression

8. **Louise is a first grade teacher. She is planning her instructional activities for the week. In considering her planning, she should keep in mind that activities for this age of child should change how often?** *(Average) (Skill 2.1)*

   A. 25–40 minutes
   B. 30–40 minutes
   C. 5–10 minutes
   D. 15–20 minutes

9. **What do cooperative learning methods all have in common?** *(Rigorous) (Skill 2.4)*

   A. Philosophy
   B. Cooperative task/cooperative reward structures
   C. Student roles and communication
   D. Teacher roles

10. **What is one component of the instructional planning model that must be given careful evaluation?** *(Rigorous) (Skill 2.4)*

    A. Students' prior knowledge and skills
    B. The script the teacher will use in instruction
    C. Future lesson plans
    D. Parent participation

11. **When planning instruction, which of the following is an organizational tool to help ensure you are providing a well-balanced set of objectives?** *(Rigorous) (Skill 2.6)*

    A. Using a taxonomy to develop objectives
    B. Determining prior knowledge skill levels
    C. Determining readiness levels
    D. Ensuring you meet the needs of diverse learners

12. **What is an example of a low order question?** *(Easy) (Skill 2.6)*

    A. "Why is it important to recycle items in your home"
    B. "Compare how glass and plastics are recycled"
    C. "What items do we recycle in our county"
    D. "Explain the importance of recycling in our county"

13. Bloom's taxonomy references six skill levels within the cognitive domain. The top three skills are known as higher-order thinking skills (HOTS). Which of the following are the three highest order skills?
(Rigorous) (Skill 2.6)

A. Comprehension, application, analysis
B. Knowledge, comprehension, evaluation
C. Application, synthesis, comprehension
D. Analysis, synthesis, and evaluation

14. Bobby, a nine-year-old, has been caught stealing frequently in the classroom. What might be a factor contributing to this behavior?
(Average) (Skill 3.2)

A. Need for the items stolen
B. Serious emotional disturbance
C. Desire to experiment
D. A normal stage of development

15. Active listening is an important skill for teachers to utilize with both students and teachers. Active listening involves all of the following strategies except…
(Rigorous) (Skill 3.4)

A. Eye Contact
B. Restating what the speaker has said
C. Clarification of speaker statements
D. Open and receptive body language

16. The process approach is a three-phase model approach that aims directly at the enhancement of self concept among students. Which of the following are components of this process approach?
(Rigorous) (Skill 3.4)

A. Sensing function, transforming function, acting function
B. Diversity model, ethnicity model, economic model
C. Problem approach, acting function, diversity model
D. Ethnicity approach, sensing model, problem approach

17. **Which of the following is an accurate description of an English Language Learner student?**
(Average) (Skill 3.5)

A. Remedial students
B. Exceptional education students
C. Are not a homogeneous group
D. Feel confident in communicating in English when with their peers

18. **What is an effective way to help an English Language Learner student succeed in class?**
(Average) (Skill 3.5)

A. Refer the child to a specialist
B. Maintain an encouraging, success-oriented atmosphere
C. Help them assimilate by making them use English exclusively
D. Help them cope with the content materials you presently use

19. **Andy shows up to class abusive and irritable. He is often late, sleeps in class, sometimes slurs his speech, and has an odor of drinking. What is the first intervention to take?**
(Rigorous) (Skill 3.7)

A. Confront him, relying on a trusting relationship you think you have
B. Do a lesson on alcohol abuse, making an example of him
C. Do nothing, it is better to err on the side of failing to identify substance abuse
D. Call administration, avoid conflict, and supervise others carefully

20. **Students who are learning English as a second language often require which of the following to process new information?**
(Rigorous) (Skill 4.1)

A. Translators
B. Reading tutors
C. Instruction in their native language
D. Additional time and repetitions

21. **How could a KWL chart be used in instruction?**
(Average) (Skill 4.5)

A. To motivate students to do a research paper
B. To assess prior knowledge of the students
C. To assist in teaching skills
D. To put events in sequential order

22. **What is a good strategy for teaching ethnically diverse students?**
(Average) (Skill 5.3)

A. Do not focus on the students' culture
B. Expect them to assimilate easily into your classroom
C. Imitate their speech patterns
D. Include ethnic studies in the curriculum

23. **Mrs. Peck wants to justify the use of personalized learning community to her principal. Which of the following reasons should she use?**
(Rigorous) (Skill 5.3)

A. They build multiculturalism
B. They provide a supportive environment to address academic and emotional needs
C. They build relationships between students that promote lifelong learning
D. They are proactive in their nature

24. **Abigail has had intermittent hearing loss from the age of 1 through age 5 when she had tubes put in her ears. What is one area of development that may be affected by this?**
(Average) (Skill 6.1)

A. Math
B. Language
C. Social skills
D. None

25. **Which of the following is a good reason to collaborate with a peer?**
(Easy) (Skill 6.4)

A. To increase your knowledge in areas where you feel you are weak, but the peer is strong
B. To increase your planning time and that of your peer by combining the classes and taking more breaks
C. To have fewer lesson plans to write
D. To teach fewer subjects

26. **What have recent studies regarding effective teachers concluded?**
(Average) (Skill 7.1)

   A. Effective teachers let students establish rules
   B. Effective teachers establish routines by the sixth week of school
   C. Effective teachers state their own policies and establish consistent class rules and procedures on the first day of class
   D. Effective teachers establish flexible routines

27. **Which of the following significantly increases appropriate behavior in the classroom?**
(Average) (Skill 7.1)

   A. Monitoring the halls
   B. Having class rules
   C. Having class rules, giving feedback, and having individual consequences
   D. Having class rules, and giving feedback

28. **What is the definition of proactive classroom management?**
(Rigorous) (Skill 7.1)

   A. Management that is constantly changing
   B. Management that is downplayed
   C. Management that gives clear and explicit instructions and rewards compliance
   D. Management that is designed by the students

29. **What is one way of effectively managing student conduct?**
(Average) (Skill 7.3)

   A. State expectations about behavior
   B. Let students discipline their peers
   C. Let minor infractions of the rules go unnoticed
   D. Increase disapproving remarks

30. **The concept of efficient use of time includes which of the following?**
(Rigorous) (Skill 7.4)

   A. Daily review, seatwork, and recitation of concepts
   B. Lesson initiation, transition, and comprehension check
   C. Review, test, and review
   D. Punctuality, management transition, and wait time avoidance

31. **Reducing off-task time and maximizing the amount of time students spend attending to academic tasks is closely related to which of the following?**
(Rigorous) (Skill 7.5)

   A. Using whole class instruction only
   B. Business-like behaviors of the teacher
   C. Dealing only with major teaching functions
   D. Giving students a maximum of two minutes to come to order

32. **How can student misconduct be redirected at times?**
(Easy) (Skill 7.5)

   A. The teacher threatens the students
   B. The teacher assigns detention to the whole class
   C. The teacher stops the activity and stares at the students
   D. The teacher effectively handles changing from one activity to another

33. **Teachers have a responsibility to help students learn how to organize their classroom environments. Which of the following is NOT an effective method of teaching responsibility to students?**
(Rigorous) (Skill 7.6)

   A. Dividing responsibilities among students
   B. Doing "spot-checks" of notebooks
   C. Cleaning up after students leave the classroom
   D. Expecting students to keep weekly calendars

34. **When considering the development of the curriculum, which of the following accurately describes the four factors which need to be considered?**
(Rigorous) (Skill 8.1)

   A. Alignment, Scope, Sequence, and Design
   B. Assessment, Instruction, Design, and Sequence
   C. Data, Alignment, Correlation, and Score
   D. Alignment, Sequence, Design, and Assessment

35. **When using a kinesthetic approach, what would be an appropriate activity?**
(Average) (Skill 8.3)

A. List
B. Match
C. Define
D. Debate

36. **Who developed the theory of multiple intelligences?**
(Average) (Skill 8.3)

A. Bruner
B. Gardner
C. Kagan
D. Cooper

37. **Norm-referenced tests:**
(Rigorous) (Skill 9.2)

A. Give information only about the local samples results
B. Provide information about how the local test takers did compared to a representative sampling of national test takers
C. Make no comparisons to national test takers
D. None of the above

38. **How are standardized tests useful in assessment?**
(Average) (Skill 9.2)

A. For teacher evaluation
B. For evaluation of the administration
C. For comparison from school to school
D. For comparison to the population on which the test was normed

39. **When a teacher wants to utilize an assessment that is subjective in nature, which of the following is the most effective method for scoring?**
(Easy) (Skill 9.4)

A. Rubric
B. Checklist
C. Alternative assessment
D. Subjective measures should not be utilized

40. **What steps are important in the review of subject matter in the classroom?**
(Rigorous) (Skill 10.1)

A. A lesson-initiating review, topic, and a lesson-end review
B. A preview of the subject matter, an in-depth discussion, and a lesson-end review
C. A rehearsal of the subject matter and a topic summary within the lesson
D. A short paragraph synopsis of the previous day's lesson and a written review at the end of the lesson

41. **What are critical elements of instructional process?**
(Rigorous) (Skill 10.1)

A. Content, goals, teacher needs
B. Means of getting money to regulate instruction
C. Content, materials, activities, goals, learner needs
D. Materials, definitions, assignments

42. **The teacher states that the lesson the students will be engaged in will consist of a review of the material from the previous day, demonstration of the scientific of an electronic circuit, and small group work on setting up an electronic circuit. What has the teacher demonstrated?**
(Rigorous) (Skill 10.2)

A. The importance of reviewing
B. Giving the general framework for the lesson to facilitate learning
C. Giving students the opportunity to leave if they are not interested in the lesson
D. Providing momentum for the lesson

43. **The use of volunteers and paraprofessionals within a classroom enriches the setting by:**
(Easy) (Skill 10.6)

A. Providing more opportunity for individual student attention
B. Offering a perceived sense of increased security for students
C. Modifying the behavior of students
D. All of the above

44. **What would improve planning for instruction?**
(Average) (Skill 12.1)

A. Describe the role of the teacher and student
B. Evaluate the outcomes of instruction
C. Rearrange the order of activities
D. Give outside assignments

45. **What should be considered when evaluating textbooks for content?**
(Easy) (Skill 12.3)

A. Type of print used
B. Number of photographs used
C. Free of cultural stereotyping
D. Outlines at the beginning of each chapter

46. **What should a teacher do when students have not responded well to an instructional activity?** *(Average) (Skill 12.5)*

   A. Reevaluate learner needs
   B. Request administrative help
   C. Continue with the activity another day
   D. Assign homework on the concept

47. **Mrs. Grant is providing her students with many extrinsic motivators in order to increase their intrinsic motivation. Which of the following best explains this relationship?** *(Rigorous) (Skill 13.1)*

   A. This is a good relationship and will increase intrinsic motivation
   B. The relationship builds animosity between the teacher and the students
   C. Extrinsic motivation does not in itself help to build intrinsic motivation
   D. There is no place for extrinsic motivation in the classroom

48. **Which statement is an example of specific praise?** *(Average) (Skill 13.2)*

   A. "John, you are the only person in class not paying attention"
   B. "William, I thought we agreed that you would turn in all of your homework"
   C. "Robert, you did a good job staying in line. See how it helped us get to music class on time"
   D. "Class, you did a great job cleaning up the art room"

49. **Which of the following is NOT a factor in student self-motivation?** *(Rigorous) (Skill 13.3)*

   A. Breaking larger tasks into more manageable steps
   B. Permitting students to turn in assignments late
   C. Offering students control over the assignment
   D. Allowing students to create dream boards

50. **Why is it important for a teacher to pose a question before calling on students to answer?** *(Rigorous) (Skill 14.4)*

   A. It helps manage student conduct
   B. It keeps the students as a group focused on the class work
   C. It allows students time to collaborate
   D. It gives the teacher time to walk among the students

51. **Wait-time has what effect?**
    (Average) (Skill 14.4)

    A. Gives structure to the class discourse
    B. Fewer chain and low-level questions are asked with more higher-level questions included
    C. Gives the students time to evaluate the response
    D. Gives the opportunity for in-depth discussion about the topic

52. **What is one benefit of amplifying a student's response?**
    (Rigorous) (Skill 14.4)

    A. It helps the student develop a positive self-image
    B. It is helpful to other students who are in the process of learning the reasoning or steps in answering the question
    C. It allows the teacher to cover more content
    D. It helps to keep the information organized

53. **What is not a way that teachers show acceptance and give value to a student response?**
    (Rigorous) (Skill 14.4)

    A. Acknowledging
    B. Correcting
    C. Discussing
    D. Amplifying

54. **What is an effective amount of wait-time?**
    (Easy) (Skill 14.4)

    A. 1 second
    B. 5 seconds
    C. 15 seconds
    D. 10 seconds

55. **Ms. Smith says, "Yes, exactly what do you mean by 'It was the author's intention to mislead you'" What does this illustrate?**
    (Rigorous) (Skill 14.4)

    A. Digression
    B. Restates response
    C. Probes a response
    D. Amplifies a response

56. **The teacher responds, "Yes, that is correct" to a student's answer. What is this an example of?**
    (Average) (Skill 14.4)

    A. Academic feedback
    B. Academic praise
    C. Simple positive response
    D. Simple negative response

57. **When are students more likely to understand complex ideas?** *(Rigorous) (Skill 14.5)*

A. If they do outside research before coming to class
B. Later when they write out the definitions of complex words
C. When they attend a lecture on the subject
D. When they are clearly defined by the teacher and are given examples and non-examples of the concept

58. **What are the two ways concepts can be taught?** *(Easy) (Skill 14.5)*

A. Factually and interpretively
B. Inductively and deductively
C. Conceptually and inductively
D. Analytically and facilitatively

59. **Which of the following is NOT a part of the hardware of a computer system?** *(Easy) (Skill 15.1)*

A. Storage device
B. Input devices
C. Software
D. Central Processing Unit

60. **What are three steps, in the correct order, for evaluating software before purchasing it for use within the classroom?** *(Rigorous) (Skill 15.1)*

A. Read the instructions to ensure it will work with the computer you have, try it out as if you were a student, and examine how the program handles errors or mistakes the student may make
B. Try the computer program as if you were a student, read any online information about the program, have a student use the program and provide feedback
C. Read the instructions and load it onto your computer, try out the program yourself as if you were a student, have a student use the program and provide feedback
D. Read the instructions, have a student use the program, try it out yourself

61. You are a classroom teacher in a building that does not have a computer lab for your class to use. However, knowing that you enjoy incorporating technology into the classroom, your principal has worked to find computers for your room. They are set up in the back of your classroom and have software loaded, but have no access to the intranet or internet within your building. Which of the following is NOT an acceptable method for using these computers within your classroom instruction?
(Rigorous) (Skill 15.4)

A. Rotating the students in small groups through the computers as centers
B. Putting students at the computers individually for skill-based review or practice
C. Dividing your classroom into three groups and putting each group at one computer and completing a whole class lesson
D. Using the computers for students to complete their writing assignments with an assigned sign-up sheet, so the students know the order in which they will type their stories

62. Which of the following are the three primary categories of instructional technology tools?
(Rigorous) (Skill 15.5)

A. Creation/design/implementation
B. Research/implementation/assessment
C. Assessment/creation/research
D. Design/research/usage

63. When a teacher is evaluating a student's technologically produced product, which of the following is considered the MOST important factor to consider?
(Rigorous) (Skill 15.7)

A. Content
B. Design
C. Audience
D. Relevance

64. Which of the following is responsible for working with the school in matters concerning the business of running a school?
(Rigorous) (Skill 16.5)

A. Curriculum coordinators
B. Administrators
C. Board of Education
D. Parent-Teacher organizations

65. Teacher's unions are involved in all of the following EXCEPT:
(Average) (Skill 16.5)

A. Updating teachers on current educational developments
B. Advocating for teacher rights
C. Matching teachers with suitable schools
D. Developing professional codes and practices

66. Mrs. Graham has taken the time to reflect, completed observations, and asked for feedback about the interactions between her and her students from her principal. It is obvious by seeking this information out that Mrs. Graham understands which of the following?
(Rigorous) (Skill 17.1)

A. The importance of clear communication with the principal
B. She needs to analyze her effectiveness of classroom interactions
C. She is clearly communicating with the principal
D. She cares about her students

67. What is a benefit of frequent self-assessment?
(Average) (Skill 17.2)

A. Opens new venues for professional development
B. Saves teachers the pressure of being observed by others
C. Reduces time spent on areas not needing attention
D. Offers a model for students to adopt in self-improvement

68. In the past, teaching has been viewed as _____ while in more current society it has been viewed as _____.
(Rigorous) (Skill 17.3)

A. isolating...collaborative
B. collaborative...isolating
C. supportive...isolating
D. isolating...supportive

69. What would happen if a school utilized an integrated approach to professional development?
(Average) (Skill 17.3)

A. All stakeholders needs are addressed
B. Teachers and administrators are on the same page
C. High-quality programs for students are developed
D. Parents drive the curriculum and instruction

70. **Which of the following should NOT be a purpose of a parent-teacher conference?**
(Average) (Skill 18.1)

A. To involve the parent in their child's education
B. To establish a friendship with the child's parents
C. To resolve a concern about the child's performance
D. To inform parents of positive behaviors by the child

71. **Mr. Brown wishes to improve his parent communication skills. Which of the following is a strategy he can utilize to accomplish this goal?**
(Easy) (Skill 18.1)

A. Hold parent-teacher conferences
B. Send home positive notes
C. Have parent nights where the parents are invited into his classroom
D. All of the above

72. **Which is NOT considered a good practice when conducting parent-teacher conferences?**
(Average) (Skill 18.1)

A. Ending the conference with an agreed plan of action
B. Figure out questions for parents during the conference
C. Prepare work samples, records of behavior, and assessment information
D. Prepare a welcoming environment, set a good mood, and be an active listener

73. **When communicating with parents for whom English is not the primary language, you should:**
(Easy) (Skill 18.1)

A. Provide materials whenever possible in their native language
B. Use an interpreter
C. Provide the same communication as you would to native English speaking parents
D. All of the above

74. Tommy is a student in your class and his parents are deaf. Tommy is struggling with math and you want to contact the parents to discuss the issues. How should you proceed?
(Easy) (Skill 18.1)

A. Limit contact because of the parent's inability to hear
B. Use a TTY phone to communicate with the parents
C. Talk to your administrator to find an appropriate interpreter to help you communicate with the parents personally
D. Both B and C, but not A

75. Which statement best reflects why family involvement is important to a student's educational success?
(Easy) (Skill 18.2)

A. Reading the class newsletter constitutes strong family involvement
B. Family involvement means to attend graduation
C. There are limited ways a parent can be active in their child's education
D. The more family members are involved, the more success a student is likely to experience

76. Which of the following is NOT an appropriate method for teachers to interact with families of diverse backgrounds?
(Easy) (Skill 18.2)

A. Show respect to parents
B. Share personal stories concerning the student
C. Display patience with parents
D. Disregard culture of student

77. A parent has left an angry message on the teacher's voicemail. The message relates to a concern about a student and is directed at the teacher. The teacher should:
(Average) (Skill 18.2)

A. Call back immediately and confront the parent
B. Cool off, plan what to discuss with the parent, then call back
C. Question the child to find out what set off the parent
D. Ignore the message, since feelings of anger usually subside after a while

78. **In successful inclusion of students with disabilities:**
(Average) (Skill 19.1)

   A. A variety of instructional arrangements are available
   B. School personnel shift the responsibility for learning outcomes to the student
   C. The physical facilities are used as they are
   D. Regular classroom teachers have sole responsibility for evaluating student progress

79. **A 16-year-old girl who has been looking sad writes an essay in which the main protagonist commits suicide. You overhear her talking about suicide. What do you do?**
(Average) (Skill 19.2)

   A. Report this immediately to school administration, talk to the girl, letting her know you will talk to her parents about it
   B. Report this immediately to authorities
   C. Report this immediately to school administration, make your own report to authorities if required by protocol in your school, and do nothing else
   D. Just give the child some extra attention, as it may just be that's all she's looking for

80. **How can a teacher use a student's permanent record?**
(Average) (Skill 19.3)

   A. To develop a better understanding of the needs of the student
   B. To record all instances of student disruptive behavior
   C. To brainstorm ideas for discussing with parents at parent-teacher conferences
   D. To develop realistic expectations of the student's performance early in the year

Sample Test with Rationales

Directions: Read each item and select the best response.

1. **What developmental patterns should a professional teacher assess to meet the needs of the student?**
    (Average) (Skill 1.1)

    A. Academic, regional, and family background
    B. Social, physical, and cognitive
    C. Academic, physical, and family background
    D. Physical, family, and ethnic background

Answer: B. Social, physical, and cognitive
The effective teacher applies knowledge of physical, social, and cognitive developmental patterns and of individual differences to meet the instructional needs of all students in the classroom. The most important premise of child development is that all domains of development (physical, social, and cognitive/academic) are integrated. The teacher has a broad knowledge and thorough understanding of the development that typically occurs during the students' current period of life. More importantly, the teacher understands how children learn best during each period of development. An examination of the student's file coupled with ongoing evaluation assures a successful educational experience for both teacher and students.

2. **How many stages of intellectual development does Piaget define?**
    (Average) (Skill 1.1)

    A. Two
    B. Four
    C. Six
    D. Eight

Answer: B. Four
The stages are:

1. <u>Sensorimotor stage</u>: from birth to age 2 years (children experience the world through movement and senses).
2. <u>Preoperational stage</u>: from ages 2 to 7(acquisition of motor skills).
3. <u>Concrete operational stage</u>: from ages 7 to 11 (children begin to think logically about concrete events).
4. <u>Formal Operational stage</u>: after age 11 (development of abstract reasoning).

3.   According to Piaget, what stage is characterized by the ability to think abstractly and to use logic?
        (Easy) (Skill 1.1)

        A. Concrete operations
        B. Pre-operational
        C. Formal operations
        D. Conservative operational

Answer: C. Formal operations
The four development stages are described in Piaget's theory as follows:

1. Sensorimotor stage: from birth to age 2 years (children experience the world through movement and senses)
2. Preoperational stage: from ages 2 to 7 (acquisition of motor skills)
3. Concrete operational stage: from ages 7 to 11 (children begin to think logically about concrete events)
4. Formal operational stage: after age 11 (development of abstract reasoning)

These chronological periods are approximate and, in light of the fact that studies have demonstrated great variation between children, cannot be seen as rigid norms. Furthermore, these stages occur at different ages, depending upon the domain of knowledge under consideration. The ages normally given for the stages reflect when each stage tends to predominate even though one might elicit examples of two, three, or even all four stages of thinking at the same time from one individual, depending upon the domain of knowledge and the means used to elicit it.

4.   At approximately what age is the average child able to define abstract terms such as honesty and justice?
        (Rigorous) (Skill 1.1)

        A. 10–12 years old
        B. 4–6 years old
        C. 14–16 years old
        D. 6–8 years old

Answer: A. 10–12 years old
The usual age for the fourth stage (the formal operational stage) as described by Piaget is from 10 to 12 years old. It is in this stage that children begin to be able to define abstract terms.

5.   **Students who can solve problems mentally have...**
      (Average) (Skill 1.1)

      A. Reached maturity
      B. Physically developed
      C. Reached the pre-operational stage of thought
      D. Achieved the ability to manipulate objects symbolically

Answer: D. Achieved the ability to manipulate objects symbolically
When students are able to solve mental problems, it is an indication to the teacher that they have achieved the ability to manipulate objects symbolically and should be instructed to continue to develop their cognitive and academic skills.

6.   **What is the most significant development emerging in children at age two?**
      (Easy) (Skill 1.2)

      A. Immune system develops
      B. Socialization occurs
      C. Language develops
      D. Perception develops

Answer: C. Language develops
Language begins to develop in an infant not long after birth. Chomsky claims that children teach themselves to speak using the people around them for resources. Several studies of the sounds infants make in their cribs seem to support this. The first stage of meaningful sounds is the uttering of a word that obviously has meaning for the child, for example "bird," when the child sees one flying through the air. Does the development of real language begin when the noun is linked with a verb ("bird fly")? When language begins and how it develops has been debated for a long time. It is useful for a teacher to investigate those theories and studies.

7. **What strategy can teachers incorporate in their classrooms that will allow students to acquire the same academic skills even though the students are at various learning levels?**
   (Rigorous) (Skill 1.3)

   A. Create learning modules
   B. Apply concrete rules to abstract theories
   C. Incorporate social learning skills
   D. Follow cognitive development progression

Answer: A. Create learning modules
Teachers should be aware of the fact that each student develops cognitively, mentally, emotionally, and physically at different levels. Each student is a unique person and may require individualized instruction. This may require for teachers to adapt their lesson plans according to a student's developmental progress.

8. **Louise is a first grade teacher. She is planning her instructional activities for the week. In considering her planning, she should keep in mind that activities for this age of child should change how often?**
   (Average) (Skill 2.1)

   A. 25–40 minutes
   B. 30–40 minutes
   C. 5–10 minutes
   D. 15–20 minutes

Answer: D.15–20 minutes
For young children, average activities should change about every twenty minutes.

9. **What do cooperative learning methods all have in common?**
(Rigorous) (Skill 2.4)

A. Philosophy
B. Cooperative task/cooperative reward structures
C. Student roles and communication
D. Teacher roles

Answer: B. Cooperative task/cooperative reward structures
Cooperative learning situations, as practiced in today's classrooms, grew out of searches conducted by several groups in the early 1970s. Cooperative learning situations can range from very formal applications such as STAD (Student Teams-Achievement Divisions) and CIRC (Cooperative Integrated Reading and Composition) to less formal groupings known variously as "group investigation," "learning together," and "discovery groups." Cooperative learning as a general term is now firmly recognized and established as a teaching and learning technique in American schools. Since cooperative learning techniques are so widely diffused in the schools, it is necessary to orient students in the skills by which cooperative learning groups can operate smoothly, and thereby enhance learning. Students who cannot interact constructively with other students will not be able to take advantage of the learning opportunities provided by the cooperative learning situations and will furthermore deprive their fellow students of the opportunity for cooperative learning.

10. **What is one component of the instructional planning model that must be given careful evaluation?**
(Rigorous) (Skill 2.4)

A. Students' prior knowledge and skills
B. The script the teacher will use in instruction
C. Future lesson plans
D. Parent participation

Answer: A. Students' prior knowledge and skills
The teacher will, of course, have certain expectations regarding where the students will be physically and intellectually when he/she plans for a new class. However, there will be wide variations in the actual classroom. If he/she does not make the extra effort to understand where there are deficiencies and where there are strengths in the individual students, the planning will probably miss the mark, at least for some members of the class. This can be obtained through a review of student records, by observation, and by testing.

11. **When planning instruction, which of the following is an organizational tool to help ensure you are providing a well-balanced set of objectives?**
    (Rigorous) (Skill 2.6)

    A. Using a taxonomy to develop objectives
    B. Determining prior knowledge skill levels
    C. Determining readiness levels
    D. Ensuring you meet the needs of diverse learners

Answer: A. Using a taxonomy to develop objectives
The use of a taxonomy, such as Bloom's, allows teachers to ensure the students are receiving instruction at a variety of different levels. It is important students are able to demonstrate skills and knowledge at a variety of different levels.

12. **What is an example of a low order question?**
    (Easy) (Skill 2.6)

    A. "Why is it important to recycle items in your home"
    B. "Compare how glass and plastics are recycled"
    C. "What items do we recycle in our county"
    D. "Explain the importance of recycling in our county"

Answer: C. "What items do we recycle in our county"
Remember that the difference between specificity and abstractness is a continuum. The most specific is something that is concrete and can be seen, heard, smelled, tasted, or felt, like cans, bottles, and newspapers. At the other end of the spectrum is an abstraction like importance. Lower-order questions are on the concrete end of the continuum; higher-order questions are on the abstract end.

13. **Bloom's taxonomy references six skill levels within the cognitive domain. The top three skills are known as higher-order thinking skills (HOTS). Which of the following are the three highest order skills?**
     (Rigorous) (Skill 2.6)

     A. Comprehension, application, analysis
     B. Knowledge, comprehension, evaluation
     C. Application, synthesis, comprehension
     D. Analysis, synthesis, and evaluation

Answer: D. Analysis, synthesis, and evaluation
The six skill levels of Bloom's taxonomy are: knowledge, comprehension, application, analysis, synthesis, and evaluation. Key instructional approaches that utilize HOTS are inquiry-based learning, problem solving, and open-ended questioning. It is crucial for students to use and refine these skills in order to apply them to everyday life and situations outside of school.

14. **Bobby, a nine-year-old, has been caught stealing frequently in the classroom. What might be a factor contributing to this behavior?**
     (Average) (Skill 3.2)

     A. Need for the items stolen
     B. Serious emotional disturbance
     C. Desire to experiment
     D. A normal stage of development

Answer: B. Serious emotional disturbance
Lying, stealing, and fighting are atypical behaviors that most children may exhibit occasionally, but if a child lies, steals, or fights regularly or blatantly, these behaviors may be indicative of emotional distress. Emotional disturbances in childhood are not uncommon and take a variety of forms. Usually these problems show up in the form of uncharacteristic behaviors. Most of the time, children respond favorably to brief treatment programs of psychotherapy. At other times, disturbances may need more intensive therapy and are harder to resolve. All stressful behaviors need to be addressed, and any type of chronic antisocial behavior needs to be examined as a possible symptom of deep-seated emotional upset.

15. **Active listening is an important skill for teachers to utilize with both students and teachers. Active listening involves all of the following strategies except...**
   (Rigorous) (Skill 3.4)

   A. Eye Contact
   B. Restating what the speaker has said
   C. Clarification of speaker statements
   D. Open and receptive body language

Answer: B. Restating what the speaker has said
While it is often taught that it is important to restate conversations during meetings, when you are active listening it is more appropriate to seek clarification rather than simply restating.

16. **The process approach is a three-phase model approach that aims directly at the enhancement of self concept among students. Which of the following are components of this process approach?**
   (Rigorous) (Skill 3.4)

   A. Sensing function, transforming function, acting function
   B. Diversity model, ethnicity model, economic model
   C. Problem approach, acting function, diversity model
   D. Ethnicity approach, sensing model, problem approach

Answer: A. Sensing function, transforming function, acting function
This three-phase approach can be simplified into the words by which the model is usually known: reach, touch, and teach. The sensing function integrates information. The transforming function conceptualizes and provides meaning and value to perceived information. The acting function chooses actions from several different alternatives to be acted upon. This three-phase approach can be applied to any situation.

17. **Which of the following is an accurate description of an English Language Learner student?**
(Average) (Skill 3.5)

A. Remedial students
B. Exceptional education students
C. Are not a homogeneous group
D. Feel confident in communicating in English when with their peers

Answer: C. Are not a homogenous group
Because ELL students are often grouped in classes that take a different approach to teaching English than those for native speakers, it is easy to assume that they all present with the same needs and characteristics. Nothing could be further from the truth, even in what they need when it comes to learning English. It is important that their backgrounds and personalities be observed just as with native speakers. It was very surprising several years ago when Vietnamese children began arriving in American schools with little training in English and went on to excel in their classes, often even beyond their American counterparts. In many schools, there were Vietnamese merit scholars in the graduating classes.

18. **What is an effective way to help an English Language Learner student succeed in class?**
(Average) (Skill 3.5)

A. Refer the child to a specialist
B. Maintain an encouraging, success-oriented atmosphere
C. Help them assimilate by making them use English exclusively
D. Help them cope with the content materials you presently use

Answer: B. Maintain an encouraging, success-oriented atmosphere
Anyone who is in an environment where his language is not the standard one feels embarrassed and inferior. The student who is in that situation expects to fail. Encouragement is even more important for these students. They need many opportunities to succeed.

19. **Andy shows up to class abusive and irritable. He is often late, sleeps in class, sometimes slurs his speech, and has an odor of drinking. What is the first intervention to take?**
(Rigorous) (Skill 3.7)

A. Confront him, relying on a trusting relationship you think you have
B. Do a lesson on alcohol abuse, making an example of him
C. Do nothing, it is better to err on the side of failing to identify substance abuse
D. Call administration, avoid conflict, and supervise others carefully

Answer: D. Call administration, avoid conflict, and supervise others carefully
Educators are not only likely to, but often do, face students who are high on something. Of course, they are not only a hazard to their own safety and those of others, but their ability to be productive learners is greatly diminished, if not non-existent. They show up instead of skip, because it is not always easy or practical for them to spend the day away from home but not in school. Unless they can stay inside they are at risk of being picked up for truancy. Some enjoy being high in school, getting a sense of satisfaction by putting something over on the system. Some just do not take drug use seriously enough to think usage at school might be inappropriate. The first responsibility of the teacher is to assure the safety of all of the children. Avoiding conflict with the student who is high and obtaining help from administration is the best course of action.

20. **Students who are learning English as a second language often require which of the following to process new information?**
(Rigorous) (Skill 4.1)

A. Translators
B. Reading tutors
C. Instruction in their native language
D. Additional time and repetitions

Answer: D. Additional time and repetitions
While there are varying thoughts and theories into the most appropriate instruction for ESL students, much ground can be gained by simply providing additional repetitions and time for new concepts. It is important to include visuals and the other senses into every aspect of this instruction.

21. **How could a KWL chart be used in instruction?**
    (Average) (Skill 4.5)

    A. To motivate students to do a research paper
    B. To assess prior knowledge of the students
    C. To assist in teaching skills
    D. To put events in sequential order

Answer: B. To assess prior knowledge of the students
To understand information, not simply repeat it, students must connect it to their previous understanding. Textbooks cannot do that. Instead, teachers—the people who know students best—have to find out what they know and how to build on that knowledge. In science, having students make predictions before conducting experiments is an obvious way of finding out what they know and having them compare their observations to those predictions helps connect new knowledge and old. In history, teachers can also ask students what they know about a topic before they begin studying it or ask them to make predictions about what they will learn. KWL charts, in which students discuss what they know, what they want to know, and (later), what they have learned, are one way to activate this prior knowledge.

22. **What is a good strategy for teaching ethnically diverse students?**
    (Average) (Skill 5.3)

    A. Do not focus on the students' culture
    B. Expect them to assimilate easily into your classroom
    C. Imitate their speech patterns
    D. Include ethnic studies in the curriculum

Answer: D. Include ethnic studies in the curriculum
Exploring a student's own cultures increases their confidence levels in the group. It is also a very useful tool when students are struggling to develop identities that they can feel comfortable with. The bonus is that this is good training for living in the world.

23. **Mrs. Peck wants to justify the use of personalized learning community to her principal. Which of the following reasons should she use?**
    (Rigorous) (Skill 5.3)

    A. They build multiculturalism
    B. They provide a supportive environment to address academic and emotional needs
    C. They build relationships between students that promote lifelong learning
    D. They are proactive in their nature

Answer: B. They provide a supportive environment to address academic and emotional needs

While professional learning communities do all of the choices provided, this question asks for a justification statement. The best justification of those choices provided for implementing a personalized learning community in a classroom is to provide a supportive environment to help address the academic and emotional needs of her students.

24. **Abigail has had intermittent hearing loss from the age of 1 through age 5 when she had tubes put in her ears. What is one area of development that may be affected by this?**
    (Average) (Skill 6.1)

    A. Math
    B. Language
    C. Social skills
    D. None

Answer: B. Language

Frequent ear infections and intermittent hearing loss can significantly impair the development of language skills.

25. **Which of the following is a good reason to collaborate with a peer?** *(Easy) (Skill 6.4)*

   A. To increase your knowledge in areas where you feel you are weak, but the peer is strong
   B. To increase your planning time and that of your peer by combining the classes and taking more breaks
   C. To have fewer lesson plans to write
   D. To teach fewer subjects

Answer: A. To increase your knowledge in areas where you feel you are weak, but the peer is strong
One of the best reasons to collaborate is to share and develop your knowledge base.

26. **What have recent studies regarding effective teachers concluded?** *(Average) (Skill 7.1)*

   A. Effective teachers let students establish rules
   B. Effective teachers establish routines by the sixth week of school
   C. Effective teachers state their own policies and establish consistent class rules and procedures on the first day of class
   D. Effective teachers establish flexible routines

Answer: C. Effective teachers state their own policies and establish consistent class rules and procedures on the first day of class
The teacher can get ahead of the game by stating clearly on the first day of school in her introductory information for the students exactly what the rules. These should be stated firmly but unemotionally. When one of those rules is broken, he/she can then refer to the rules, rendering enforcement much easier to achieve. It is extremely difficult to achieve goals with students who are out of control. Establishing limits early and consistently enforcing them enhances learning. It is also helpful for the teacher to display prominently the classroom rules. This will serve as a visual reminder of the students' expected behaviors. In a study of classroom management procedures, it was established that the combination of conspicuously displayed rules, frequent verbal references to the rules, and appropriate consequences for appropriate behaviors led to increased levels of on-task behavior.

27.   Which of the following significantly increases appropriate behavior
       in the classroom?
       (Average) (Skill 7.1)

       A. Monitoring the halls
       B. Having class rules
       C. Having class rules, giving feedback, and having individual
           consequences
       D. Having class rules, and giving feedback

**Answer: C. Having class rules, giving feedback, and having individual
consequences**
Clear, consistent class rules go a long way to preventing inappropriate behavior.
Effective teachers give immediate feedback to students regarding their behavior
or misbehavior. If there are consequences, they should be as close as possible
to the outside world, especially for adolescents. Consistency, especially with
adolescents, reduces the occurrence of power struggles and teaches them that
predictable consequences follow for their choice of actions.

28.   What is the definition of proactive classroom management?
       (Rigorous) (Skill 7.1)

       A. Management that is constantly changing
       B. Management that is downplayed
       C. Management that gives clear and explicit instructions and rewards
           compliance
       D. Management that is designed by the students

**Answer: C. Management that gives clear and explicit instructions and
rewards compliance**
Classroom management plans should be in place when the school year begins.
Developing a management plan takes a proactive approach—that is, decide what
behaviors will be expected of the class as a whole, anticipate possible problems,
and teach the behaviors early in the school year. Involving the students in the
development of the classroom rules lets the students know the rationale for the
rules allows them to assume responsibility in the rules because they had a part in
developing them.

29. **What is one way of effectively managing student conduct? (Average) (Skill 7.3)**

A. State expectations about behavior
B. Let students discipline their peers
C. Let minor infractions of the rules go unnoticed
D. Increase disapproving remarks

Answer: A. State expectations about behavior
The effective teacher demonstrates awareness of what the entire class is doing and is in control of the behavior of all students even when the teacher is working with only a small group of the children. In an attempt to prevent student misbehaviors the teacher makes clear, concise statements about what is happening in the classroom directing attention to content and the students' accountability for their work rather than focusing the class on the misbehavior. It is also effective for the teacher to make a positive statement about the appropriate behavior that is observed. If deviant behavior does occur, the effective teacher will specify who the deviant is, what he or she is doing wrong, and why this is unacceptable conduct or what the proper conduct would be. This can be a difficult task to accomplish as the teacher must maintain academic focus and flow while addressing and desisting misbehavior. The teacher must make clear, brief statements about the expectations without raising his/her voice and without disrupting instruction.

30. **The concept of efficient use of time includes which of the following? (Rigorous) (Skill 7.4)**

A. Daily review, seatwork, and recitation of concepts
B. Lesson initiation, transition, and comprehension check
C. Review, test, and review
D. Punctuality, management transition, and wait time avoidance

Answer: D. Punctuality, management transition, and wait time avoidance
The "benevolent boss" concept applies here. One who succeeds in managing a business follows these rules; so does the successful teacher.

31. **Reducing off-task time and maximizing the amount of time students spend attending to academic tasks is closely related to which of the following?**
    (Rigorous) (Skill 7.5)

    A. Using whole class instruction only
    B. Business-like behaviors of the teacher
    C. Dealing only with major teaching functions
    D. Giving students a maximum of two minutes to come to order

Answer: B. Business-like behaviors of the teacher
The effective teacher continually evaluates his/her own physical/mental/social/emotional well-being with regard to the students in his/her classroom. There is always the tendency to satisfy social and emotional needs through relationships with the students. A good teacher genuinely likes his/her students, and that is a positive thing. However, if students are not convinced that the teacher's purpose for being there is to get a job done, the atmosphere in the classroom becomes difficult to control. This is the job of the teacher. Maintaining a business-like approach in the classroom yields many positive results. It is a little like a benevolent boss.

32. **How can student misconduct be redirected at times?**
    (Easy) (Skill 7.5)

    A. The teacher threatens the students
    B. The teacher assigns detention to the whole class
    C. The teacher stops the activity and stares at the students
    D. The teacher effectively handles changing from one activity to another

Answer: D. The teacher effectively handles changing from one activity to another
Appropriate verbal techniques include a soft non-threatening voice void of undue roughness, anger, or impatience regardless of whether the teacher is instructing, providing student alerts, or giving a behavior reprimand. Verbal techniques that may be effective in modifying student behavior include simply stating the student's name, explaining briefly and succinctly what the student is doing that is inappropriate and what the student should be doing. Verbal techniques for reinforcing behavior include both encouragement and praise delivered by the teacher. In addition, for verbal techniques to positively affect student behavior and learning, the teacher must give clear, concise directives while implying her warmth toward the students.

33. **Teachers have a responsibility to help students learn how to organize their classroom environments. Which of the following is NOT an effective method of teaching responsibility to students?** *(Rigorous) (Skill 7.6)*

    A. Dividing responsibilities among students
    B. Doing "spot-checks" of notebooks
    C. Cleaning up after students leave the classroom
    D. Expecting students to keep weekly calendars

Answer: C. Cleaning up after students leave the classroom
Teachers of young children can help students learn how to behave appropriately and take care of their surroundings by providing them with opportunities to practice ownership, chores, and leadership. By allowing students to leave a messy and disorganized class at the end of the day does not teach them responsibility.

34. **When considering the development of the curriculum, which of the following accurately describes the four factors which need to be considered?** *(Rigorous) (Skill 8.1)*

    A. Alignment, Scope, Sequence, and Design
    B. Assessment, Instruction, Design, and Sequence
    C. Data, Alignment, Correlation, and Score
    D. Alignment, Sequence, Design, and Assessment

Answer: A. Alignment, Scope, Sequence, and Design
When developing curriculum, it is important to first start with alignment. Alignment to state, national, or other standards is the first step. Next, the scope of the curriculum involves looking at the amount of material covered within a grade level or subject. Next, the sequence of material needs to be considered. Finally, it is important to look at the design of the units individually from beginning to end.

35. **When using a kinesthetic approach, what would be an appropriate activity?**
(Average) (Skill 8.3)

A. List
B. Match
C. Define
D. Debate

Answer: B. Match

Brain lateralization theory emerged in the 1970s and demonstrated that the left hemisphere appeared to be associated with verbal and sequential abilities whereas the right hemisphere appeared to be associated with emotions and with spatial, holistic processing. Although those particular conclusions continue to be challenged, it is clear that people concentrate, process, and remember new and difficult information under very different conditions. For example, auditory and visual perceptual strengths, passivity, and self-oriented or authority-oriented motivation often correlate with high academic achievement, whereas tactual and kinesthetic strengths, a need for mobility, nonconformity, and peer motivation often correlate with school underachievement (Dunn & Dunn, 1992, 1993). Understanding how students perceive the task of learning new information differently is often helpful in tailoring the classroom experience for optimal success.

36. **Who developed the theory of multiple intelligences?**
(Average) (Skill 8.3)

A. Bruner
B. Gardner
C. Kagan
D. Cooper

Answer: B. Gardner

Howard Gardner's most famous work is probably *Frames of Mind*, which details seven dimensions of intelligence (visual/spatial intelligence, musical intelligence, verbal intelligence, logical/mathematical intelligence, interpersonal intelligence, intrapersonal intelligence, and bodily/kinesthetic intelligence). Gardner's claim that pencil and paper IQ tests do not capture the full range of human intelligences has garnered much praise within the field of education but has also met criticism, largely from psychometricians. Since the publication of *Frames of Mind*, Gardner has additionally identified the 8th dimension of intelligence: naturalist intelligence, and is still considering a possible ninth—existentialist intelligence.

37. **Norm-referenced tests:**
(Rigorous) (Skill 9.2)

   A. Give information only about the local samples results
   B. Provide information about how the local test takers did compared to a representative sampling of national test takers
   C. Make no comparisons to national test takers
   D. None of the above

Answer: B. Provide information about how the local test takers did compared to a representative sampling of national test takers
This is the definition of a norm-referenced test.

38. **How are standardized tests useful in assessment?**
(Average) (Skill 9.2)

   A. For teacher evaluation
   B. For evaluation of the administration
   C. For comparison from school to school
   D. For comparison to the population on which the test was normed

Answer: D. For comparison to the population on which the test was normed
While the efficacy of the standardized tests that are being used nationally has come under attack recently, they are actually the only device for comparing where an individual student stands with a wide range of peers. They also provide a measure for a program or a school to evaluate how their own students are doing as compared to the populace at large.

39. **When a teacher wants to utilize an assessment that is subjective in nature, which of the following is the most effective method for scoring?**
(Easy) (Skill 9.4)

   A. Rubric
   B. Checklist
   C. Alternative assessment
   D. Subjective measures should not be utilized

Answer: A. Rubric
Rubrics are the most effective tool for assessing items that can be considered subjective. They provide the students with a clearer picture of teacher expectations and provide the teacher with a more consistent method of comparing this type of assignment.

40. **What steps are important in the review of subject matter in the classroom?**
    (Rigorous) (Skill 10.1)

    A. A lesson-initiating review, topic, and a lesson-end review
    B. A preview of the subject matter, an in-depth discussion, and a lesson-end review
    C. A rehearsal of the subject matter and a topic summary within the lesson
    D. A short paragraph synopsis of the previous day's lesson and a written review at the end of the lesson

Answer: A. A lesson-initiating review, topic, and a lesson-end review
The effective teacher utilizes all three of these together with comprehension checks to make sure the students are processing the information. Lesson-end reviews are restatements (by the teacher or teacher and students) of the content of discussion at the end of a lesson. Subject matter retention increases when lessons include an outline at the beginning of the lesson and a summary at the end of the lesson. This type of structure is utilized in successful classrooms. Moreover, when students know what is coming next and what is expected of them, they feel more a part of their learning environment, and deviant behavior is lessened.

41. **What are critical elements of instructional process?**
    (Rigorous) (Skill 10.1)

    A. Content, goals, teacher needs
    B. Means of getting money to regulate instruction
    C. Content, materials, activities, goals, learner needs
    D. Materials, definitions, assignments

Answer: C. Content, materials, activities, goals, learner needs
Goal-setting is a vital component of the instructional process. The teacher will, of course, have overall goals for her class, both short-term and long-term. However, perhaps even more important than that is the setting of goals that take into account the individual learner's needs, background, and stage of development. Making an educational program child-centered involves building on the natural curiosity children bring to school and asking children what they want to learn. Student-centered classrooms contain not only textbooks, workbooks, and literature but also rely heavily on a variety of audiovisual equipment and computers. There are tape recorders, language masters, filmstrip projectors, and laser disc players to help meet the learning styles of the students. Planning for instructional activities entails identification or selection of the activities the teacher and students will engage in during a period of instruction.

42. The teacher states that the lesson the students will be engaged in will consist of a review of the material from the previous day, demonstration of the scientific of an electronic circuit, and small group work on setting up an electronic circuit. What has the teacher demonstrated?
(Rigorous) (Skill 10.2)

A. The importance of reviewing
B. Giving the general framework for the lesson to facilitate learning
C. Giving students the opportunity to leave if they are not interested in the lesson
D. Providing momentum for the lesson

Answer: B. Giving the general framework for the lesson to facilitate learning
If children know where they're going, they're more likely to be engaged in getting there. It's important to give them a road map whenever possible for what is coming in their classes.

43. The use of volunteers and paraprofessionals within a classroom enriches the setting by:
(Easy) (Skill 10.6)

A. Providing more opportunity for individual student attention
B. Offering a perceived sense of increased security for students
C. Modifying the behavior of students
D. All of the above

Answer: D. All of the above
Research has shown that volunteers and paraprofessionals involvement in the educational process positively impacts the attitude and conduct of children in the classroom. Always be cautious in choosing classroom helpers that you trust and are competent.

44.   **What would improve planning for instruction?**
       (Average) (Skill 12.1)

    A. Describe the role of the teacher and student
    B. Evaluate the outcomes of instruction
    C. Rearrange the order of activities
    D. Give outside assignments

Answer: B. Evaluate the outcomes of instruction
Important as it is to plan content, materials, activities, goals taking into account learner needs and to base what goes on in the classroom on the results of that planning, it makes no difference if students are not able to demonstrate improvement in the skills being taught. An important part of the planning process is for the teacher to constantly adapt all aspects of the curriculum to what is actually happening in the classroom. Planning frequently misses the mark or fails to allow for unexpected factors. Evaluating the outcomes of instruction regularly and making adjustments accordingly will have a positive impact on the overall success of a teaching methodology.

45.   **What should be considered when evaluating textbooks for content?**
       (Easy) (Skill 12.3)

    A. Type of print used
    B. Number of photographs used
    C. Free of cultural stereotyping
    D. Outlines at the beginning of each chapter

Answer: C. Free of cultural stereotyping
While textbook writers and publishers have responded to the need to be culturally diverse in recent years, a few texts are still being offered that do not meet these standards. When teachers have an opportunity to be involved in choosing textbooks, they can be watchdogs for the community in keeping the curriculum free of matter that reinforces bigotry and discrimination.

46.   What should a teacher do when students have not responded well to
      an instructional activity?
      (Average) (Skill 12.5)

      A. Reevaluate learner needs
      B. Request administrative help
      C. Continue with the activity another day
      D. Assign homework on the concept

Answer: A. Reevaluate learner needs
The value of teacher observations cannot be underestimated. It is through the
use of observations that the teacher is able to informally assess the needs of the
students during instruction. These observations will drive the lesson and
determine the direction that the lesson will take based on student activity and
behavior. After a lesson is carefully planned, teacher observation is the single
most important component of an instructional presentation. If the teacher
observes that a particular student is not on task, she will change the method of
instruction accordingly. She may change from a teacher-directed approach to a
more interactive approach. Questioning will increase in order to increase the
participation of the students. If appropriate, the teacher will introduce
manipulative materials to the lesson. In addition, teachers may switch to a
cooperative group activity, thereby removing the responsibility of instruction from
the teacher and putting it on the students.

47.   Mrs. Grant is providing her students with many extrinsic motivators
      in order to increase their intrinsic motivation. Which of the following
      best explains this relationship?
      (Rigorous) (Skill 13.1)

      A. This is a good relationship and will increase intrinsic motivation
      B. The relationship builds animosity between the teacher and the
         students
      C. Extrinsic motivation does not in itself help to build intrinsic motivation
      D. There is no place for extrinsic motivation in the classroom

**Answer: C. Extrinsic motivation does not in itself help to build intrinsic
motivation**
There are some cases where it is necessary to utilize extrinsic motivation;
however, the use of extrinsic motivation is not alone a strategy to use to build
intrinsic motivation. Intrinsic motivation comes from within the student
themselves, while extrinsic motivation comes from outside parties.

48. **Which statement is an example of specific praise?**
(Average) (Skill 13.2)

   A. "John, you are the only person in class not paying attention"
   B. "William, I thought we agreed that you would turn in all of your homework"
   C. "Robert, you did a good job staying in line. See how it helped us get to music class on time"
   D. "Class, you did a great job cleaning up the art room"

Answer: C. "Robert, you did a good job staying in line. See how it helped us get to music class on time"
Praise is a powerful tool in obtaining and maintaining order in a classroom. In addition, it is an effective motivator. It is even more effective if the positive results of good behavior are included.

49. **Which of the following is NOT a factor in student self-motivation?**
(Rigorous) (Skill 13.3)

   A. Breaking larger tasks into more manageable steps
   B. Permitting students to turn in assignments late
   C. Offering students control over the assignment
   D. Allowing students to create dream boards

Answer: B. Permitting students to turn in assignments late
Student motivation in the classroom is an essential component of teaching. Highly motivated students actively engage more in the learning process than less motivated students. Teachers should have a firm understanding of the diverse aspects that influence student motivation and then incorporate strategies for encouraging motivation in the classroom.

50. **Why is it important for a teacher to pose a question before calling on students to answer?**
(Rigorous) (Skill 14.4)

   A. It helps manage student conduct
   B. It keeps the students as a group focused on the class work
   C. It allows students time to collaborate
   D. It gives the teacher time to walk among the students

Answer: B. It keeps the students as a group focused on the class work
It does not take much distraction for a class's attention to become diffused. Once this happens, effectively teaching a principle or a skill is very difficult. The teacher should plan presentations that will keep students focused on the lesson. A very useful tool is effective, well thought-out, pointed questions.

51. **Wait-time has what effect?**
(Average) (Skill 14.4)

A. Gives structure to the class discourse
B. Fewer chain and low-level questions are asked with more high-level questions included
C. Gives the students time to evaluate the response
D. Gives the opportunity for in-depth discussion about the topic

Answer: B. Fewer chain and low-level questions are asked with more high-level questions included

One part of the questioning process for the successful teacher is *wait-time*: the time between the question and either the student response or a follow-up. Many teachers vaguely recommend some general amount of wait-time (until the student starts to get uncomfortable or is clearly perplexed), but here the focus is on wait-time as a specific and powerful communicative tool that speaks through its structured silences. Embedded in wait-time are subtle clues about judgments of a student's abilities and expectations of individuals and groups. For example, the more time a student is allowed to mull through a question, the more the teacher trusts his or her ability to answer that question without getting flustered. As a rule, the practice of prompting is not a problem. Giving support and helping students reason through difficult conundrums is part of being an effective teacher.

52. **What is one benefit of amplifying a student's response?**
(Rigorous) (Skill 14.4)

A. It helps the student develop a positive self-image
B. It is helpful to other students who are in the process of learning the reasoning or steps in answering the question
C. It allows the teacher to cover more content
D. It helps to keep the information organized

Answer: B. It is helpful to other students who are in the process of learning the reasoning or steps in answering the question

Not only does the teacher show acceptance and give value to student responses by acknowledging, amplifying, discussing, or restating the comment or question, she also helps the rest of the class learn to reason. If a student response is allowed, even if it is blurted out, it must be acknowledged and the student made aware of the quality of the response. A teacher acknowledges a student response by commenting on it. For example, the teacher states the definition of a noun, and then asks for examples of nouns in the classroom. A student responds, "My pencil is a noun." The teacher answers, "Okay, let us list that on the board." By this response and the action of writing "pencil" on the board, the teacher has just incorporated the student's response into the lesson.

53.   **What is not a way that teachers show acceptance and give value to a student response?**
        (Rigorous) (Skill 14.4)

        A. Acknowledging
        B. Correcting
        C. Discussing
        D. Amplifying

Answer: B. Correcting
There are ways to treat every answer as worthwhile even if it happens to be wrong. The objective is to keep students involved in the dialogue. If their efforts to participate are "rewarded" with what seems to them to be a rebuke or that leads to embarrassment, they will be less willing to respond the next time.

54.   **What is an effective amount of wait-time?**
        (Easy) (Skill 14.4)

        A. 1 second
        B. 5 seconds
        C. 15 seconds
        D. 10 seconds

Answer: B. 5 seconds
One part of the questioning process for the successful teacher is *wait-time*: the time between the question and either the student response or a follow-up. Many teachers vaguely recommend some general amount of wait-time (until the student starts to get uncomfortable or is clearly perplexed), but here the focus is on wait-time as a specific and powerful communicative tool that speaks through its structured silences. Embedded in wait-time are subtle clues about judgments of a student's abilities and expectations of individuals and groups. For example, the more time a student is allowed to mull through a question, the more the teacher trusts his or her ability to answer that question without getting flustered. As a rule, the practice of prompting is not a problem. Giving support and helping students reason through difficult conundrums is part of being an effective teacher.

55.   Ms. Smith says, "Yes, exactly what do you mean by 'It was the author's intention to mislead you'" What does this illustrate?
(Rigorous) (Skill 14.4)

A. Digression
B. Restates response
C. Probes a response
D. Amplifies a response

Answer: C. Probes a response

From ancient times, notable teachers such as Socrates and Jesus have employed oral-questioning to enhance their discourse, to stimulate thinking, and/or to stir emotion among their audiences. Educational researchers and practitioners virtually all agree that teachers' effective use of questioning promotes student learning. Effective teachers continually develop their questioning skills.

56.   The teacher responds, "Yes, that is correct" to a student's answer. What is this an example of?
(Average) (Skill 14.4)

A. Academic feedback
B. Academic praise
C. Simple positive response
D. Simple negative response

Answer: C. Simple positive response

The reason for praise in the classroom is to increase the desirable in order to eliminate the undesirable. This refers to both conduct and academic focus. It further states that effective praise should be authentic, it should be used in a variety of ways, and it should be low-keyed. Academic praise is a group of specific statements that give information about the value of the response or its implications. For example, a teacher using academic praise would respond, "That is an excellent analysis of Twain's use of the river in Huckleberry Finn." Whereas a simple positive response to the same question would be, "That's correct."

57. **When are students more likely to understand complex ideas?**
    (Rigorous) (Skill 14.5)

    A. If they do outside research before coming to class
    B. Later when they write out the definitions of complex words
    C. When they attend a lecture on the subject
    D. When they are clearly defined by the teacher and are given examples and non-examples of the concept

Answer: D. When they are clearly defined by the teacher and are given examples and non-examples of the concept
Several studies have been carried out to determine the effectiveness of giving examples as well as the difference in effectiveness of various types of examples. It was found conclusively that the most effective method of concept presentation included giving a definition along with examples and non-examples and also providing an explanation of them. These same studies indicate that boring examples were just as effective as interesting examples in promoting learning. Additional studies have been conducted to determine the most effective number of examples that will result in maximum student learning. These studies concluded that a few thoughtfully selected examples are just as effective as many examples. It was determined that the actual number of examples necessary to promote student learning was relative to the learning characteristics of the learners. It was again ascertained that learning is facilitated when examples are provided along with the definition.

58. **What are the two ways concepts can be taught?**
    (Easy) (Skill 14.5)

    A. Factually and interpretively
    B. Inductively and deductively
    C. Conceptually and inductively
    D. Analytically and facilitatively

Answer: B. Inductively and deductively
Induction is reasoning from the particular to the general—that is, looking at a feature that exists in several examples and drawing a conclusion about that feature. Deduction is the reverse; it is the statement of the generality and then supporting it with specific examples.

TEACHER CERTIFICATION STUDY GUIDE

59.   Which of the following is NOT a part of the hardware of a computer system?
      (Easy) (Skill 15.1)

      A. Storage device
      B. Input devices
      C. Software
      D. Central Processing Unit

Answer: C. Software
Software is not a part of the hardware of a computer but instead consists of all of the programs which allow the computer to run. Software is either an operating system or an application program.

60.   What are three steps, in the correct order, for evaluating software before purchasing it for use within the classroom?
      (Rigorous) (Skill 15.1)

      A. Read the instructions to ensure it will work with the computer you have, try it out as if you were a student, and examine how the program handles errors or mistakes the students may make
      B. Try the computer program as if you were a student, read any online information about the program, have a student use the program and provide feedback
      C. Read the instructions and load it onto your computer, try out the program yourself as if you were a student, have a student use the program and provide feedback
      D. Read the instructions, have a student use the program, try it out yourself

Answer: A. Read the instructions to ensure it will work with the computer you have, try it out as if you were a student, and examine how the program handles errors or mistakes the students may make
You should not have students use the program until you have read all of the material related to the use, tried it out yourself as if you were a student and made many different types of mistakes when using it. You should try to make as many different types of errors as possible, so that you can see how the program responds and ensure it is how you want your students errors handled.

NYSTCE ATS-W Elementary 90   240

61. You are a classroom teacher in a building that does not have a computer lab for your class to use. However, knowing that you enjoy incorporating technology into the classroom, your principal has worked to find computers for your room. They are set up in the back of your classroom and have software loaded, but have no access to the intranet or internet within your building. Which of the following is NOT an acceptable method for using these computers within your classroom instruction?
    (Rigorous) (Skill 15.4)

    A. Rotating the students in small groups through the computers as centers
    B. Putting students at the computers individually for skill-based review or practice
    C. Dividing your classroom into three groups and putting each group at one computer and completing a whole class lesson
    D. Using the computers for students to complete their writing assignments with an assigned sign-up sheet, so the students know the order in which they will type their stories

Answer: C. Dividing your classroom into three groups and putting each group at one computer and completing a whole class lesson
Three computers are not enough for a typical class size across the country. This would involve too many students at one computer and could result in behavioral issues. Additionally, it would be difficult for the students to all have the ability to interact in a meaningful way with the software. If you would like to complete a whole class lesson using the technology, it would be best to find a projector that connects to the computer so all students have equal opportunity to participate and see.

62. Which of the following are the three primary categories of instructional technology tools?
    (Rigorous) (Skill 15.5)

    A. Creation/design/implementation
    B. Research/implementation/assessment
    C. Assessment/creation/research
    D. Design/research/usage

Answer: C. Assessment/creation/research
Assessment programs may not necessarily teach students about technology but are very clear-cut and simple programs to use. Creation is the category where students can practice their technology skills. Teachers can permit students to utilize their researching skills by allowing classroom time to research the topics they are studying. This also allows them to keep them abreast of technological advances.

63. **When a teacher is evaluating a student's technologically produced product, which of the following is considered the MOST important factor to consider?**
(Rigorous) (Skill 15.7)

    A. Content
    B. Design
    C. Audience
    D. Relevance

Answer: D. Relevance
All of the above are important; however, relevance is of utmost importance. It is imperative that students are aware of how to design a technologically based assignment and also to incorporate effective content. However, if the content is not relevant and pertinent to the topic studied, it is not considered an effective learning strategy.

64. **Which of the following is responsible for working with the school in matters concerning the business of running a school?**
(Rigorous) (Skill 16.5)

    A. Curriculum coordinators
    B. Administrators
    C. Board of Education
    D. Parent-Teacher organizations

Answer: C. Board of Education
The Board of Education is elected by the district to offer direction for the students and their schools. Among its many responsibilities, the Board establishes a long-term vision for the district and designs their policies and goals. The administrator carries out the school district's policies and manages the day-to-day operations of the school.

65.   Teacher's unions are involved in all of the following EXCEPT:
       (Average) (Skill 16.5)

       A. Updating teachers on current educational developments
       B. Advocating for teacher rights
       C. Matching teachers with suitable schools
       D. Developing professional codes and practices

Answer: C. Matching teachers with suitable schools
The role of teachers unions is to work with teachers to develop and improve the profession of teaching by advocating for higher wages and improved conditions for teachers, developing professional codes and practices and keeping teachers up to date on current educational developments. It is not the role of Teacher Unions to find suitable employment for teachers.

66.   Mrs. Graham has taken the time to reflect, completed observations, and asked for feedback about the interactions between her and her students from her principal. It is obvious by seeking this information out that Mrs. Graham understands which of the following? *(Rigorous) (Skill 17.1)*

       A. The importance of clear communication with the principal
       B. She needs to analyze her effectiveness of classroom interactions
       C. She is clearly communicating with the principal
       D. She cares about her students

Answer: B. She needs to analyze her effectiveness of classroom interactions
By utilizing reflection, observations, and feedback from peers or supervisors, teachers can help to build their own understanding of how they interact with students. In this way, they can better analyze their effectiveness at building appropriate relationships with students.

67.   **What is a benefit of frequent self-assessment?**
      (Average) (Skill 17.2)

      A. Opens new venues for professional development
      B. Saves teachers the pressure of being observed by others
      C. Reduces time spent on areas not needing attention
      D. Offers a model for students to adopt in self-improvement

Answer: A. Opens new venues for professional development
When a teacher is involved in the process of self-reflection and self-assessment, one of the common outcomes is that the teacher comes to identify areas of skill or knowledge that require more research or improvement on her part. She may become interested in overcoming a particular weakness in her performance or may decide to attend a workshop or consult with a mentor to learn more about a particular area of concern.

68.   **In the past, teaching has been viewed as _____ while in more current society it has been viewed as _____.**
      (Rigorous) (Skill 17.3)

      A. isolating…collaborative
      B. collaborative…isolating
      C. supportive…isolating
      D. isolating…supportive

Answer: A. isolating…collaborative
In the past, teachers often walked into their own classrooms and closed the door. They were not involved in any form of collaboration and were responsible for only the students within their classrooms. However, in today's more modern schools, teachers work in collaborative teams and are responsible for all of the children in a school setting.

69. **What would happen if a school utilized an integrated approach to professional development?**
(Average) (Skill 17.3)

A. All stakeholders needs are addressed
B. Teachers and administrators are on the same page
C. High-quality programs for students are developed
D. Parents drive the curriculum and instruction

Answer: C. High-quality programs for students are developed
The implementation of an integrated approach to professional development is a critical component to ensuring success of programs for students. It involves teachers, parents, and other community members working together to develop appropriate programs to ensure students are receiving the necessary instruction to be successful in the future workforce.

70. **Which of the following should NOT be a purpose of a parent-teacher conference?**
(Average) (Skill 18.1)

A. To involve the parent in their child's education
B. To establish a friendship with the child's parents
C. To resolve a concern about the child's performance
D. To inform parents of positive behaviors by the child

Answer: B. To establish a friendship with the child's parents
The purpose of a parent-teacher conference is to involve parents in their child's education, address concerns about the child's performance, and share positive aspects of the student's learning with the parents. It would be unprofessional to allow the conference to degenerate into a social visit to establish a friendship.

71. **Mr. Brown wishes to improve his parent communication skills. Which of the following is a strategy he can utilize to accomplish this goal?**
(Easy) (Skill 18.1)

A. Hold parent-teacher conferences
B. Send home positive notes
C. Have parent nights where the parents are invited into his classroom
D. All of the above

Answer: D. All of the above
Increasing parent communication skills is important for teachers. All of the listed strategies are methods a teacher can utilize to increase his skills.

72. **Which is NOT considered a good practice when conducting parent-teacher conferences?**
(Average) (Skill 18.1)

A. Ending the conference with an agreed plan of action
B. Figure out questions for parents during the conference
C. Prepare work samples, records of behavior, and assessment information
D. Prepare a welcoming environment, set a good mood, and be an active listener

Answer: B. Figure out questions for parents during the conference
Choices A, C, and D all reflect effective practices for holding a successful parent teacher conference. Teachers should prepare questions and comments for parents prior to the conference so they are optimally prepared.

73. **When communicating with parents for whom English is not the primary language, you should:**
(Easy) (Skill 18.1)

A. Provide materials whenever possible in their native language
B. Use an interpreter
C. Provide the same communication as you would to native English speaking parents
D. All of the above

Answer: D. All of the above
When communicating with non-English speaking parents, it is important to treat them as you would any other parent and utilize any means necessary to ensure they have the ability to participate in their child's educational process.

74. **Tommy is a student in your class and his parents are deaf. Tommy is struggling with math and you want to contact the parents to discuss the issues. How should you proceed?**
(Easy) (Skill 18.1)

   A. Limit contact because of the parent's inability to hear
   B. Use a TTY phone to communicate with the parents
   C. Talk to your administrator to find an appropriate interpreter to help you communicate with the parents personally
   D. Both B and C, but not A

Answer: D. Both B and C, but not A
You should never avoid communicating with parents for any reason; instead you should find strategies to find an effective way to communicate in various methods, just as you would with any other student in your classroom.

75. **Which statement best reflects why family involvement is important to a student's educational success?**
(Easy) (Skill 18.2)

   A. Reading the class newsletter constitutes strong family involvement
   B. Family involvement means to attend graduation
   C. There are limited ways a parent can be active in their child's education
   D. The more family members are involved, the more success a student is likely to experience

Answer: D. The more family members are involved, the more success a student is likely to experience
Although reading the class newsletter and coming to graduation are obvious parts of parental involvement, it is not the sole involvement for which teachers hope. Unlike the statement in choice C, there are many unique ways parents can participate and share talents toward their child's education. Parents are invited in to assist with workshops, attend class trips, participate as a room parents, organize special events, read to the class, speak of an occupation, help with classroom housekeeping, and more. Parents can also be involved by volunteering for the PTO/A, library help, office help, and other tasks. Some teachers plan a few events a year in the classroom for special parties, presentations and events. Therefore, choice D is correct.

76. **Which of the following is NOT an appropriate method for teachers to interact with families of diverse backgrounds?**
(Easy) (Skill 18.2)

    A. Show respect to parents
    B. Share personal stories concerning the student
    C. Display patience with parents
    D. Disregard culture of student

Answer: D. Disregard culture of student
The culture of the student must be taken into account when interacting with families of diverse background. Teachers must show respect to all parents and families, and they need to realize that various cultures have different views of how children should be educated—this must be taken into consideration when dealing with families.

77. **A parent has left an angry message on the teacher's voicemail. The message relates to a concern about a student and is directed at the teacher. The teacher should:**
(Average) (Skill 18.2)

    A. Call back immediately and confront the parent
    B. Cool off, plan what to discuss with the parent, then call back
    C. Question the child to find out what set off the parent
    D. Ignore the message, since feelings of anger usually subside after a while

Answer: B. Cool off, plan what to discuss with the parent, then call back
It is professional for a teacher to keep her head in the face of emotion and respond to an angry parent in a calm and objective manner. The teacher should give herself time to cool off and plan the conversation with the parents with the purpose of understanding the concern and resolving it, rather than putting the parent in his or her place. Above all, the teacher should remember that parent-teacher interactions should aim to benefit the student.

78. **In successful inclusion of students with disabilities:**
(Average) (Skill 19.1)

A. A variety of instructional arrangements are available
B. School personnel shift the responsibility for learning outcomes to the student
C. The physical facilities are used as they are
D. Regular classroom teachers have sole responsibility for evaluating student progress

Answer: A. A variety if instructional arrangements are available
The regular teacher believes the student can succeed. School personnel are committed to accepting responsibility for the learning outcomes of students with disabilities. School personnel and the students in the class have been prepared to receive a student with disabilities.

79. **A 16-year-old girl who has been looking sad writes an essay in which the main protagonist commits suicide. You overhear her talking about suicide. What do you do?**
(Average) (Skill 19.2)

A. Report this immediately to school administration, talk to the girl, letting her know you will talk to her parents about it
B. Report this immediately to authorities
C. Report this immediately to school administration, make your own report to authorities if required by protocol in your school, and do nothing else
D. Just give the child some extra attention, as it may just be that's all she's looking for

Answer: C. Report this immediately to school administration, make your own report to authorities if required by protocol in your school, and do nothing else
A child who is suicidal is beyond any help that can be offered in a classroom. The first step is to report the situation to administration. If your school protocol calls for it, the situation should also be reported to authorities.

80. **How can a teacher use a student's permanent record?**
(Average) (Skill 19.3)

   A. To develop a better understanding of the needs of the student
   B. To record all instances of student disruptive behavior
   C. To brainstorm ideas for discussing with parents at parent-teacher conferences
   D. To develop realistic expectations of the student's performance early in the year

Answer: A. To develop a better understanding of the needs of the student
The purpose of a student's permanent record is to give the teacher a better understanding of the student's educational history and provide her with relevant information to support the student's learning. Permanent records may not be used to arrive at preconceived judgments or to build a case against the student. Above all, the contents of a student's permanent record are confidential.

ANSWER KEY

1. B	28. C	55. C
2. B	29. A	56. C
3. C	30. D	57. D
4. A	31. B	58. B
5. D	32. D	59. C
6. C	33. C	60. A
7. A	34. A	61. C
8. D	35. B	62. C
9. B	36. B	63. D
10. A	37. B	64. C
11. A	38. D	65. C
12. C	39. A	66. B
13. D	40. A	67. A
14. B	41. C	68. A
15. B	42. B	69. C
16. A	43. D	70. B
17. C	44. B	71. D
18. B	45. C	72. B
19. D	46. A	73. D
20. D	47. C	74. D
21. B	48. C	75. D
22. D	49. B	76. D
23. B	50. B	77. B
24. B	51. B	78. A
25. A	52. B	79. C
26. C	53. B	80. A
27. C	54. B	

RIGOR TABLE

Easy
3, 6, 12, 25, 32, 39, 43, 45, 54, 58, 59, 71, 73, 74, 75, 76

Average
1, 2, 5, 8, 14, 17, 18, 21, 22, 24, 27, 29, 35, 36, 38, 44, 46, 48, 51, 56, 65, 67, 69, 70, 72, 77, 78, 79, 80

Rigorous
4, 7, 9, 10, 11, 13, 15, 16, 19, 20, 23, 26, 28, 30, 31, 33, 34, 37, 40, 41, 42, 47, 49, 50, 52, 53, 55, 57, 60, 61, 62, 63, 64, 66, 68

CPSIA information can be obtained
at www.ICGtesting.com
Printed in the USA
JSHW031239091021
19450JS00003B/104

9 781607 873051